THE ROUTLEDGE ATLAS OF AMERICAN HISTORY

OTHER BOOKS BY MARTIN GILBERT

The Churchill biography
Volume III, 'The Challenge of War', 1914–1916
Volume III, Documents, Parts I and II
Volume IV, 'The Stricken World', 1917–1922
Volume IV, Documents, Parts I II and III
Volume V, 'The Prophet of Truth', 1922–1939
The Exchequer Years, Documents, 1922–1929
The Wilderness Years, Documents, 1929–1935
The Coming of War, Documents, 1936–1939
Volume VI, 'Finest Hours', 1939–1941
At the Admiralty, Documents, September 1939–May 1940
Volume VII, 'Road to Victory', 1941–1945
Volume VIII, 'Never Despair', 1945–1965
Never Surrender, Documents, May–December 1940

Historical works
The Appeasers (with Richard Gott)
The European Powers, 1900–1945
The Roots of Appeasement
Britain and Germany Between the Wars (documents)
Plough My Own Furrow: the Life of Lord Allen of Hurtwood (documents)
Servant of India: Diaries of the Viceroy's Private Secretary (documents)
Sir Horace Rumbold: Portrait of a Diplomat
Churchill: a Photographic Portrait
Churchill's Political Philosophy
Auschwitz and the Allies
Exile and Return: the Struggle for Jewish Statehood
The Jews of Hope: the Plight of Soviet Jewry Today
Shcharansky: Hero of our Time
Jerusalem: Rebirth of a City, 1838–1898
Final Journey: the Fate of the Jews in Nazi Europe
The Holocaust: the Jewish Tragedy
First World War
Second World War
The Day the War Ended, 8 May 1945
Churchill, A Life

Atlases
The Routledge Atlas of the Arab–Israeli Conflict
The Routledge Atlas of British History
The Routledge Atlas of the First World War
The Routledge Atlas of the Holocaust
The Routledge Atlas of Jewish History
The Routledge Atlas of Recent History (*in preparation*)
The Routledge Atlas of Russian History
The Jews of Arab Lands: Their History in Maps
The Jews of Russia: Their History in Maps
Jerusalem: Illustrated History Atlas
Children's Illustrated Bible Atlas

THE ROUTLEDGE ATLAS OF
AMERICAN HISTORY

Third edition

Martin Gilbert

Fellow of Merton College, Oxford

CRM c-1

LONDON AND NEW YORK

First published as *The Dent Atlas of American History*
in 1968 by J.M. Dent Ltd
Revised edition 1985
Third edition 1993

Reprinted 1995, 2001
by Routledge
11 New Fetter Lane, London EC4P 4EE
29 West 35th Street, New York, NY 10001

Routledge is an imprint of the Taylor & Francis Group

Printed and bound in Great Britain by
Bell & Bain Ltd., Glasgow

British Library Cataloguing in Publication Data
A catalogue record for this book is available from the British Library

Library of Congress Cataloguing in Publication Data
A catalogue record for this book is available from the Library of Congress

ISBN 0–415–13623–7 (hbk)
ISBN 0–415–13624–5 (pbk)

Preface

The idea for this atlas came to me while I was teaching at the University of South Carolina. Its aim is to provide a short but informative visual guide to American history. I have tried to make use of maps in the widest possible way, designing each one individually, and seeking to transform statistics and facts into something easily seen and grasped. My material has been obtained from a wide range of historical works, encyclopaedias, and newspaper and Government reports.

More than twenty-five years have passed since the first publication of this atlas. It was a period marked first by the intensification and then by the ending of the Vietnam war, with more than 55,000 American dead. It was also a period marked by a substantial increase in the population of the United States, and continued immigration. This same period has seen the development of outer space as a region of defence policy. New maps cover these recent developments.

Since the revised edition was published in 1985, the pattern of events has led me to draw twenty-six new maps, to cover, among recent developments, the continuing growth of immigration, new ethnic and population changes, and the military and humanitarian actions of the United States overseas, culminating in the Gulf War (1991), aid to Somalia (1992), and air drops to Bosnia (1993). New domestic maps show the natural and accidental disasters of the past two decades, the continuing high death rate from motor accidents (more than a million dead in twenty years), murder (a quarter of a million dead in a single decade), and the new scourge of Aids (170,000 deaths in a decade).

The United States has also been the pioneer in exploring the solar system and in defence preparedness in space, for both of which I have drawn a special map. United States' arms sales, and economic help to poorer countries, as well as the ending of the Cold War confrontation, also required new maps, as did pollution. The continuing United States' presence in the Pacific, and her defence preparedness at home and abroad, are also mapped.

I have been helped considerably in the task of updating this atlas by Abe Eisenstat and Kay Thomson. Many individuals and institutions have provided extra material for the maps. I am particularly grateful to:

Martin Adams, Bureau of Political-Military Affairs, State Department, Washington DC
James T. Hackett, Member of the President's General Advisory Committee on Arms Control
Louan Hall, National Highway Traffic Safety Administration
Michael Hoeffer, Statistics Division, Immigration and Naturalisation Services
John Richter, Agency for International Development, State Department
Joshua Gilbert (for help on the space map)

For the first and second edition of this atlas, my draft maps were turned into clear and striking artwork by Arthur Banks and Terry Bicknell. For this new edition, I am grateful to the cartographic skills of Tim Aspden. At my publishers, JM Dent, David Swarbrick has made it possible to realise my ambition to re-issue all of my historical atlases updated. It is my hope that they will be of interest and service to teachers, students, and the general reader for whom the past is not a forbidden planet, but an integral part of today's world.

MARTIN GILBERT
Merton College, Oxford

14 June 1993

Maps

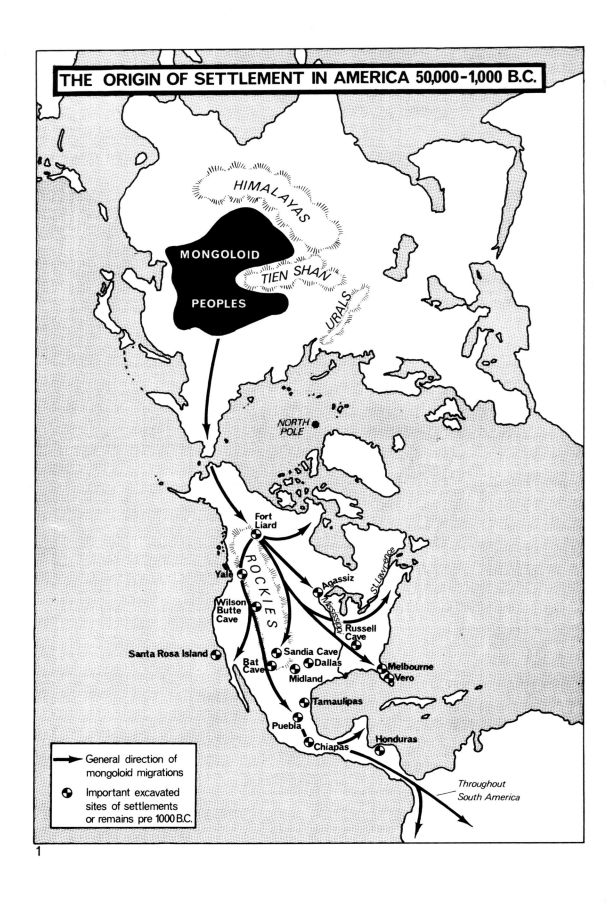

THE ORIGIN OF SETTLEMENT IN AMERICA 50,000–1,000 B.C.

HIMALAYAS

MONGOLOID

TIEN SHAN

PEOPLES

URALS

NORTH POLE

Fort Liard

ROCKIES

Yale

Agassiz

St. Lawrence

Wilson Butte Cave

Mississippi

Russell Cave

Santa Rosa Island

Sandia Cave

Bat Cave

Dallas

Midland

Melbourne

Vero

Tamaulipas

Puebla

Chiapas

Honduras

Throughout South America

General direction of mongoloid migrations

Important excavated sites of settlements or remains pre 1000 B.C.

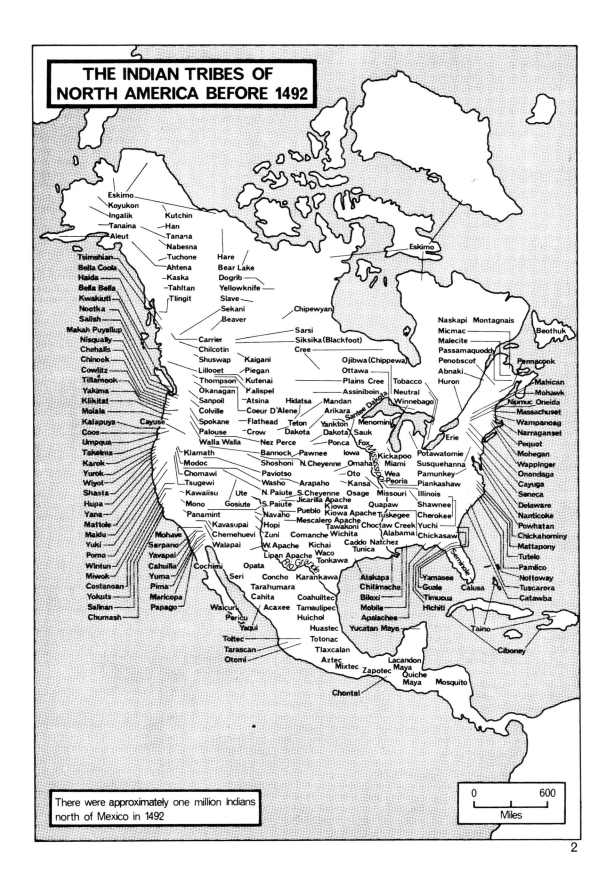

THE INDIAN TRIBES OF NORTH AMERICA BEFORE 1492

Eskimo
Koyukon
Ingalik   Kutchin
Tanaina   Han
Aleut   Tanana
                 Nabesna
Tsimshian   Tuchone   Hare
Bella Coola   Ahtena   Bear Lake
Haida   Kaska   Dogrib
Bella Bella   Tahltan   Yellowknife
Kwakiutl   Tlingit   Slave
Nootka   Sekani
Salish   Beaver   Chipewyan
Makah Puyallup
Nisqually   Carrier   Sarsi
Chehalis   Chilcotin   Siksika (Blackfoot)
Chinook   Shuswap   Cree
Cowlitz   Lillooet   Kaigani
Tillamook   Thompson   Piegan
Yakima   Okanagan   Kutenai
Klikitat   Sanpoil   Kalispel
Molala   Colville   Atsina   Hidatsa   Mandan
Kalapuya   Spokane   Coeur D'Alene Arikara
Cayuse   Palouse   Flathead   Teton   Yankton
Coos   Crow   Dakota
Umpqua   Walla Walla   Nez Perce   Ponca   Sauk
Takelma   Klamath   Bannock   Pawnee   Iowa
Karok   Modoc   Shoshoni   N.Cheyenne Omaha
Yurok   Chomawi   Paviotso   Oto
Wiyot   Tsugewi   Washo   Arapaho   Kansa
Shasta   Kawaiisu   N. Paiute S.Cheyenne Osage   Missouri
Hupa   Mono   Ute   S. Paiute Jicarilla Apache   Quapaw
Yana   Gosiute   Pueblo   Kiowa
Mattole   Panamint   Navaho   Kiowa Apache
Maidu   Kavasupai Hopi   Mescalero Apache
Yuki   Mohave   Chemehuevi Zuni   Comanche Wichita
Pomo   Serrano   Walapai   W. Apache Kichai
Wintun   Yavapai   Lipan Apache Waco   Tonkawa
Miwok   Cahuilla Cochimi   Opata   Karankawa
Costanoan   Yuma   Seri   Concho
Yokuts   Pima   Tarahumara
Salinan   Maricopa   Cahita   Coahuiltec
Chumash   Papago   Acaxee   Tamaulipec
                 Walcuri   Huichol
                 Pericu   Coahuiltec
                 Yaqui   Huastec
                 Toltec   Totonac
                 Tarascan   Tlaxcalan
                 Otomi   Aztec
                               Mixtec   Zapotec
                 Chontal

Eskimo

Naskapi Montagnais
Micmac
Malecite   Beothuk
Passamaquoddy
Penobscot   Pennacook
Abnaki
Huron   Mahican
Tobacco   Mohawk
Neutral   Nipmuc Oneida
Winnebago   Massachuset
                       Wampanoset
Menomini   Narraganset
             Erie   Pequot
                       Mohegan
Potawatomie   Wappinger
Kickapoo   Onondaga
Miami   Cayuga
Susquehanna   Seneca
Pamunkey   Delaware
Wea   Nanticoke
Peoria   Powhatan
Piankashaw   Chickahominy
Illinois   Mattapony
                       Tutelo
Shawnee   Pamlico
Tuskegee   Nottoway
Cherokee   Tuscarora
Yuchi   Catawba
Choctaw Creek
         Alabama
Chickasaw

Caddo Natchez
       Tunica

Atakapa   Yamasee
Chitimacha   Guale
Biloxi   Timucua   Calusa
Mobile   Hichiti
Apalaches
Yucatan Maya
                  Taino
                           Ciboney
Lacandon
Maya
Quiche
Maya   Mosquito

Mississippi
Santee Dakota
Rio Grande
Seminole

0   600
        Miles

There were approximately one million Indians
north of Mexico in 1492

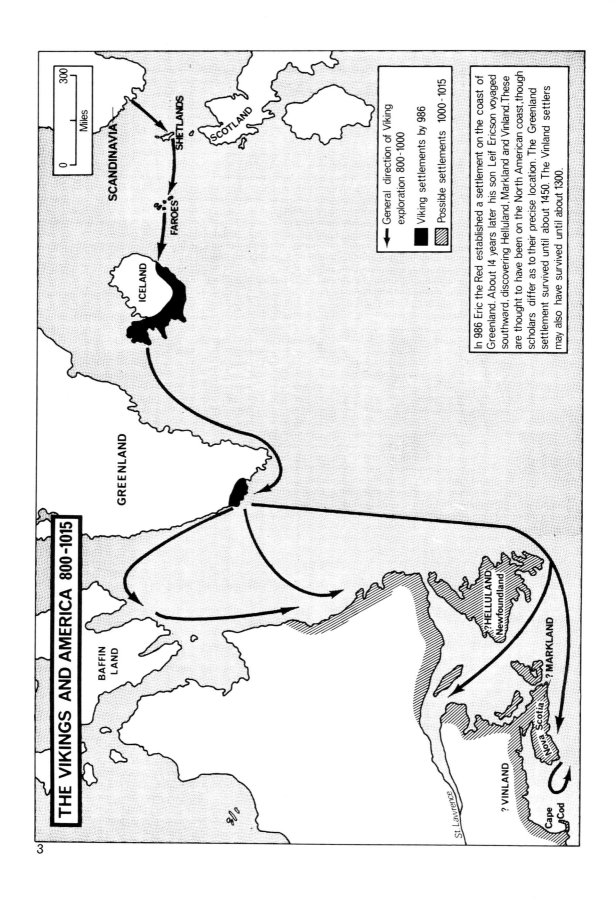

THE VIKINGS AND AMERICA 800-1015

SCANDINAVIA

SHETLANDS

SCOTLAND

FAROES

ICELAND

GREENLAND

BAFFIN LAND

St. Lawrence

?HELLULAND
Newfoundland

? MARKLAND

? VINLAND

Nova Scotia

Cape Cod

0 300
Miles

→ General direction of Viking exploration 800-1000

■ Viking settlements by 986

▨ Possible settlements 1000-1015

In 986 Eric the Red established a settlement on the coast of Greenland. About 14 years later his son Leif Ericson voyaged southward, discovering Helluland, Markland and Vinland. These are thought to have been on the North American coast, though scholars differ as to their precise location. The Greenland settlement survived until about 1450. The Vinland settlers may also have survived until about 1300.

3

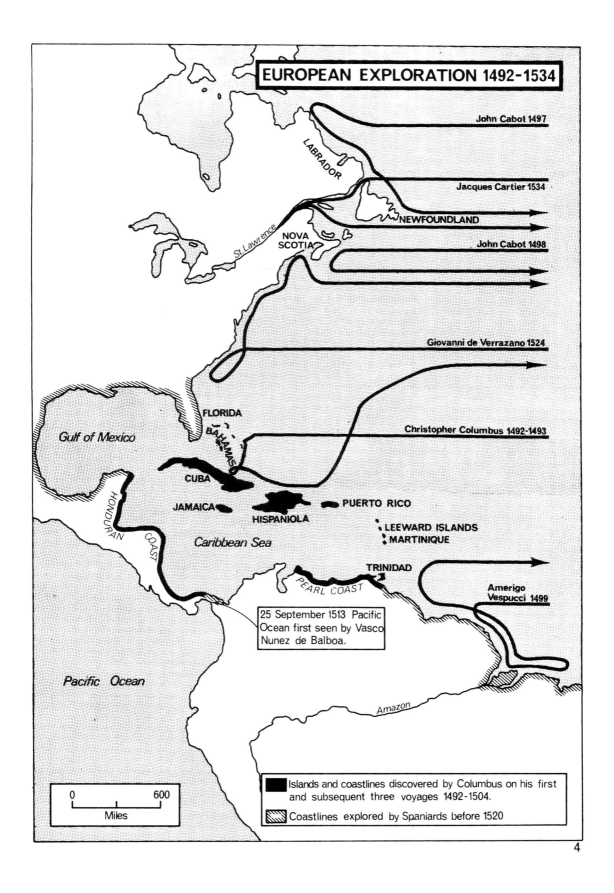

EUROPEAN EXPLORATION 1492–1534

John Cabot 1497

LABRADOR

Jacques Cartier 1534

NEWFOUNDLAND

John Cabot 1498

NOVA SCOTIA

St. Lawrence

Giovanni de Verrazano 1524

FLORIDA

BAHAMAS

Gulf of Mexico

Christopher Columbus 1492-1493

CUBA

JAMAICA

HISPANIOLA

PUERTO RICO

LEEWARD ISLANDS

MARTINIQUE

HONDURAN COAST

Caribbean Sea

TRINIDAD

PEARL COAST

25 September 1513 Pacific Ocean first seen by Vasco Nunez de Balboa.

Amerigo Vespucci 1499

Pacific Ocean

Amazon

0   600
Miles

Islands and coastlines discovered by Columbus on his first and subsequent three voyages 1492-1504.

Coastlines explored by Spaniards before 1520

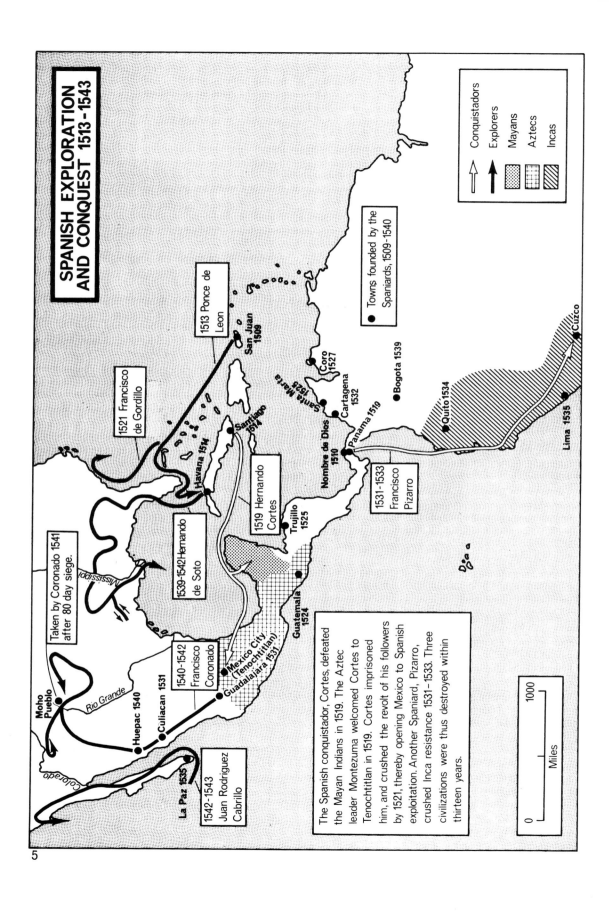

SPANISH EXPLORATION AND CONQUEST 1513-1543

Conquistadors →
Explorers →
Mayans
Aztecs
Incas

● Towns founded by the Spaniards, 1509-1540

1513 Ponce de Leon

1521 Francisco de Gordillo

San Juan 1509

Coro 1527

Santa Maria 1525

Cartagena 1532

Bogota 1539

Quito 1534

Cuzco

Lima 1535

Havana 1514

Santiago 1514

Nombre de Dios 1510

Panama 1519

1519 Hernando Cortes

Trujillo 1525

1531-1533 Francisco Pizarro

1539-1542 Hernando de Soto

Taken by Coronado 1541 after 80 day siege.

Mississippi

Guatemala 1524

1540-1542 Francisco Coronado

Mexico City (Tenochtitlan)

Guadalajara 1531

Culiacan 1531

Moho Pueblo 1540

Rio Grande

Huepac 1540

Colorado

La Paz 1535

1542-1543 Juan Rodriguez Cabrillo

The Spanish conquistador, Cortes, defeated the Mayan Indians in 1519. The Aztec leader Montezuma welcomed Cortes to Tenochtitlan in 1519. Cortes imprisoned him, and crushed the revolt of his followers by 1521, thereby opening Mexico to Spanish exploitation. Another Spaniard, Pizarro, crushed Inca resistance 1531–1533. Three civilizations were thus destroyed within thirteen years.

Miles

0   1000

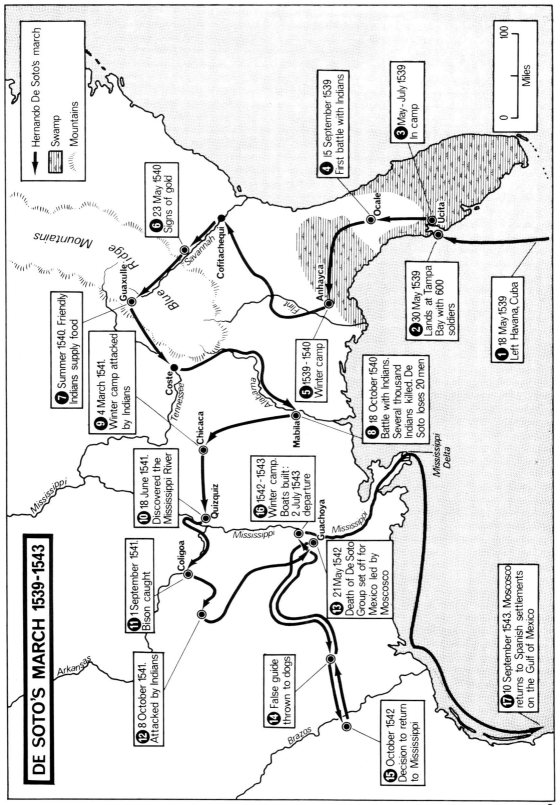

DE SOTO'S MARCH 1539-1543

Legend:
- → Hernando De Soto's march
- Swamp
- Mountains

Scale: 0 — 100 Miles

1 18 May 1539 Left Havana, Cuba

2 30 May 1539 Lands at Tampa Bay with 600 soldiers

3 May–July 1539 In camp

4 15 September 1539 First battle with Indians

5 1539–1540 Winter camp

6 23 May 1540 Signs of gold

7 Summer 1540. Friendly Indians supply food

8 18 October 1540 Battle with Indians. Several thousand Indians killed. De Soto loses 20 men

9 4 March 1541. Winter camp attacked by Indians

10 18 June 1541. Discovered the Mississippi River

11 1 September 1541. Bison caught

12 8 October 1541. Attacked by Indians

13 21 May 1542 Death of De Soto Group set off for Mexico led by Moscosco

14 False guide thrown to dogs

15 October 1542 Decision to return to Mississippi

16 1542–1543 Winter camp. Boats built: 2 July 1543 departure

17 10 September 1543. Moscosco returns to Spanish settlements on the Gulf of Mexico

Places: Ucita, Ocale, Anhayca, Cofitachequi, Guaxulle, Savannah, Blue Ridge, Mountains, Coste, Tennessee, Chicaca, Mabila, Alabama, Flint, Quizquiz, Coligoa, Guachoya, Mississippi, Mississippi Delta, Arkansas, Brazos, Mississippi

6

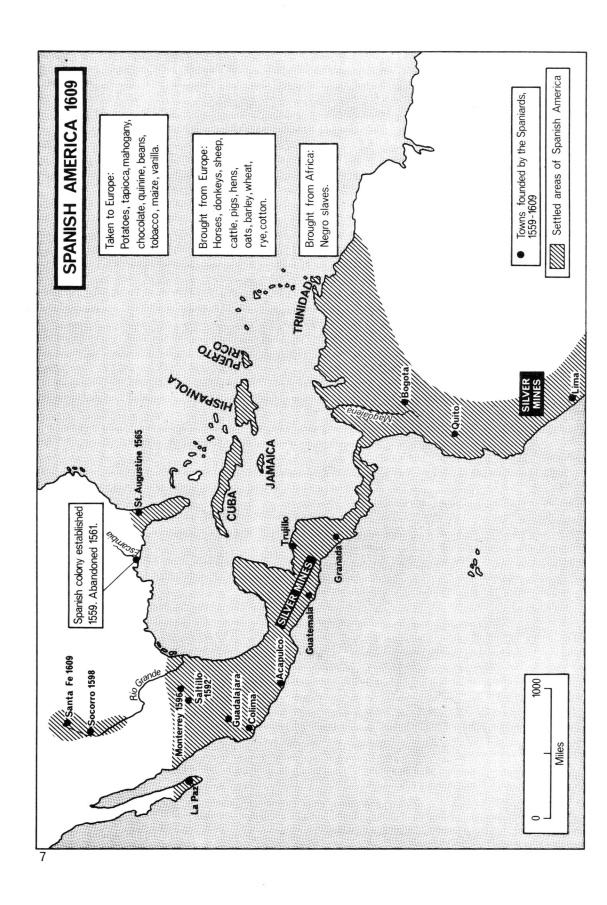

SPANISH AMERICA 1609

Taken to Europe:
Potatoes, tapioca, mahogany, chocolate, quinine, beans, tobacco, maize, vanilla.

Brought from Europe:
Horses, donkeys, sheep, cattle, pigs, hens, oats, barley, wheat, rye, cotton.

Brought from Africa:
Negro slaves.

● Towns founded by the Spaniards, 1559-1609

▨ Settled areas of Spanish America

Spanish colony established 1559. Abandoned 1561.

● Santa Fe 1609
● Socorro 1598

● Monterrey 1596
● Saltillo 1592

● Guadalajara
● Colima
● Acapulco
● Guatemala

● La Paz

St. Augustine 1565

Escambia
Rio Grande

CUBA
JAMAICA
HISPANIOLA
PUERTO RICO
TRINIDAD

● Trujillo
● Granada

SILVER MINES

Magdalena
● Bogota
● Quito
● Lima

SILVER MINES

1000

0
Miles

7

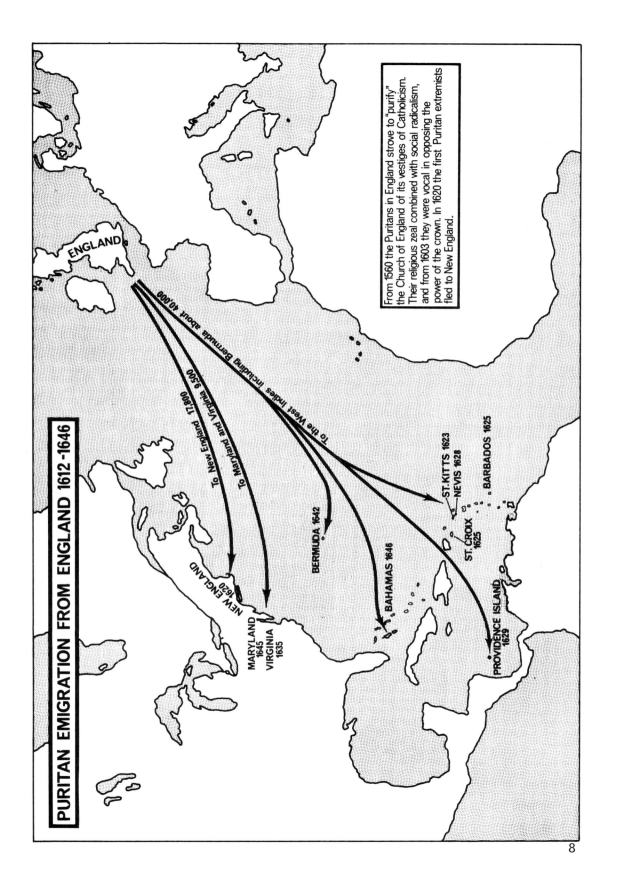

PURITAN EMIGRATION FROM ENGLAND 1612-1646

ENGLAND

From 1560 the Puritans in England strove to "purify" the Church of England of its vestiges of Catholicism. Their religious zeal combined with social radicalism, and from 1603 they were vocal in opposing the power of the crown. In 1620 the first Puritan extremists fled to New England.

To New England 17,800

To Maryland and Virginia 9,500

To the West Indies including Bermuda about 40,000

NEW ENGLAND 1620

MARYLAND 1645
VIRGINIA 1635

BERMUDA 1642

BAHAMAS 1646

ST.KITTS 1623
NEVIS 1628
BARBADOS 1625
ST.CROIX 1625

PROVIDENCE ISLAND 1629

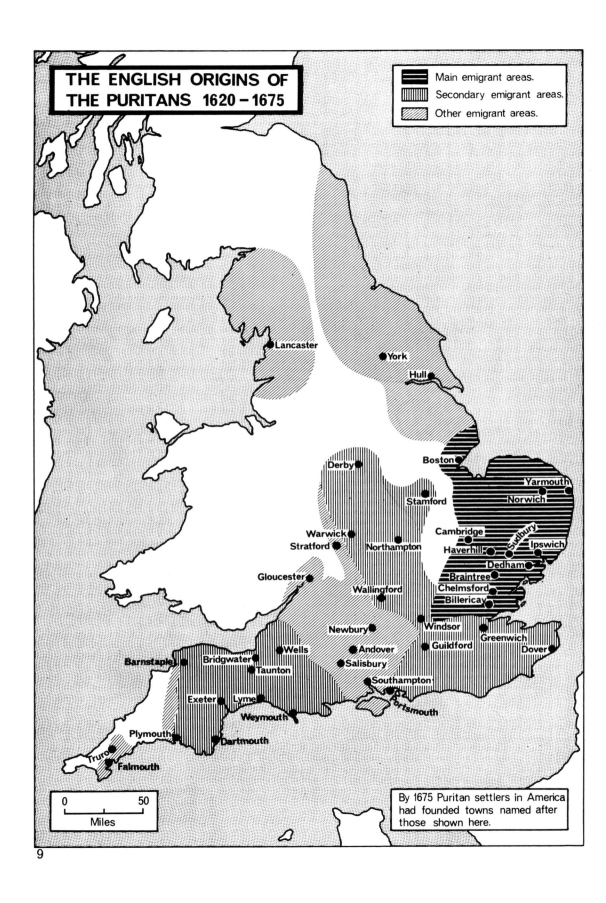

THE ENGLISH ORIGINS OF THE PURITANS 1620 – 1675

Main emigrant areas.
Secondary emigrant areas.
Other emigrant areas.

Lancaster
York
Hull
Derby
Boston
Yarmouth
Norwich
Stamford
Cambridge
Sudbury
Warwick
Ipswich
Stratford
Northampton
Haverhill
Dedham
Gloucester
Braintree
Chelmsford
Wallingford
Billericay
Newbury
Windsor
Greenwich
Wells
Andover
Guildford
Dover
Barnstaple
Bridgwater
Salisbury
Taunton
Southampton
Exeter
Lyme
Portsmouth
Weymouth
Plymouth
Dartmouth
Truro
Falmouth

0   50
Miles

By 1675 Puritan settlers in America
had founded towns named after
those shown here.

9

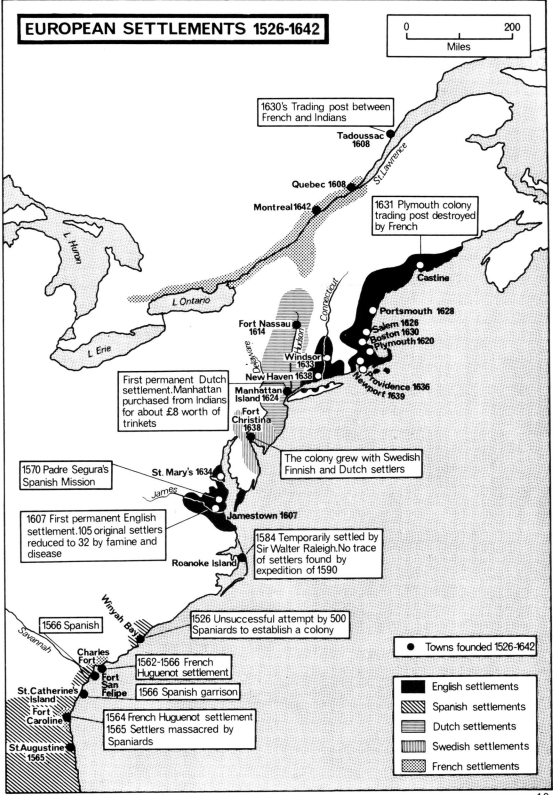

EUROPEAN SETTLEMENTS 1526-1642

0   200
Miles

1630's Trading post between French and Indians

Tadoussac 1608

Quebec 1608

St. Lawrence

Montreal 1642

1631 Plymouth colony trading post destroyed by French

Castine

L. Huron

L. Ontario

L. Erie

Fort Nassau 1614

Hudson

Connecticut

Portsmouth 1628
Salem 1626
Boston 1630
Plymouth 1620

Windsor 1633

Delaware

New Haven 1638

Providence 1636
Newport 1639

First permanent Dutch settlement. Manhattan purchased from Indians for about £8 worth of trinkets

Manhattan Island 1624

Fort Christina 1638

The colony grew with Swedish Finnish and Dutch settlers

1570 Padre Segura's Spanish Mission

St. Mary's 1634

James

1607 First permanent English settlement. 105 original settlers reduced to 32 by famine and disease

Jamestown 1607

1584 Temporarily settled by Sir Walter Raleigh. No trace of settlers found by expedition of 1590

Roanoke Island

Winyah Bay

1566 Spanish

Savannah

1526 Unsuccessful attempt by 500 Spaniards to establish a colony

Charles Fort

1562-1566 French Huguenot settlement

Fort San Felipe

1566 Spanish garrison

St. Catherine's Island

Fort Caroline

St. Augustine 1565

1564 French Huguenot settlement 1565 Settlers massacred by Spaniards

● Towns founded 1526-1642

■ English settlements
▨ Spanish settlements
▤ Dutch settlements
▥ Swedish settlements
▦ French settlements

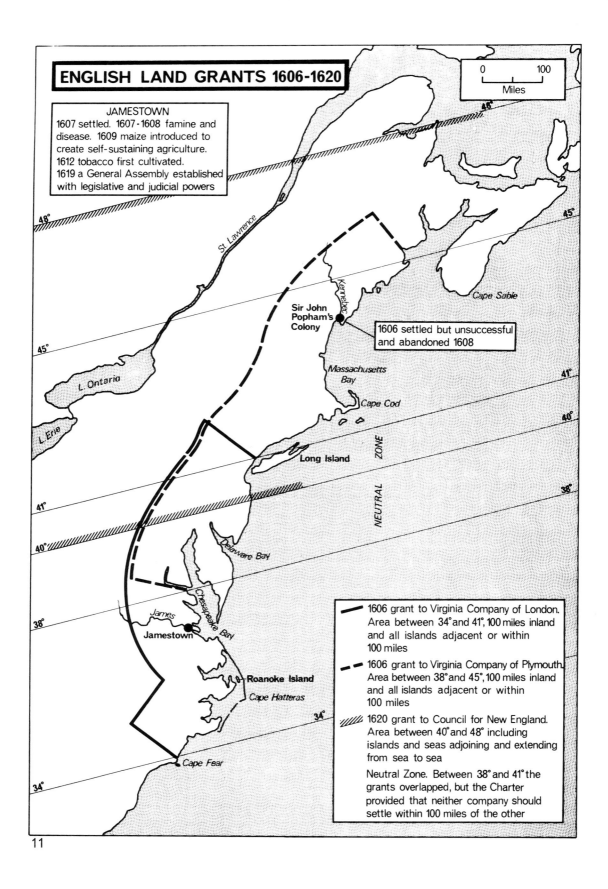

ENGLISH LAND GRANTS 1606-1620

0   100
Miles

JAMESTOWN
1607 settled. 1607-1608 famine and
disease. 1609 maize introduced to
create self-sustaining agriculture.
1612 tobacco first cultivated.
1619 a General Assembly established
with legislative and judicial powers

48°

45°

45°

Cape Sable

St. Lawrence

Kennebec

45°

Sir John
Popham's
Colony

1606 settled but unsuccessful
and abandoned 1608

Massachusetts
Bay

41°

L. Ontario

Cape Cod

40°

L. Erie

Long Island

Z
O
N
E

38°

41°

N
E
U
T
R
A
L

40°

Delaware Bay

Chesapeake Bay

38°

James

Jamestown

Roanoke Island

Cape Hatteras

34°

—— 1606 grant to Virginia Company of London.
Area between 34° and 41°, 100 miles inland
and all islands adjacent or within
100 miles

– – – 1606 grant to Virginia Company of Plymouth.
Area between 38° and 45°, 100 miles inland
and all islands adjacent or within
100 miles

////// 1620 grant to Council for New England.
Area between 40° and 48° including
islands and seas adjoining and extending
from sea to sea

Neutral Zone. Between 38° and 41° the
grants overlapped, but the Charter
provided that neither company should
settle within 100 miles of the other

34°

Cape Fear

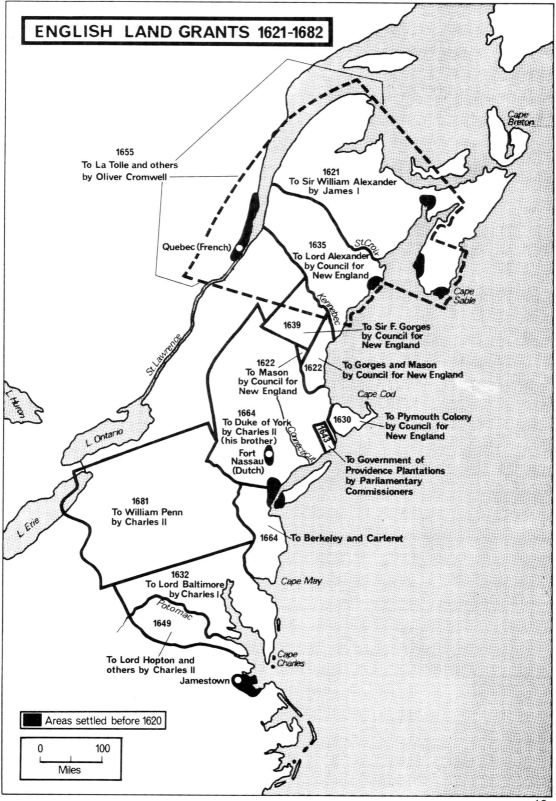

ENGLISH LAND GRANTS 1621-1682

1655
To La Tolle and others
by Oliver Cromwell

1621
To Sir William Alexander
by James I

Cape
Breton

1635
To Lord Alexander
by Council for
New England

St Croix

Quebec (French)

Kennebec

Cape
Sable

1639

To Sir F. Gorges
by Council for
New England

St. Lawrence

1622
To Mason
by Council for
New England

1622

To Gorges and Mason
by Council for New England

Cape Cod

L. Huron

1664
To Duke of York
by Charles II
(his brother)

1630

To Plymouth Colony
by Council for
New England

L. Ontario

Connecticut

1643

Fort
Nassau
(Dutch)

To Government of
Providence Plantations
by Parliamentary
Commissioners

1681
To William Penn
by Charles II

L. Erie

1664   To Berkeley and Carteret

1632
To Lord Baltimore
by Charles I

Cape May

Potomac

1649

*Cape
Charles*

To Lord Hopton and
others by Charles II
Jamestown

■ Areas settled before 1620

0   100
└──┴──┴──┘
     Miles

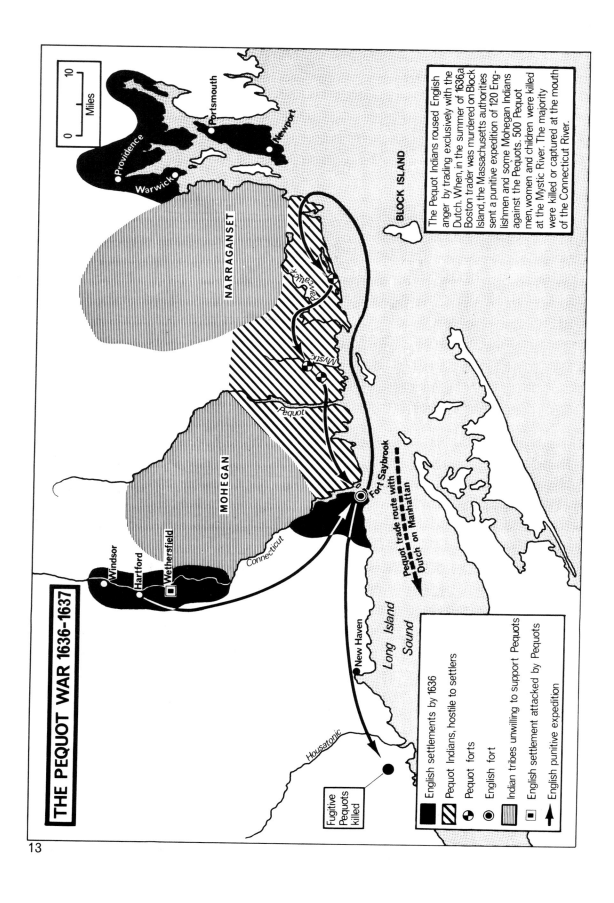

THE PEQUOT WAR 1636-1637

The Pequot Indians roused English anger by trading exclusively with the Dutch. When, in the summer of 1636, a Boston trader was murdered on Block Island, the Massachusetts authorities sent a punitive expedition of 120 Englishmen and some Mohegan Indians against the Pequots. 500 Pequot men, women and children were killed at the Mystic River. The majority were killed or captured at the mouth of the Connecticut River.

BLOCK ISLAND

NARRAGANSET

MOHEGAN

Providence
Warwick
Portsmouth
Newport

Windsor
Hartford
Wethersfield

Connecticut

Fort Saybrook

Pawcatuck
Mystic
Pequot

Long Island Sound

New Haven

Housatonic

Pequot trade route with
Dutch on Manhattan

Fugitive
Pequots
killed

0   10
Miles

■ English settlements by 1636
▨ Pequot Indians, hostile to settlers
☗ Pequot forts
◉ English fort
▥ Indian tribes unwilling to support Pequots
□ English settlement attacked by Pequots
↑ English punitive expedition

13

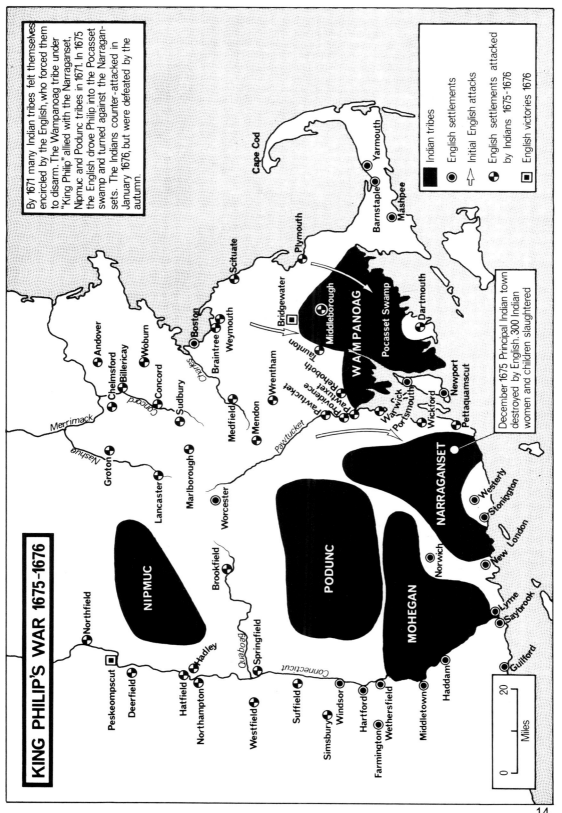

KING PHILIP'S WAR 1675–1676

By 1671 many Indian tribes felt themselves encircled by the English, who forced them to disarm. The Wampanoag tribe under "King Philip" allied with the Narraganset, Nipmuc and Podunc tribes in 1671. In 1675 the English drove Philip into the Pocasset swamp and turned against the Narragansets. The Indians counter-attacked in January 1676, but were defeated by the autumn.

Key:
- Indian tribes
- ◉ English settlements
- ⇨ Initial English attacks
- ◓ English settlements attacked by Indians 1675–1676
- ▣ English victories 1676

December 1675 Principal Indian town destroyed by English. 300 Indian women and children slaughtered

Cape Cod

Yarmouth
Mashpee
Barnstaple
Plymouth
Scituate
Bridgewater
Boston
Weymouth
Braintree
Middleborough
WAMPANOAG
Pocasset Swamp
Dartmouth
Taunton
Rehoboth
Wrentham
Medfield
Mendon
Pawtucket
Providence
Pawtucket
Newport
Pettaquamscut
Warwick
Portsmouth
Wickford
Merrimack
Chelmsford
Billericay
Woburn
Concord
Andover
Sudbury
Charles
Concord
Nashua
Groton
Marlborough
Worcester
Lancaster
NARRAGANSET
Westerly
Stonington
Norwich
New London
Brookfield
PODUNC
MOHEGAN
Lyme
Saybrook
Northfield
NIPMUC
Peskeompscut
Deerfield
Hadley
Hatfield
Northampton
Westfield
Quaboag
Springfield
Suffield
Simsbury
Windsor
Hartford
Farmington
Wethersfield
Middletown
Haddam
Guilford
Connecticut

0   20
Miles

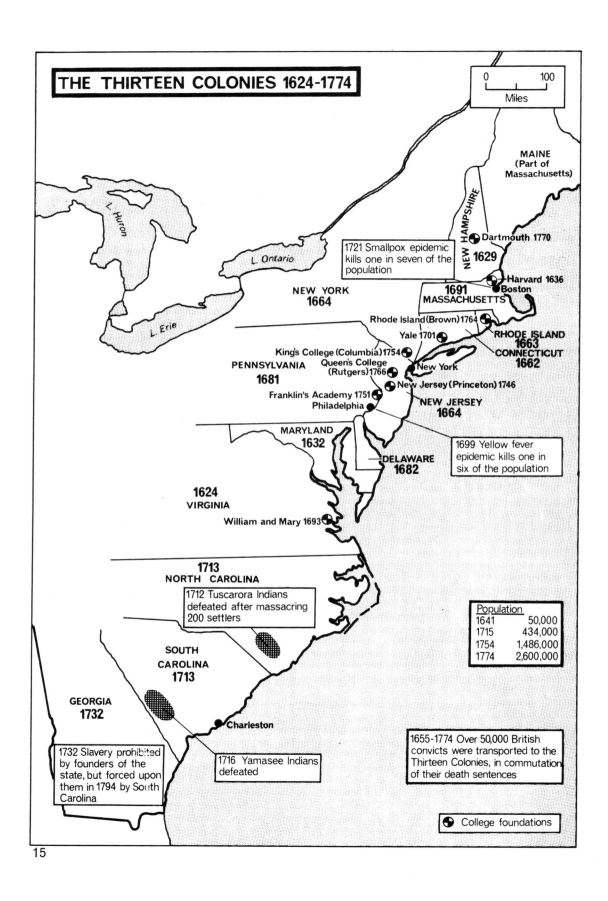

THE THIRTEEN COLONIES 1624-1774

0   100
Miles

L. Huron

L. Ontario

L. Erie

MAINE
(Part of
Massachusetts)

Dartmouth 1770

NEW HAMPSHIRE
1629

1721 Smallpox epidemic
kills one in seven of the
population

NEW YORK
1664

Harvard 1636
Boston

1691
MASSACHUSETTS

Rhode Island (Brown) 1764

Yale 1701

RHODE ISLAND
1663
CONNECTICUT
1662

King's College (Columbia) 1754
Queen's College
(Rutgers) 1766

PENNSYLVANIA
1681

New York

New Jersey (Princeton) 1746

Franklin's Academy 1751
Philadelphia

NEW JERSEY
1664

MARYLAND
1632

DELAWARE
1682

1699 Yellow fever
epidemic kills one in
six of the population

1624
VIRGINIA

William and Mary 1693

1713
NORTH CAROLINA

1712 Tuscarora Indians
defeated after massacring
200 settlers

SOUTH
CAROLINA
1713

Population	
1641	50,000
1715	434,000
1754	1,486,000
1774	2,600,000

GEORGIA
1732

Charleston

1732 Slavery prohibited
by founders of the
state, but forced upon
them in 1794 by South
Carolina

1716 Yamasee Indians
defeated

1655-1774 Over 50,000 British
convicts were transported to the
Thirteen Colonies, in commutation
of their death sentences

College foundations

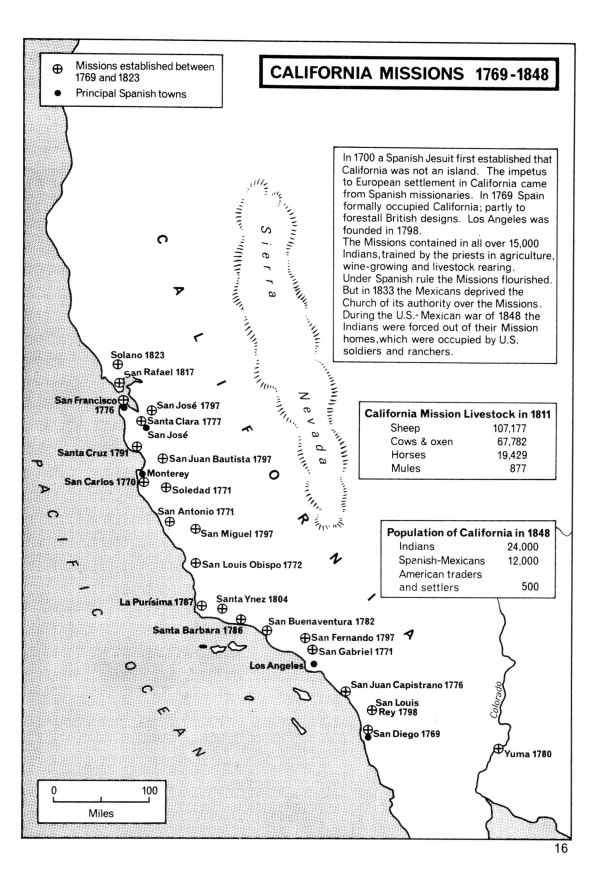

CALIFORNIA MISSIONS 1769-1848

⊕ Missions established between 1769 and 1823

● Principal Spanish towns

In 1700 a Spanish Jesuit first established that California was not an island. The impetus to European settlement in California came from Spanish missionaries. In 1769 Spain formally occupied California; partly to forestall British designs. Los Angeles was founded in 1798.
The Missions contained in all over 15,000 Indians, trained by the priests in agriculture, wine-growing and livestock rearing.
Under Spanish rule the Missions flourished. But in 1833 the Mexicans deprived the Church of its authority over the Missions. During the U.S.-Mexican war of 1848 the Indians were forced out of their Mission homes, which were occupied by U.S. soldiers and ranchers.

California Mission Livestock in 1811

Sheep	107,177
Cows & oxen	67,782
Horses	19,429
Mules	877

Population of California in 1848

Indians	24,000
Spanish-Mexicans	12,000
American traders and settlers	500

Solano 1823
San Rafael 1817
San Francisco 1776
San José 1797
Santa Clara 1777
San José
Santa Cruz 1791
San Juan Bautista 1797
San Carlos 1770
Monterey
Soledad 1771
San Antonio 1771
San Miguel 1797
San Louis Obispo 1772
Santa Ynez 1804
La Purísima 1787
San Buenaventura 1782
Santa Barbara 1786
San Fernando 1797
San Gabriel 1771
Los Angeles
San Juan Capistrano 1776
San Louis Rey 1798
San Diego 1769
Yuma 1780

Sierra Nevada
CALIFORNIA
PACIFIC OCEAN
Colorado

0   100
Miles

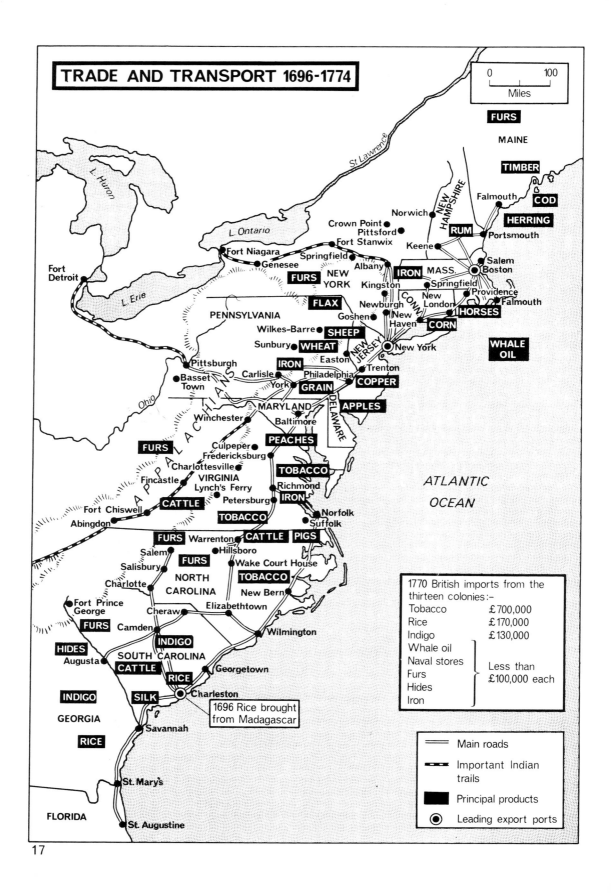

TRADE AND TRANSPORT 1696-1774

0   100
Miles

FURS

MAINE

TIMBER

St.Lawrence

Falmouth

COD

Norwich

HERRING

Crown Point
Pittsford

NEW
HAMPSHIRE

RUM

Portsmouth

Keene

Fort Niagara

L. Ontario

Fort Stanwix

Springfield

Salem
Boston

Fort
Detroit

L. Erie

Genesee

Albany

IRON

MASS.

FURS

NEW
YORK

Kingston

Springfield

Providence

Falmouth

Newburgh

New
London

FLAX

PENNSYLVANIA

Goshen

New
Haven

HORSES

Wilkes-Barre

SHEEP

CORN

Sunbury

WHEAT

NEW
JERSEY

New York

**WHALE
OIL**

Pittsburgh

Easton

Basset
Town

Carlisle

Trenton

Ohio

IRON

Philadelphia

COPPER

York

GRAIN

MARYLAND

Winchester

DELAWARE

APPLES

Baltimore

Culpeper

FURS

PEACHES

Fredericksburg

Charlottesville

TOBACCO

Fincastle

VIRGINIA

Lynch's Ferry

Richmond

**ATLANTIC
OCEAN**

Fort Chiswell

Petersburg

IRON

CATTLE

Abingdon

TOBACCO

Norfolk

Suffolk

FURS

Warrenton

CATTLE

PIGS

Hillsboro

Salem

FURS

Wake Court House

Salisbury

NORTH
CAROLINA

TOBACCO

Charlotte

New Bern

Fort Prince
George

Cheraw

Elizabethtown

FURS

Camden

Wilmington

HIDES

INDIGO

Augusta

SOUTH CAROLINA

CATTLE

Georgetown

RICE

INDIGO

SILK

Charleston

GEORGIA

1696 Rice brought
from Madagascar

RICE

Savannah

St.Mary's

FLORIDA

St. Augustine

1770 British imports from the
thirteen colonies:-
Tobacco   £700,000
Rice   £170,000
Indigo   £130,000
Whale oil
Naval stores
Furs   Less than
Hides   £100,000 each
Iron

Main roads

Important Indian
trails

Principal products

Leading export ports

17

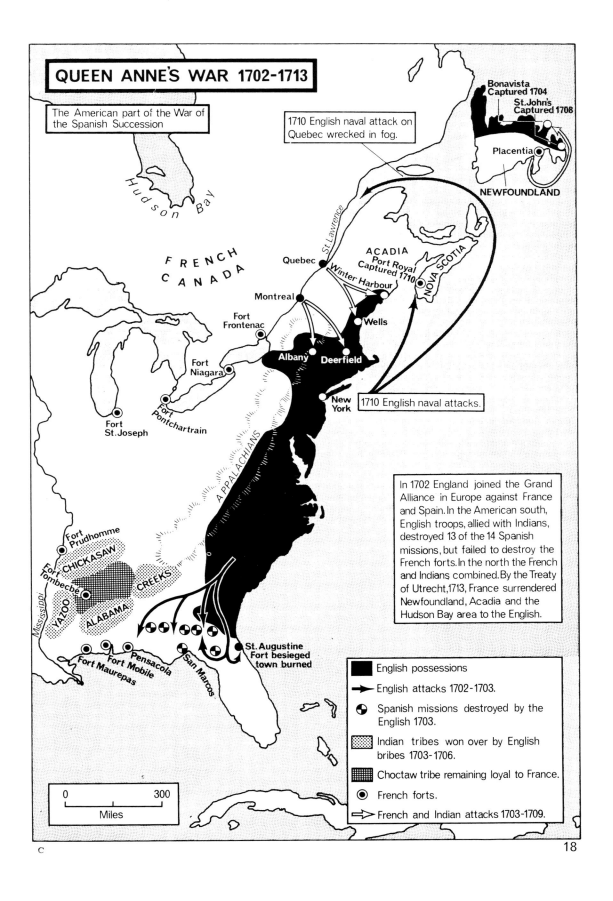

QUEEN ANNE'S WAR 1702-1713

The American part of the War of the Spanish Succession

Bonavista Captured 1704
St.John's Captured 1708
Placentia
NEWFOUNDLAND

1710 English naval attack on Quebec wrecked in fog.

Hudson Bay

F R E N C H
C A N A D A

St. Lawrence

Quebec
ACADIA
Port Royal Captured 1710
Winter Harbour
NOVA SCOTIA

Montreal

Fort Frontenac

Wells

Fort Niagara

Albany Deerfield

Fort St.Joseph

Fort Pontchartrain

A P P A L A C H I A N S

New York

1710 English naval attacks.

In 1702 England joined the Grand Alliance in Europe against France and Spain. In the American south, English troops, allied with Indians, destroyed 13 of the 14 Spanish missions, but failed to destroy the French forts. In the north the French and Indians combined. By the Treaty of Utrecht, 1713, France surrendered Newfoundland, Acadia and the Hudson Bay area to the English.

Fort Prudhomme
CHICKASAW
Fort Tombecbe
CREEKS
YAZOO
ALABAMA

Mississippi

Pensacola
Fort Mobile
Fort Maurepas
San Marcos

St. Augustine Fort besieged town burned

■ English possessions
➔ English attacks 1702-1703.
◕ Spanish missions destroyed by the English 1703.
▨ Indian tribes won over by English bribes 1703-1706.
▦ Choctaw tribe remaining loyal to France.
◉ French forts.
⇨ French and Indian attacks 1703-1709.

0   300
Miles

c

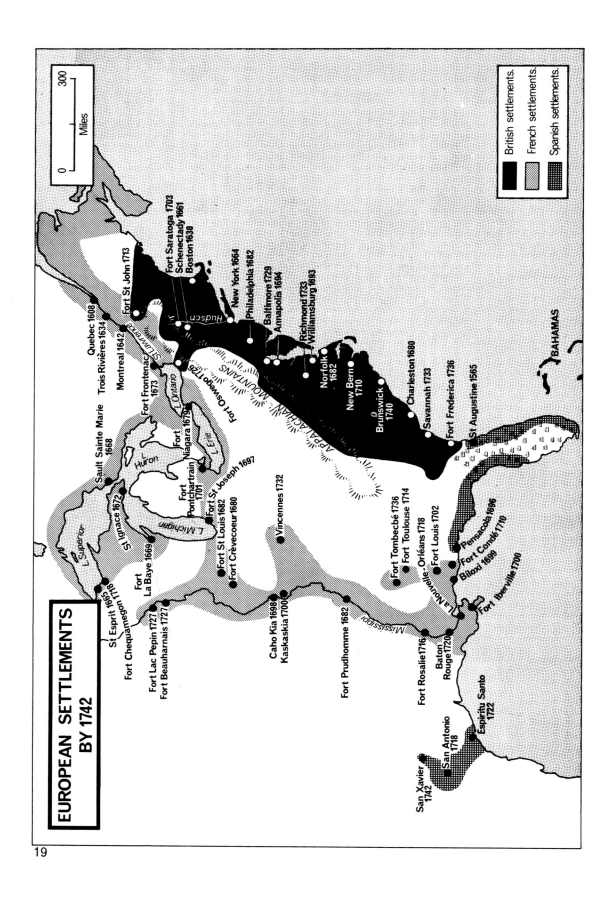

EUROPEAN SETTLEMENTS BY 1742

British settlements.
French settlements.
Spanish settlements.

300 Miles

Quebec 1608
Trois Rivières 1634
Montreal 1642
Fort Frontenac 1673
Fort St John 1713
Fort Saratoga 1703
Schenectady 1661
Boston 1630
New York 1664
Philadelphia 1682
Baltimore 1729
Annapolis 1694
Richmond 1733
Williamsburg 1693
Norfolk 1682
New Bern 1710
Brunswick 1740
Charleston 1680
Savannah 1733
Fort Frederica 1736
St Augustine 1565

Hudson
St Lawrence
L. Ontario
L. Erie
L. Huron
L. Michigan
L. Superior
APPALACHIAN MOUNTAINS
Fort Oswego 1726
Fort Niagara 1679
Sault Sainte Marie 1668
St Ignace 1672
St Esprit 1665
St Chequamegon 1718
Fort La Baye 1669
Fort Lac Pepin 1727
Fort Beauharnais 1727
Fort Pontchartrain 1701
Fort St Joseph 1697
Fort St Louis 1682
Fort Crèvecoeur 1680
Vincennes 1732
Caho Kia 1698
Kaskaskia 1700
Fort Prudhomme 1682
Fort Rosalie 1716
Baton Rouge 1720
Fort Tombecbé 1736
Fort Toulouse 1714
La Nouvelle-Orléans 1718
Fort Louis 1702
Fort Condé 1710
Biloxi 1699
Pensacola 1696
Fort Iberville 1700
Mississippi
Espiritu Santo 1722
San Antonio 1718
San Xavier 1742
BAHAMAS

19

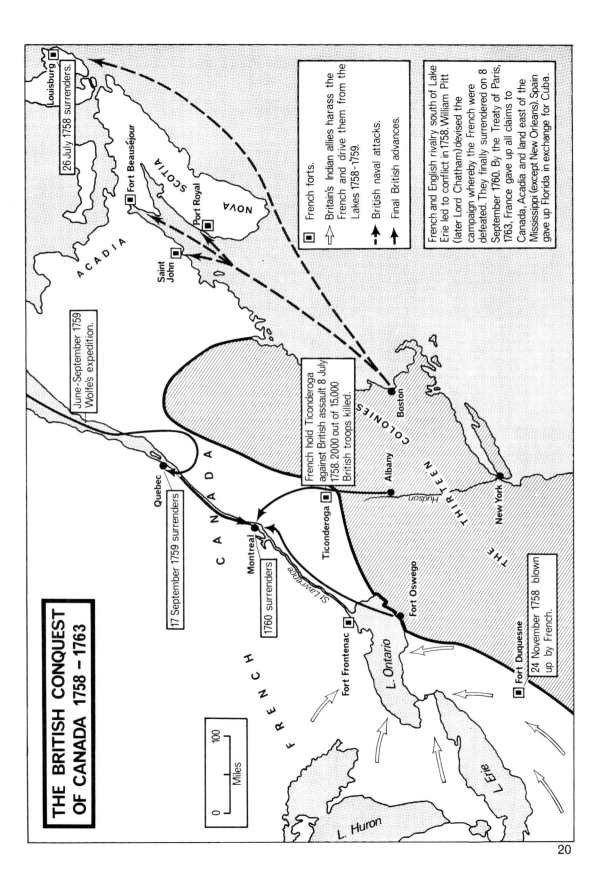

THE BRITISH CONQUEST OF CANADA 1758 – 1763

Louisburg surrenders.
26 July 1758 surrenders.

Fort Beauséjour

Port Royal

NOVA SCOTIA

ACADIA

Saint John

French forts.

Britain's Indian allies harass the French and drive them from the Lakes 1758-1759.

British naval attacks.

Final British advances.

French and English rivalry south of Lake Erie led to conflict in 1758. William Pitt (later Lord Chatham) devised the campaign whereby the French were defeated. They finally surrendered on 8 September 1760. By the Treaty of Paris, 1763, France gave up all claims to Canada. Acadia and land east of the Mississippi (except New Orleans). Spain gave up Florida in exchange for Cuba.

June-September 1759 Wolfe's expedition.

French hold Ticonderoga against British assault 8 July 1758. 2000 out of 15,000 British troops killed.

Boston

Albany

Hudson

THE THIRTEEN COLONIES

New York

CANADA

Quebec
17 September 1759 surrenders

Montreal
1760 surrenders

Ticonderoga

St Lawrence

Fort Oswego

Fort Frontenac

L. Ontario

FRENCH

Fort Duquesne
24 November 1758 blown up by French.

L. Erie

0 100

Miles

L. Huron

20

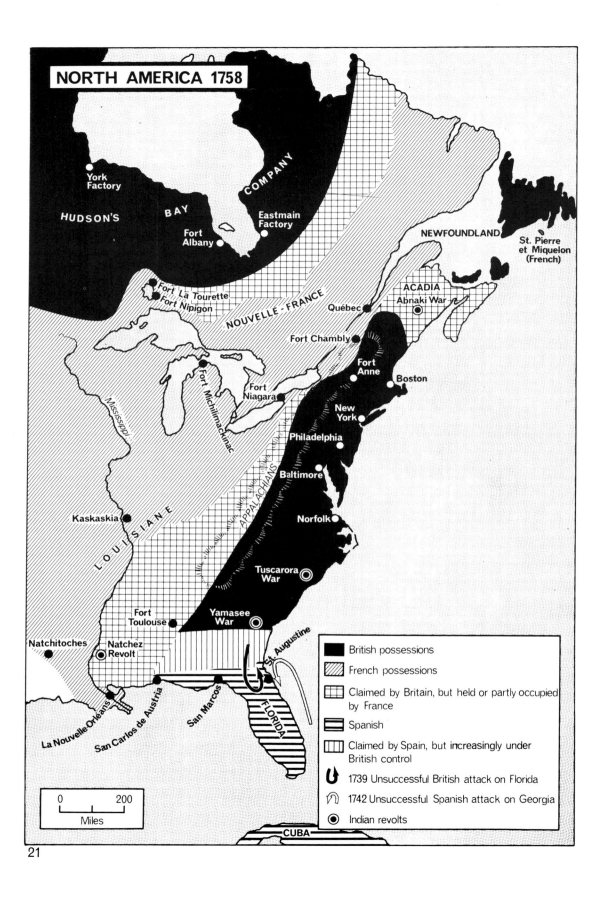

NORTH AMERICA 1758

HUDSON'S BAY COMPANY

York Factory

Fort Albany

Eastmain Factory

NEWFOUNDLAND

St. Pierre et Miquelon (French)

Fort La Tourette

Fort Nipigon

NOUVELLE-FRANCE

ACADIA
Abnaki War

Québec

Fort Chambly

Fort Michilimackinac

Mississippi

Fort Niagara

Fort Anne

Boston

New York

Philadelphia

Baltimore

Kaskaskia

L O U I S I A N E

APPALACHIANS

Norfolk

Tuscarora War

Fort Toulouse

Yamasee War

Natchitoches

Natchez Revolt

La Nouvelle Orléans

San Carlos de Austria

San Marcos

St. Augustine

FLORIDA

0   200
Miles

CUBA

Legend:

■ British possessions

▨ French possessions

▦ Claimed by Britain, but held or partly occupied by France

▤ Spanish

▥ Claimed by Spain, but increasingly under British control

↺ 1739 Unsuccessful British attack on Florida

⌂ 1742 Unsuccessful Spanish attack on Georgia

◉ Indian revolts

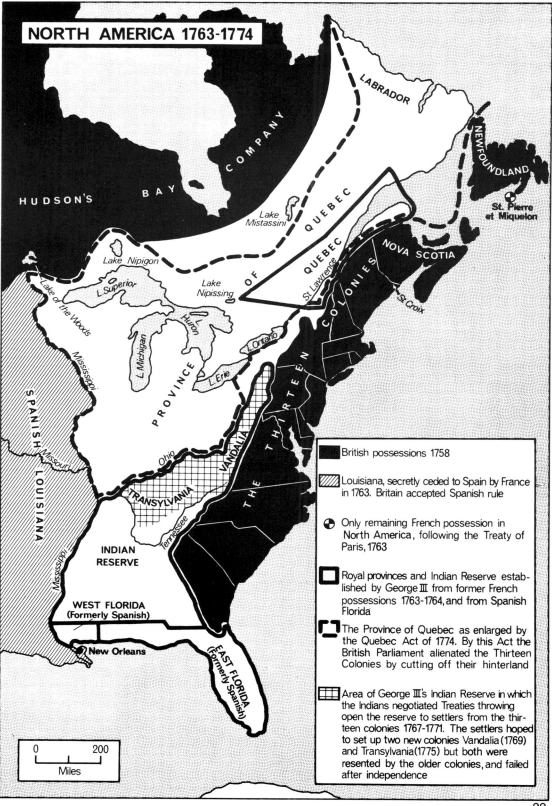

NORTH AMERICA 1763-1774

LABRADOR

HUDSON'S BAY COMPANY

NEWFOUNDLAND

St. Pierre et Miquelon

Lake Mistassini

PROVINCE OF QUEBEC

QUEBEC

St. Lawrence

NOVA SCOTIA

St. Croix

Lake Nipigon

Lake Nipissing

L. Superior

L. Michigan

L. Huron

L. Ontario

L. Erie

Lake of the Woods

Mississippi

Missouri

SPANISH LOUISIANA

Ohio

VANDALIA

TRANSYLVANIA

Tennessee

THE THIRTEEN COLONIES

INDIAN RESERVE

WEST FLORIDA (Formerly Spanish)

Mississippi

New Orleans

EAST FLORIDA (Formerly Spanish)

0   200
Miles

British possessions 1758

Louisiana, secretly ceded to Spain by France in 1763. Britain accepted Spanish rule

Only remaining French possession in North America, following the Treaty of Paris, 1763

Royal provinces and Indian Reserve established by George III from former French possessions 1763-1764, and from Spanish Florida

The Province of Quebec as enlarged by the Quebec Act of 1774. By this Act the British Parliament alienated the Thirteen Colonies by cutting off their hinterland

Area of George III's Indian Reserve in which the Indians negotiated Treaties throwing open the reserve to settlers from the thirteen colonies 1767-1771. The settlers hoped to set up two new colonies Vandalia (1769) and Transylvania (1775) but both were resented by the older colonies, and failed after independence

22

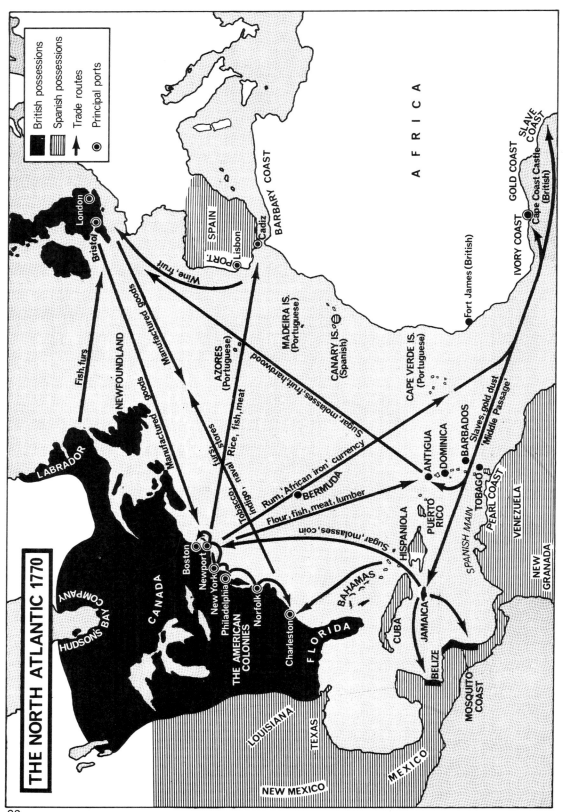

THE NORTH ATLANTIC 1770

British possessions
Spanish possessions
Trade routes
Principal ports

AFRICA

SLAVE COAST
GOLD COAST
Cape Coast Castle (British)
IVORY COAST
Fort James (British)

BARBARY COAST
SPAIN
PORT.
Lisbon
Cadiz

London
Bristol

Wine, fruit

Manufactured goods
Manufactured goods

NEWFOUNDLAND

Fish, furs

LABRADOR

HUDSON'S BAY COMPANY

CANADA

AZORES (Portuguese)

MADEIRA IS. (Portuguese)
CANARY IS. (Spanish)
CAPE VERDE IS. (Portuguese)

furs, naval stores
Tobacco, Rice, fish, meat
indigo, naval stores
Sugar, molasses, fruit, hardwood

Rum, 'African iron' currency

Boston
Newport
New York
Philadelphia
Norfolk
Charleston

THE AMERICAN COLONIES

FLORIDA

BERMUDA

Flour, fish, meat, lumber

Sugar, molasses, coin

BAHAMAS
CUBA
JAMAICA
BELIZE
HISPANIOLA
PUERTO RICO
ANTIGUA
DOMINICA
BARBADOS
TOBAGO
PEARL COAST

Slaves, gold dust
'Middle Passage'

SPANISH MAIN

VENEZUELA
NEW GRANADA

MOSQUITO COAST

LOUISIANA
TEXAS
MEXICO
NEW MEXICO

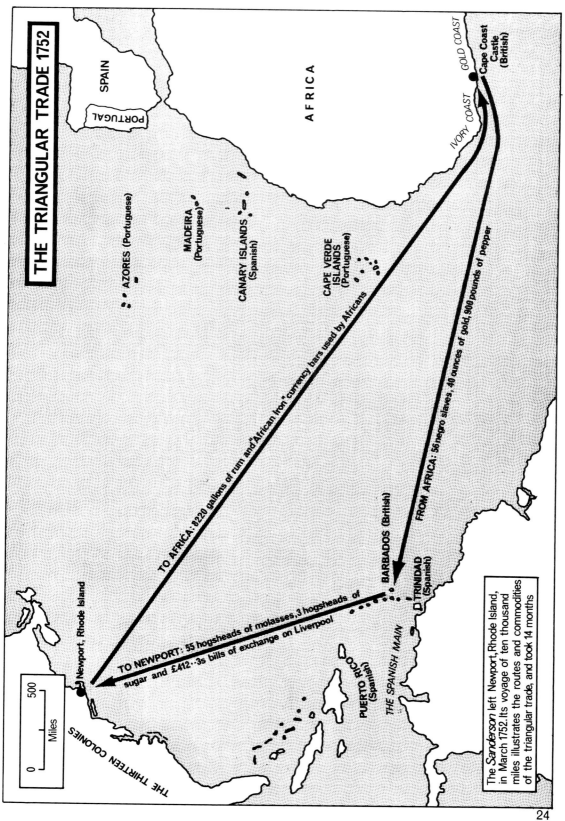

THE TRIANGULAR TRADE 1752

SPAIN

PORTUGAL

AFRICA

GOLD COAST

Cape Coast Castle (British)

IVORY COAST

AZORES (Portuguese)

MADEIRA (Portuguese)

CANARY ISLANDS (Spanish)

CAPE VERDE ISLANDS (Portuguese)

TO AFRICA: 8220 gallons of rum and "African Iron" currency bars used by Africans

FROM AFRICA: 56 negro slaves, 40 ounces of gold, 900 pounds of pepper

BARBADOS (British)

TRINIDAD (Spanish)

Newport, Rhode Island

TO NEWPORT: 55 hogsheads of molasses, 3 hogsheads of sugar and £412··3s bills of exchange on Liverpool

PUERTO RICO (Spanish)

THE SPANISH MAIN

THE THIRTEEN COLONIES

Miles
0   500

The *Sanderson* left Newport, Rhode Island, in March 1752. Its voyage of ten thousand miles illustrates the routes and commodities of the triangular trade, and took 14 months

24

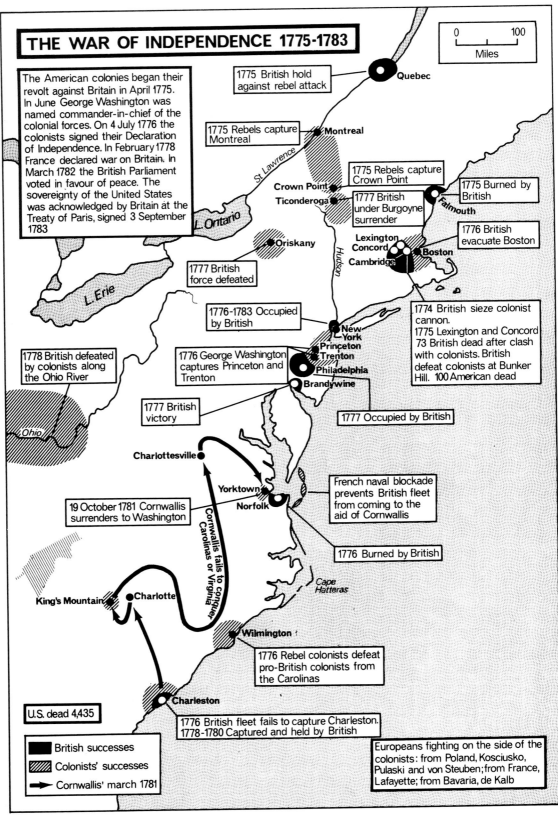

THE WAR OF INDEPENDENCE 1775-1783

The American colonies began their revolt against Britain in April 1775. In June George Washington was named commander-in-chief of the colonial forces. On 4 July 1776 the colonists signed their Declaration of Independence. In February 1778 France declared war on Britain. In March 1782 the British Parliament voted in favour of peace. The sovereignty of the United States was acknowledged by Britain at the Treaty of Paris, signed 3 September 1783

0   100
Miles

1775 British hold against rebel attack

Quebec

1775 Rebels capture Montreal

Montreal

1775 Rebels capture Crown Point

Crown Point

Ticonderoga

1777 British under Burgoyne surrender

1775 Burned by British

Falmouth

1776 British evacuate Boston

Lexington
Concord
Cambridge

Boston

L. Ontario

Oriskany

1777 British force defeated

Hudson

L. Erie

1776-1783 Occupied by British

New York
Princeton
Trenton
Philadelphia

1774 British sieze colonist cannon.
1775 Lexington and Concord 73 British dead after clash with colonists. British defeat colonists at Bunker Hill. 100 American dead

1778 British defeated by colonists along the Ohio River

1776 George Washington captures Princeton and Trenton

Brandywine

1777 British victory

1777 Occupied by British

Ohio

Charlottesville

Yorktown
Norfolk

French naval blockade prevents British fleet from coming to the aid of Cornwallis

19 October 1781 Cornwallis surrenders to Washington

Cornwallis fails to conquer Carolinas or Virginia

1776 Burned by British

Cape Hatteras

King's Mountain

Charlotte

Wilmington

1776 Rebel colonists defeat pro-British colonists from the Carolinas

U.S. dead 4,435

Charleston

1776 British fleet fails to capture Charleston.
1778-1780 Captured and held by British

■ British successes
▨ Colonists' successes
→ Cornwallis' march 1781

Europeans fighting on the side of the colonists: from Poland, Kosciusko, Pulaski and von Steuben; from France, Lafayette; from Bavaria, de Kalb

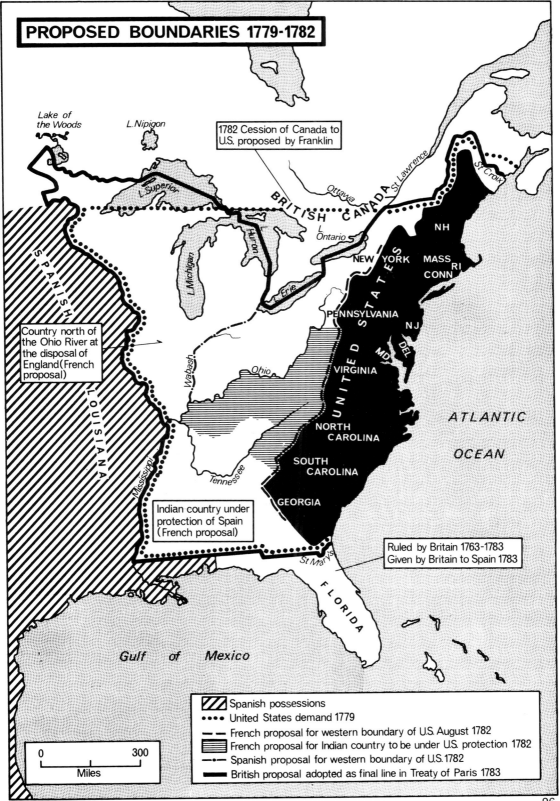

PROPOSED BOUNDARIES 1779-1782

Lake of the Woods

L. Nipigon

1782 Cession of Canada to U.S. proposed by Franklin

Ottawa

St. Lawrence

BRITISH CANADA

St. Croix

L. Superior

L. Huron

L. Michigan

L. Ontario

Erie

NEW YORK

NH

MASS

RI

CONN

Country north of the Ohio River at the disposal of England (French proposal)

SPANISH LOUISIANA

PENNSYLVANIA

NJ

DEL

MD

VIRGINIA

Wabash

Ohio

UNITED STATES

NORTH CAROLINA

Tennessee

Mississippi

Indian country under protection of Spain (French proposal)

SOUTH CAROLINA

GEORGIA

ATLANTIC

OCEAN

Ruled by Britain 1763-1783 Given by Britain to Spain 1783

St. Mary's

FLORIDA

Gulf of Mexico

Spanish possessions
United States demand 1779
French proposal for western boundary of U.S. August 1782
French proposal for Indian country to be under U.S. protection 1782
Spanish proposal for western boundary of U.S. 1782
British proposal adopted as final line in Treaty of Paris 1783

0   300
Miles

26

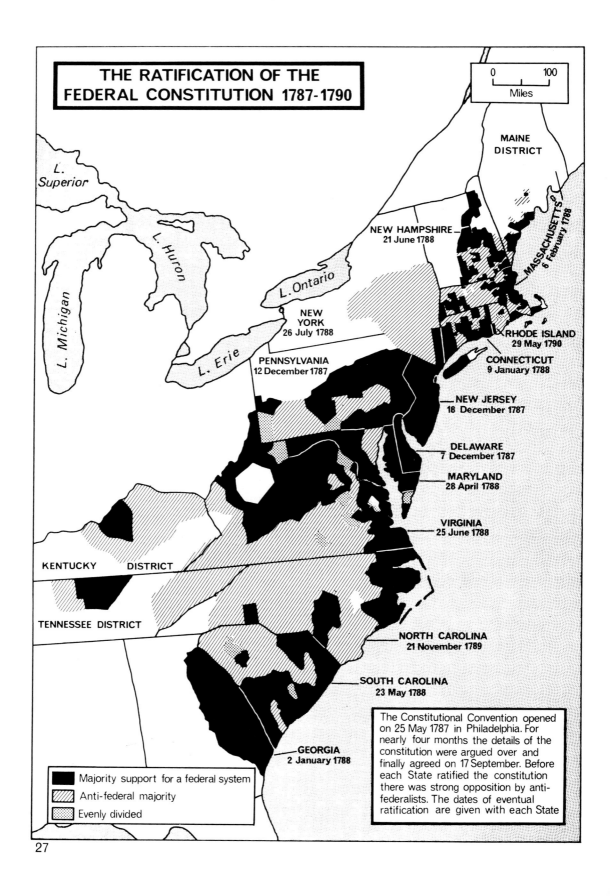

THE RATIFICATION OF THE FEDERAL CONSTITUTION 1787-1790

0 ___ 100
Miles

L. Superior

L. Huron

L. Michigan

L. Ontario

L. Erie

MAINE DISTRICT

NEW HAMPSHIRE
21 June 1788

MASSACHUSETTS
6 February 1788

NEW YORK
26 July 1788

RHODE ISLAND
29 May 1790

CONNECTICUT
9 January 1788

PENNSYLVANIA
12 December 1787

NEW JERSEY
18 December 1787

DELAWARE
7 December 1787

MARYLAND
28 April 1788

VIRGINIA
25 June 1788

KENTUCKY   DISTRICT

TENNESSEE DISTRICT

NORTH CAROLINA
21 November 1789

SOUTH CAROLINA
23 May 1788

GEORGIA
2 January 1788

■ Majority support for a federal system
▨ Anti-federal majority
▦ Evenly divided

The Constitutional Convention opened on 25 May 1787 in Philadelphia. For nearly four months the details of the constitution were argued over and finally agreed on 17 September. Before each State ratified the constitution there was strong opposition by anti-federalists. The dates of eventual ratification are given with each State

27

NORTH AMERICA 1783

Legend:
- The United States of America.
- British claims not finally ceded to U.S. until the Jay Treaty of 1795.
- British possessions.
- Spanish possessions.
- Disputed and unsettled frontiers

ALASKA

Kodiak

1784 Russian settlement founded

UNEXPLORED

TERRITORY

Northern limit of Spanish claims

Columbia

Snake

CALIFORNIA

Rio Grande

TEXAS

MEXICO

BAFFIN LAND

HUDSON BAY

NEW SOUTH WALES

NEW BRITAIN

LABRADOR

NEWFOUNDLAND

CANADA

ACADIA

NOVA SCOTIA

Mississippi

THE UNITED STATES

FLORIDA

BAHAMAS

CUBA

JAMAICA

BELIZE

MOSQUITO COAST

PANAMA

By the Treaty of Paris, 3 September 1783, Britain recognised the independence of the United States, withdrew all military and naval forces, agreed to fix the boundary of Canada by negotiation, and returned Florida to Spain.

0   1000
Miles

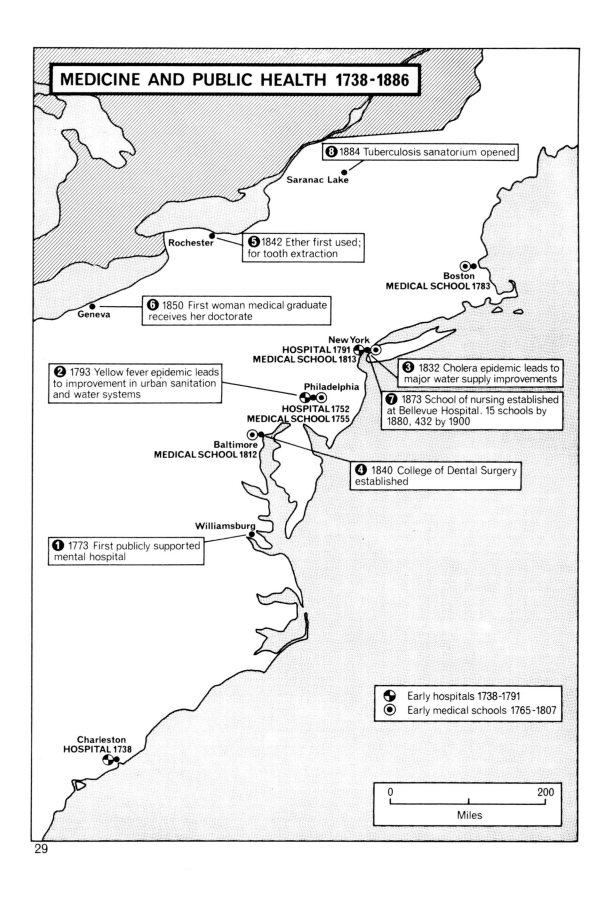

MEDICINE AND PUBLIC HEALTH 1738-1886

8 1884 Tuberculosis sanatorium opened

Saranac Lake

5 1842 Ether first used; for tooth extraction

Rochester

Boston
MEDICAL SCHOOL 1783

6 1850 First woman medical graduate receives her doctorate

Geneva

New York
HOSPITAL 1791
MEDICAL SCHOOL 1813

2 1793 Yellow fever epidemic leads to improvement in urban sanitation and water systems

3 1832 Cholera epidemic leads to major water supply improvements

Philadelphia
HOSPITAL 1752
MEDICAL SCHOOL 1755

7 1873 School of nursing established at Bellevue Hospital. 15 schools by 1880, 432 by 1900

Baltimore
MEDICAL SCHOOL 1812

4 1840 College of Dental Surgery established

Williamsburg

1 1773 First publicly supported mental hospital

Charleston
HOSPITAL 1738

Early hospitals 1738-1791
Early medical schools 1765-1807

0	200

Miles

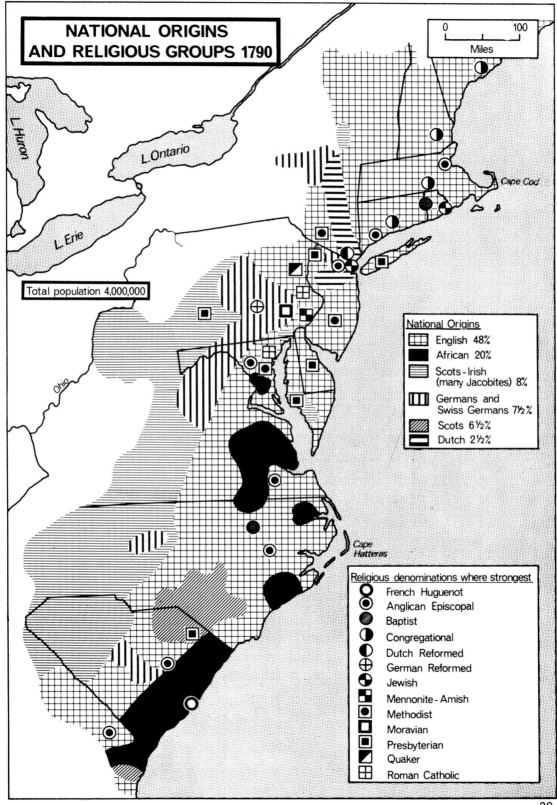

NATIONAL ORIGINS AND RELIGIOUS GROUPS 1790

0   100
Miles

L.Huron

L.Ontario

L. Erie

Ohio

Total population 4,000,000

Cape Cod

Cape Hatteras

National Origins
▦	English 48%
■	African 20%
▤	Scots - Irish (many Jacobites) 8%
▥	Germans and Swiss Germans 7½%
▨	Scots 6½%
▭	Dutch 2½%

Religious denominations where strongest
◯	French Huguenot
◉	Anglican Episcopal
◍	Baptist
◐	Congregational
◑	Dutch Reformed
⊕	German Reformed
⊞	Jewish
▣	Mennonite - Amish
⊡	Methodist
□	Moravian
▪	Presbyterian
◪	Quaker
⊞	Roman Catholic

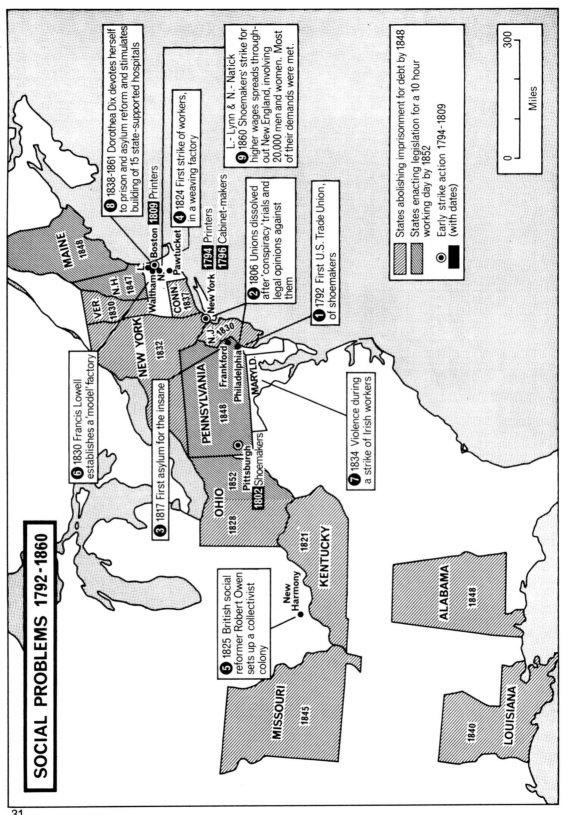

SOCIAL PROBLEMS 1792-1860

8 1838-1861 Dorothea Dix devotes herself to prison and asylum reform and stimulates building of 15 state-supported hospitals

1809 Printers

4 1824 First strike of workers, in a weaving factory

L - Lynn & N - Natick

9 1860 Shoemakers' strike for higher wages spreads throughout New England, involving 20,000 men and women. Most of their demands were met.

MAINE 1848

Boston
Waltham
Pawtucket

L.
N.

N.H. 1847

VER 1830

CONN 1837

Printers **1794**
Cabinet-makers **1796**

2 1806 Unions dissolved after 'conspiracy' trials and legal opinions against them

New York

1 1792 First U.S. Trade Union, of shoemakers

6 1830 Francis Lowell establishes a 'model' factory

NEW YORK 1832

3 1817 First asylum for the insane

N.J. 1830

Frankford

PENNSYLVANIA 1848

Philadelphia

MARYLD.

Shoemakers

Pittsburgh **1802**

OHIO 1828

1852

7 1834 Violence during a strike of Irish workers

5 1825 British social reformer Robert Owen sets up a collectivist colony

New Harmony

KENTUCKY 1821

MISSOURI 1845

ALABAMA 1848

LOUISIANA 1840

States abolishing imprisonment for debt by 1848

States enacting legislation for a 10 hour working day by 1852

Early strike action 1794-1809 (with dates)

0   300
Miles

31

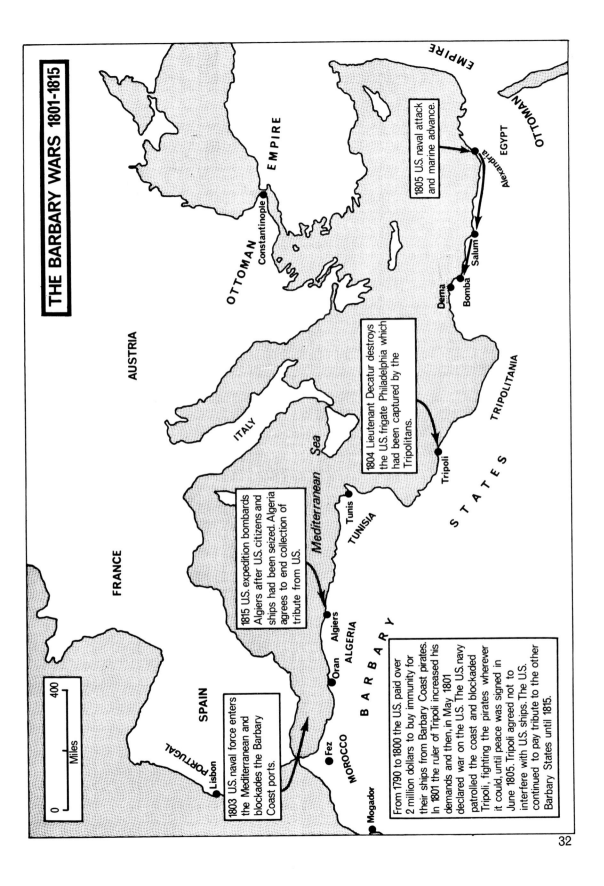

THE BARBARY WARS 1801-1815

OTTOMAN EMPIRE

OTTOMAN EMPIRE

Constantinople

AUSTRIA

FRANCE

SPAIN

PORTUGAL

Lisbon

ITALY

Mediterranean Sea

MOROCCO

Fez

Mogador

B A R B A R Y

ALGERIA

Oran

Algiers

TUNISIA

Tunis

S T A T E S

Tripoli

TRIPOLITANIA

Derna

Bomba

Salum

Alexandria

EGYPT

1805 U.S. naval attack and marine advance.

1804 Lieutenant Decatur destroys the U.S. frigate Philadelphia which had been captured by the Tripolitans.

1815 U.S. expedition bombards Algiers after U.S. citizens and ships had been seized. Algeria agrees to end collection of tribute from U.S.

1803 U.S. naval force enters the Mediterranean and blockades the Barbary Coast ports.

From 1790 to 1800 the U.S. paid over 2 million dollars to buy immunity for their ships from Barbary Coast pirates. In 1801 the ruler of Tripoli increased his demands and then, in May 1801 declared war on the U.S. The U.S. navy patrolled the coast and blockaded Tripoli, fighting the pirates wherever it could, until peace was signed in June 1805. Tripoli agreed not to interfere with U.S. ships. The U.S. continued to pay tribute to the other Barbary States until 1815.

Miles

0   400

32

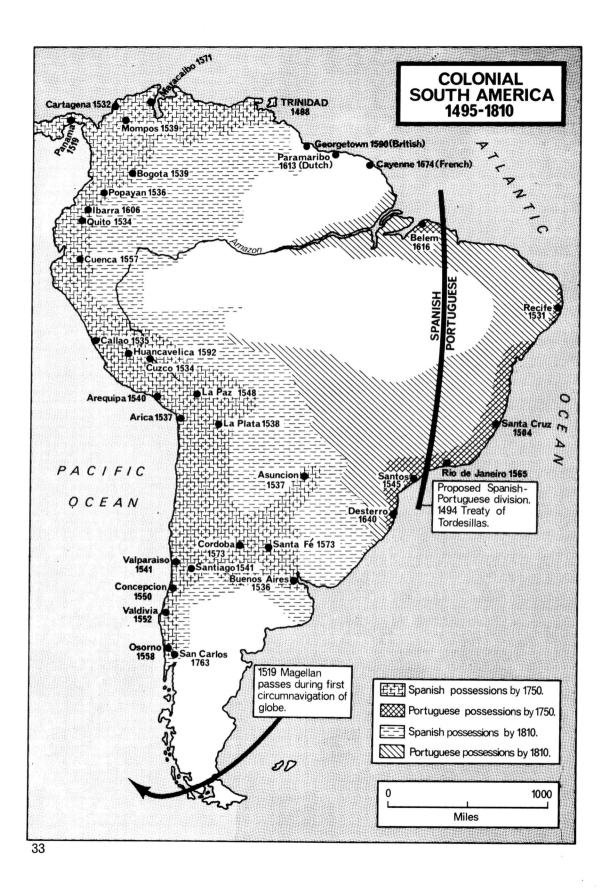

COLONIAL
SOUTH AMERICA
1495-1810

Cartagena 1532

Maracaibo 1571

TRINIDAD
1488

Mompos 1539

Georgetown 1590 (British)

Paramaribo
1613 (Dutch)

Cayenne 1674 (French)

Panama
1519

Bogota 1539

Popayan 1536

Ibarra 1606
Quito 1534

Amazon

Belem
1616

Cuenca 1557

Recife
1531

SPANISH

PORTUGUESE

Callao 1535
Huancavelica 1592
Cuzco 1534

La Paz 1548

Arequipa 1540

Arica 1537

La Plata 1538

Santa Cruz
1504

PACIFIC

OCEAN

Asuncion
1537

Santos
1545

Rio de Janeiro 1565

Desterro
1640

Proposed Spanish-
Portuguese division.
1494 Treaty of
Tordesillas.

Cordoba
1573

Santa Fé 1573

Valparaiso
1541

Santiago 1541

Concepcion
1550

Buenos Aires
1536

Valdivia
1552

Osorno
1558

San Carlos
1763

1519 Magellan
passes during first
circumnavigation of
globe.

ATLANTIC

OCEAN

Spanish possessions by 1750.

Portuguese possessions by 1750.

Spanish possessions by 1810.

Portuguese possessions by 1810.

0   1000

Miles

INDEPENDENT SOUTH AMERICA 1810-1938

PANAMA

COLOMBIA

VENEZUELA

1811-1821 War against Spain

1811-1821 War against Spain. 1831-1861 Civil War. 1903 Secession of Panama

1822 Joins Colombia. 1830 Independent

ECUADOR

TRINIDAD (British)

BRITISH

DUTCH

FRENCH

GUIANA

Amazon

PERU

1821 Independent from Spain. 1864-1866 War against Spain

BOLIVIA

1809-1825 War against Spain. 1825 Independent. 1879-1883 War against Chile

BRAZIL

1820 Revolution against Portuguese rule. 1822 Independent Empire. 1865-1870 War against Paraguay. 1888 Emancipation of 700,000 slaves. 1889 Republic

1811 Independent from Spain

PARAGUAY

1810-1818 Civil War. 1818 Independent from Spain

CHILE

ARGENTINA

1810 Independent from Spain. 1843-1851 War against Uruguay. 1865-1870 War against Paraguay

URUGUAY

Montevideo

1810-1830 War against Portugal. 1843-1851 Argentina besieges Montevideo

Land gained after frontier disputes

European possessions

Falkland Islands

1833 British. Claimed by Argentina

0   1000

Miles

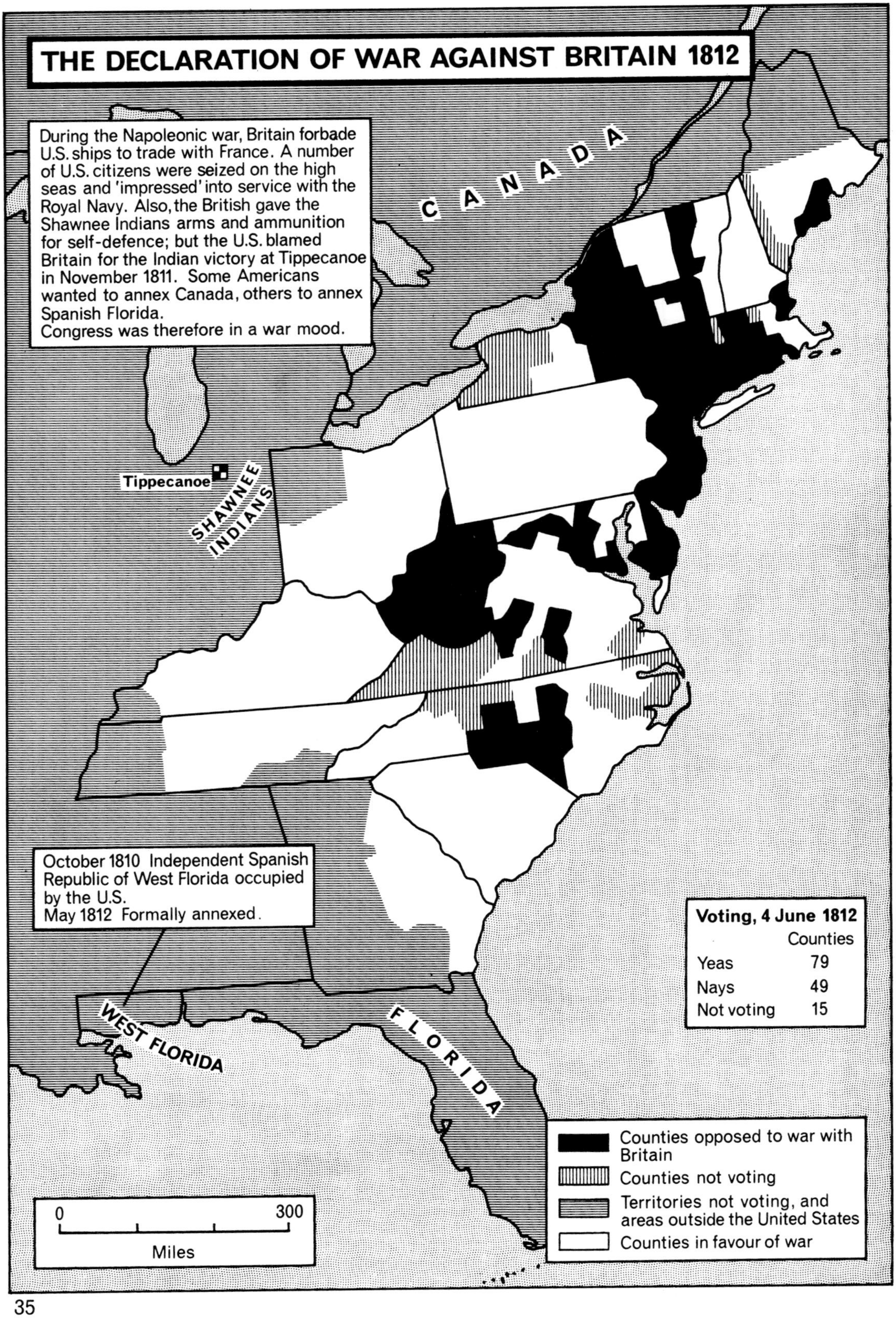

THE DECLARATION OF WAR AGAINST BRITAIN 1812

During the Napoleonic war, Britain forbade U.S. ships to trade with France. A number of U.S. citizens were seized on the high seas and 'impressed' into service with the Royal Navy. Also, the British gave the Shawnee Indians arms and ammunition for self-defence; but the U.S. blamed Britain for the Indian victory at Tippecanoe in November 1811. Some Americans wanted to annex Canada, others to annex Spanish Florida.
Congress was therefore in a war mood.

CANADA

Tippecanoe

SHAWNEE INDIANS

October 1810 Independent Spanish Republic of West Florida occupied by the U.S.
May 1812 Formally annexed.

WEST FLORIDA

FLORIDA

Voting, 4 June 1812

	Counties
Yeas	79
Nays	49
Not voting	15

■ Counties opposed to war with Britain
▨ Counties not voting
▨ Territories not voting, and areas outside the United States
□ Counties in favour of war

0 _____ 300
Miles

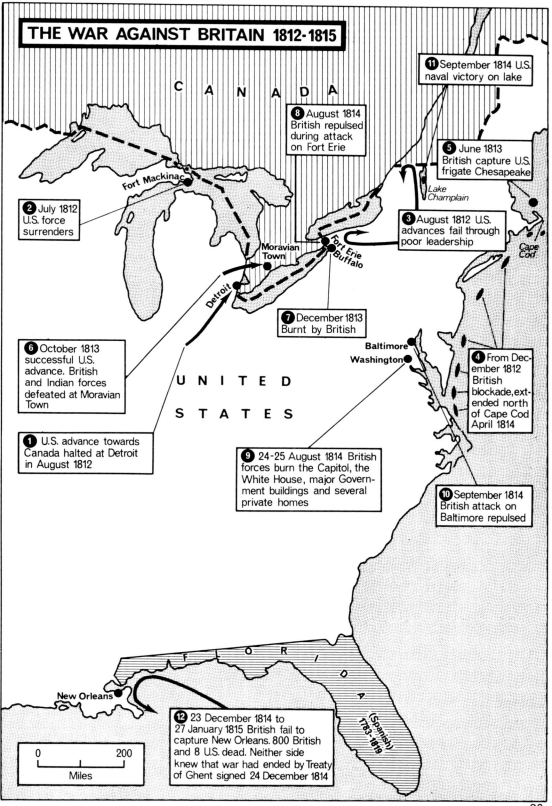

THE WAR AGAINST BRITAIN 1812-1815

C A N A D A

11 September 1814 U.S. naval victory on lake

8 August 1814 British repulsed during attack on Fort Erie

5 June 1813 British capture U.S. frigate Chesapeake

Fort Mackinac

2 July 1812 U.S. force surrenders

Lake Champlain

3 August 1812 U.S. advances fail through poor leadership

Cape Cod

Moravian Town

Fort Erie
Buffalo

Detroit

7 December 1813 Burnt by British

6 October 1813 successful U.S. advance. British and Indian forces defeated at Moravian Town

Baltimore
Washington

4 From December 1812 British blockade, extended north of Cape Cod April 1814

U N I T E D

S T A T E S

1 U.S. advance towards Canada halted at Detroit in August 1812

9 24-25 August 1814 British forces burn the Capitol, the White House, major Government buildings and several private homes

10 September 1814 British attack on Baltimore repulsed

F L O R I D A

(Spanish) 1783-1819

New Orleans

12 23 December 1814 to 27 January 1815 British fail to capture New Orleans. 800 British and 8 U.S. dead. Neither side knew that war had ended by Treaty of Ghent signed 24 December 1814

0   200
Miles

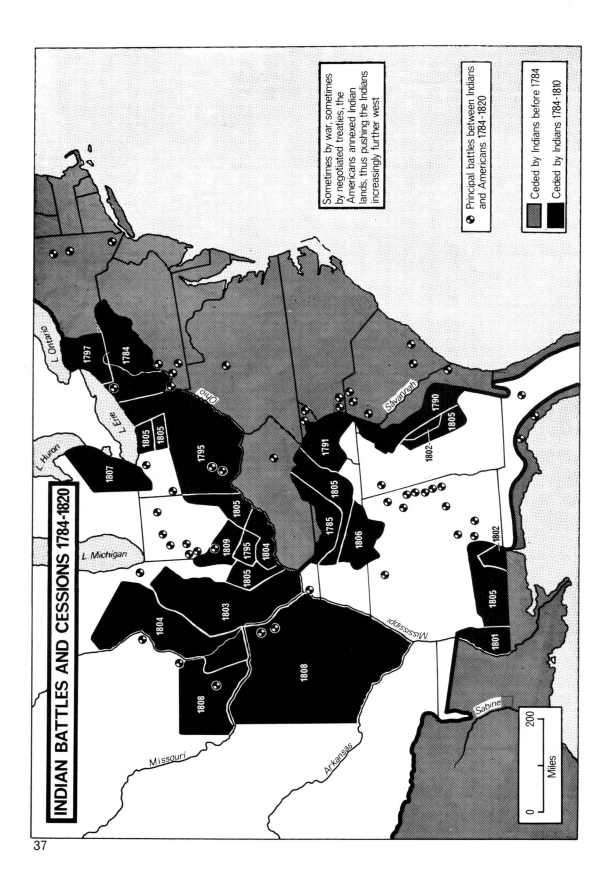

INDIAN BATTLES AND CESSIONS 1784-1820

Sometimes by war, sometimes by negotiated treaties, the Americans annexed Indian lands, thus pushing the Indians increasingly further west

⊕ Principal battles between Indians and Americans 1784-1820

Ceded by Indians before 1784

Ceded by Indians 1784-1810

L. Ontario

L. Erie

L. Huron

L. Michigan

Ohio

Savannah

Mississippi

Missouri

Arkansas

Sabine

1797
1784
1807
1795
1805
1805
1805
1809
1795
1804
1805
1803
1804
1808
1808
1791
1785
1805
1806
1802
1790
1805
1805
1801
1802

0   200
Miles

37

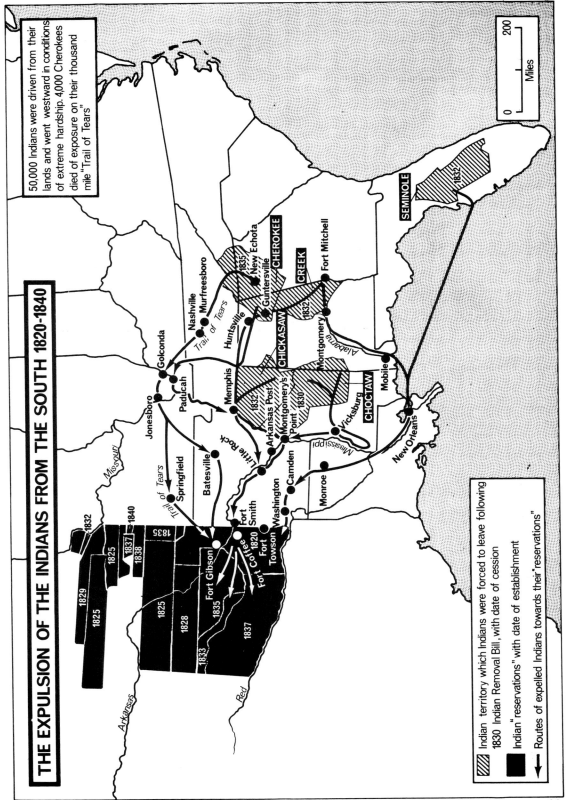

THE EXPULSION OF THE INDIANS FROM THE SOUTH 1820-1840

50,000 Indians were driven from their lands and went westward in conditions of extreme hardship. 4,000 Cherokees died of exposure on their thousand mile "Trail of Tears"

200

Miles

0

SEMINOLE

1832

CHEROKEE

New Echota

1835

Guntersville

Murfreesboro

Nashville

Huntsville

CREEK

Fort Mitchell

1832

CHICKASAW

Montgomery

Trail of Tears

Memphis

Alabama

CHOCTAW

1830

Vicksburg

Mobile

Montgomery's
Point

1832

Arkansas Post

Paducah

Golconda

Mississippi

New Orleans

Jonesboro

Little Rock

Camden

Batesville

Monroe

Springfield

Washington

Trail of Tears

Fort
Smith

Missouri

1832

1840

Fort Gibson

Fort Coffee

1820

Fort
Towson

1835

1825

1837

1838

1829

1825

1828

1825

1835

1833

1837

Red

Arkansas

Indian territory which Indians were forced to leave following 1830 Indian Removal Bill, with date of cession

Indian "reservations" with date of establishment

Routes of expelled Indians towards their "reservations"

38

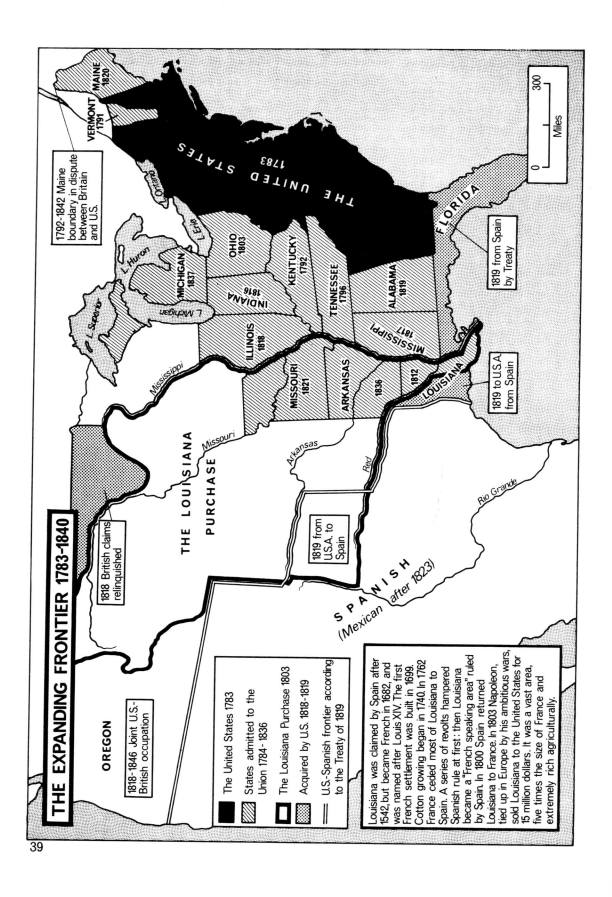

THE EXPANDING FRONTIER 1783-1840

THE UNITED STATES 1783

1792-1842 Maine boundary in dispute between Britain and U.S.

MAINE 1820

VERMONT 1791

MICHIGAN 1837

OHIO 1803

KENTUCKY 1792

INDIANA 1816

TENNESSEE 1796

ILLINOIS 1818

ALABAMA 1819

MISSISSIPPI 1817

MISSOURI 1821

ARKANSAS 1836

1836

1812

LOUISIANA

FLORIDA

1819 from Spain by Treaty

1819 to U.S.A from Spain

L. Superior

L. Huron

L. Michigan

L. Ontario

L. Erie

Mississippi

Missouri

Arkansas

Red

Rio Grande

THE LOUISIANA PURCHASE

1819 from U.S.A. to Spain

1818 British claims relinquished

SPANISH
(Mexican after 1823)

OREGON

1818-1846 Joint U.S.-British occupation

The United States 1783

States admitted to the Union 1784-1836

The Louisiana Purchase 1803

Acquired by U.S. 1818-1819

U.S.-Spanish frontier according to the Treaty of 1819

Louisiana was claimed by Spain after 1542, but became French in 1682, and was named after Louis XIV. The first French settlement was built in 1699. Cotton growing began in 1740. In 1762 France ceded most of Louisiana to Spain. A series of revolts hampered Spanish rule at first: then Louisiana became a "French speaking area" ruled by Spain. In 1800 Spain returned Louisiana to France. In 1803 Napoleon, tied up in Europe by his ambitious wars, sold Louisiana to the United States for 15 million dollars. It was a vast area, five times the size of France and extremely rich agriculturally.

0 300
Miles

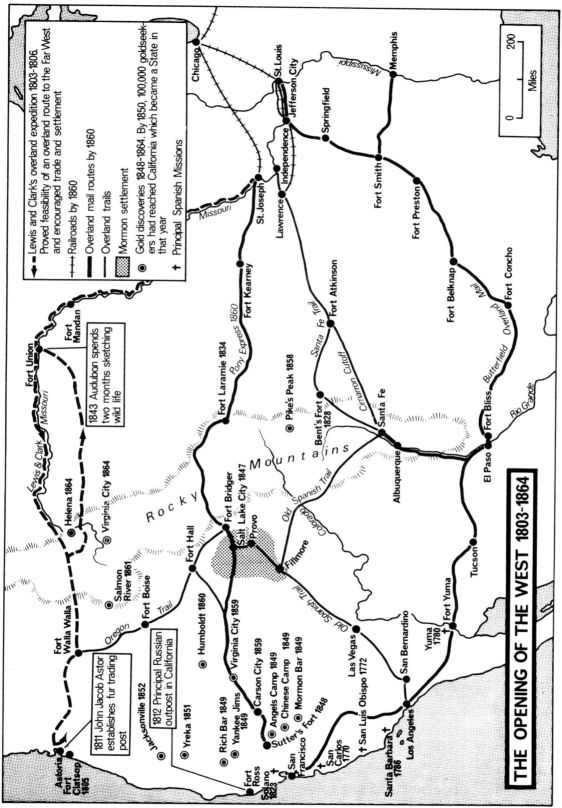

THE OPENING OF THE WEST 1803-1864

Legend:
- Lewis and Clark's overland expedition 1803-1806.
- Proved feasibility of an overland route to the Far West and encouraged trade and settlement
- Railroads by 1860
- Overland mail routes by 1860
- Overland trails
- Mormon settlement
- Gold discoveries 1848-1864. By 1850, 100,000 goldseekers had reached California which became a State in that year
- Principal Spanish Missions

1843 Audubon spends two months sketching wild life

1811 John Jacob Astor establishes fur trading post

1812 Principal Russian outpost in California

Fort Union
Fort Mandan
Helena 1864
Virginia City 1864
Salmon River 1861
Fort Boise
Fort Walla Walla
Astoria Fort Clatsop 1805
Jacksonville 1852
Yreka 1851
Rich Bar 1849
Yankee Jims 1849
Angels Camp 1849
Chinese Camp 1849
Mormon Bar 1849
Sutter's Fort 1848
San Francisco
Fort Ross
Solano 1823
Humboldt 1860
Virginia City 1859
Carson City 1859
San Carlos 1770
San Luis Obispo 1772
Santa Barbara 1786
Los Angeles
San Bernardino
Las Vegas
Yuma 1780
Fort Yuma
Tucson
Fort Hall
Fort Bridger
Salt Lake City 1847
Provo
Fillmore
Rocky Mountains
Pike's Peak 1858
Bent's Fort 1828
Santa Fe
Albuquerque
El Paso
Fort Bliss
Fort Concho
Fort Belknap
Fort Preston
Fort Smith
Fort Atkinson
Fort Kearney
Fort Laramie 1834
Lawrence
St. Joseph
Independence
Jefferson City
St. Louis
Springfield
Chicago
Memphis

Lewis & Clark
Missouri
Oregon Trail
Pony Express 1860
Santa Fe Trail
Cimarron Cutoff
Old Spanish Trail
Old Spanish Trail
Colorado
Rio Grande
Butterfield
Overland Mail
Mississippi

0   200   Miles

40

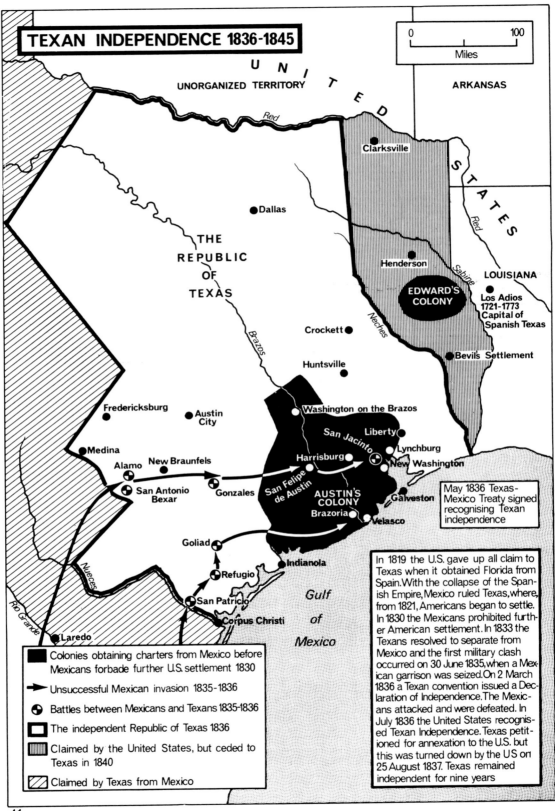

TEXAN INDEPENDENCE 1836-1845

0   100
Miles

UNITED

UNORGANIZED TERRITORY

ARKANSAS

STATES

Red

•Clarksville

•Dallas

THE
REPUBLIC
OF
TEXAS

•Henderson

LOUISIANA

Los Adios
1721-1773
Capital of
Spanish Texas

EDWARD'S
COLONY

Crockett•

Bevils Settlement

Huntsville•

Fredericksburg•   •Austin
City

Washington on the Brazos

San Jacinto   Liberty

•Medina

Harrisburg   Lynchburg

Alamo   New Braunfels

New Washington

San Antonio
Bexar   Gonzales   San Felipe
de Austin   AUSTIN'S
COLONY   Galveston

May 1836 Texas-
Mexico Treaty signed
recognising Texan
independence

Brazoria   Velasco

Goliad

Indianola

Refugio

Gulf
of
Mexico

San Patricio

Corpus Christi

Laredo

In 1819 the U.S. gave up all claim to
Texas when it obtained Florida from
Spain. With the collapse of the Spanish Empire, Mexico ruled Texas, where,
from 1821, Americans began to settle.
In 1830 the Mexicans prohibited further American settlement. In 1833 the
Texans resolved to separate from
Mexico and the first military clash
occurred on 30 June 1835, when a Mexican garrison was seized. On 2 March
1836 a Texan convention issued a Declaration of Independence. The Mexicans attacked and were defeated. In
July 1836 the United States recognised Texan Independence. Texas petit-
ioned for annexation to the U.S. but
this was turned down by the US on
25 August 1837. Texas remained
independent for nine years

■ Colonies obtaining charters from Mexico before
Mexicans forbade further U.S. settlement 1830

➔ Unsuccessful Mexican invasion 1835-1836

⊕ Battles between Mexicans and Texans 1835-1836

☐ The independent Republic of Texas 1836

▥ Claimed by the United States, but ceded to
Texas in 1840

▨ Claimed by Texas from Mexico

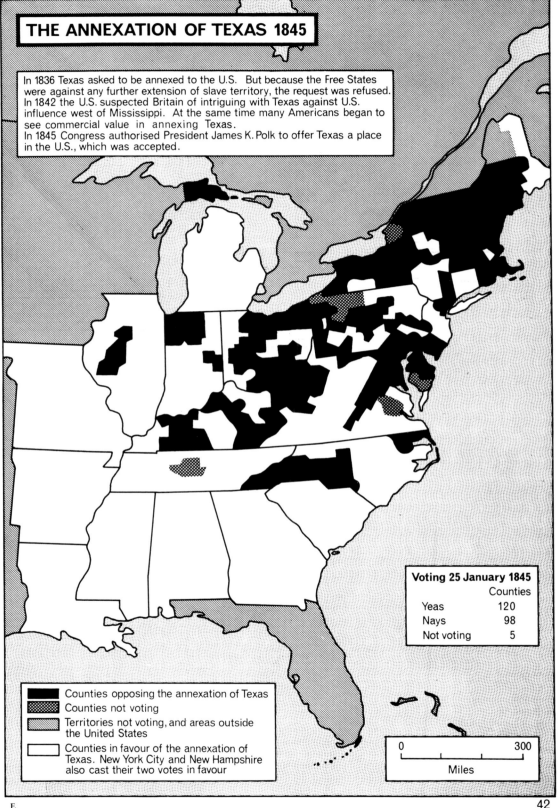

THE ANNEXATION OF TEXAS 1845

In 1836 Texas asked to be annexed to the U.S. But because the Free States were against any further extension of slave territory, the request was refused. In 1842 the U.S. suspected Britain of intriguing with Texas against U.S. influence west of Mississippi. At the same time many Americans began to see commercial value in annexing Texas.
In 1845 Congress authorised President James K. Polk to offer Texas a place in the U.S., which was accepted.

Voting 25 January 1845

	Counties
Yeas	120
Nays	98
Not voting	5

Counties opposing the annexation of Texas

Counties not voting

Territories not voting, and areas outside the United States

Counties in favour of the annexation of Texas. New York City and New Hampshire also cast their two votes in favour

0   300

Miles

E

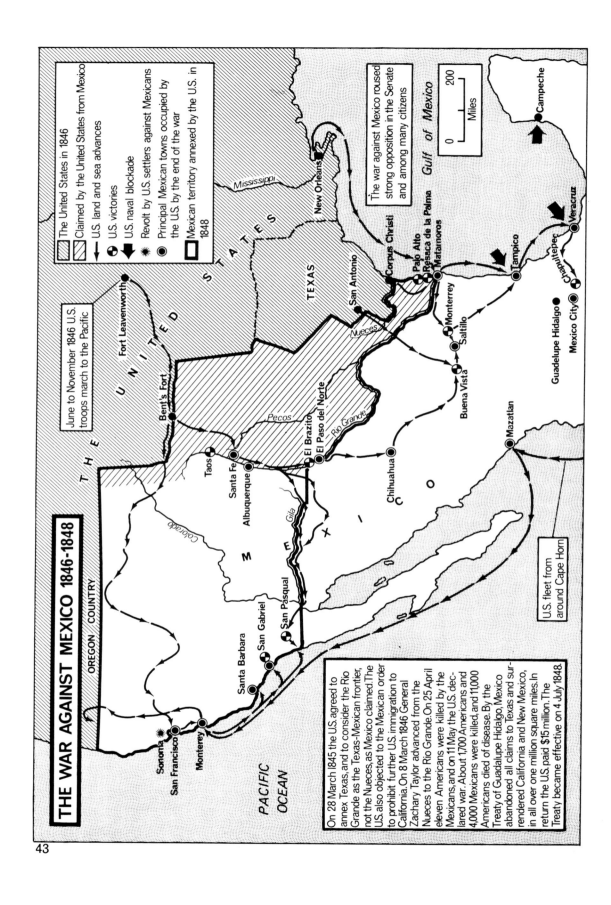

THE WAR AGAINST MEXICO 1846-1848

Legend:

- The United States in 1846
- Claimed by the United States from Mexico
- ↓ U.S. land and sea advances
- ☢ U.S. victories
- ⬇ U.S. naval blockade
- ✴ Revolt by U.S. settlers against Mexicans
- ◉ Principal Mexican towns occupied by the U.S. by the end of the war
- ☐ Mexican territory annexed by the U.S. in 1848

June to November 1846 U.S. troops march to the Pacific

The war against Mexico roused strong opposition in the Senate and among many citizens

Gulf of Mexico

0   200
Miles

OREGON COUNTRY

THE UNITED STATES

PACIFIC OCEAN

Mississippi

New Orleans

Fort Leavenworth

Bent's Fort

TEXAS

San Antonio

Nueces

Corpus Christi
Palo Alto
Resaca de la Palma
Matamoros

Monterrey
Saltillo
Buena Vista

Tampico

Guadelupe Hidalgo
Chapultepec
Veracruz

Mexico City

Taos
Santa Fe
Albuquerque
El Brazito
El Paso del Norte

Pecos
Rio Grande
Colorado
Gila

Chihuahua

M E X I C O

Mazatlan

San Gabriel
San Pasqual
Santa Barbara
Monterey
San Francisco
Sonoma

Campeche

U.S. fleet from around Cape Horn

On 28 March 1845 the U.S. agreed to annex Texas, and to consider the Rio Grande as the Texas-Mexican frontier, not the Nueces, as Mexico claimed. The U.S. also objected to the Mexican order to prohibit further U.S. immigration to California. On 8 March 1846 General Zachary Taylor advanced from the Nueces to the Rio Grande. On 25 April eleven Americans were killed by the Mexicans, and on 11 May the U.S. declared war. About 1,700 Americans and 4,000 Mexicans were killed, and 11,000 Americans died of disease. By the Treaty of Guadalupe Hidalgo, Mexico abandoned all claims to Texas and surrendered California and New Mexico, in all over one million square miles. In return the U.S. paid $15 million. The Treaty became effective on 4 July 1848.

43

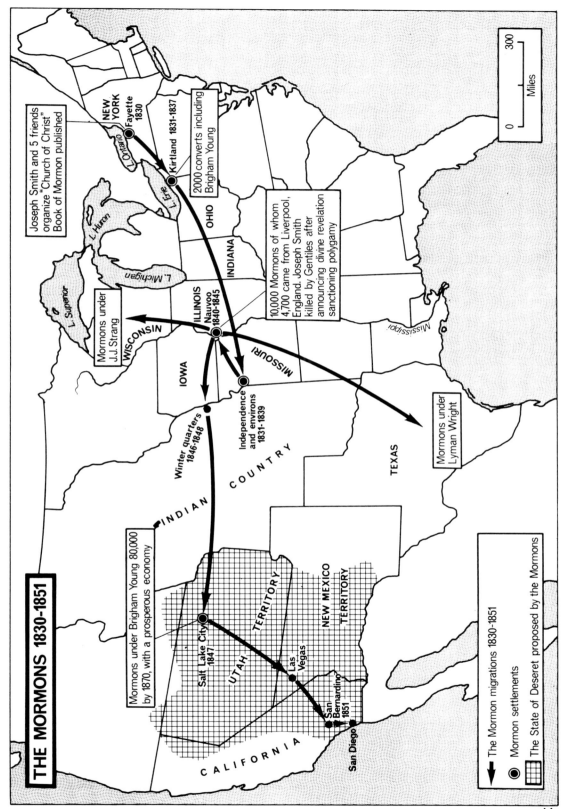

THE MORMONS 1830-1851

Joseph Smith and 5 friends organize "Church of Christ" Book of Mormon published

NEW YORK
Fayette 1830

Kirtland 1831-1837

2000 converts including Brigham Young

OHIO

INDIANA

10,000 Mormons of whom 4,700 came from Liverpool, England. Joseph Smith killed by Gentiles after announcing divine revelation sanctioning polygamy

Mormons under J.J. Strang

WISCONSIN

ILLINOIS
Nauvoo 1840-1845

IOWA

MISSOURI

Winter quarters 1846-1848

Independence and environs 1831-1839

INDIAN COUNTRY

Mormons under Lyman Wright

TEXAS

Mormons under Brigham Young 80,000 by 1870, with a prosperous economy

Salt Lake City 1847

UTAH TERRITORY

NEW MEXICO TERRITORY

Las Vegas

San Bernardino 1851

CALIFORNIA

San Diego

L. Ontario

L. Erie

L. Huron

L. Michigan

L. Superior

Mississippi

0 — 300 Miles

The Mormon migrations 1830-1851
● Mormon settlements
The State of Deseret proposed by the Mormons

44

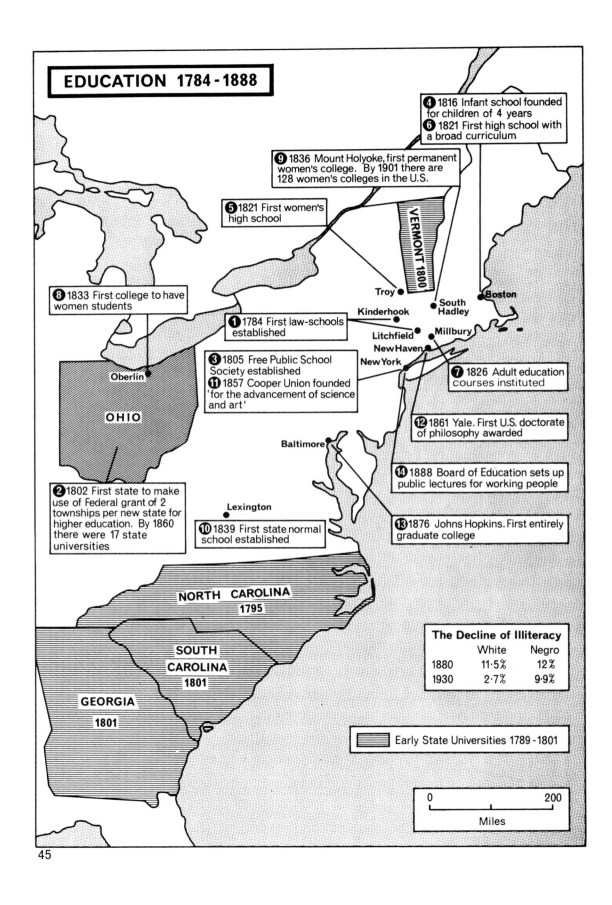

EDUCATION 1784-1888

4 1816 Infant school founded for children of 4 years

6 1821 First high school with a broad curriculum

9 1836 Mount Holyoke, first permanent women's college. By 1901 there are 128 women's colleges in the U.S.

5 1821 First women's high school

VERMONT 1800

8 1833 First college to have women students

1 1784 First law-schools established

3 1805 Free Public School Society established

11 1857 Cooper Union founded 'for the advancement of science and art'

7 1826 Adult education courses instituted

12 1861 Yale. First U.S. doctorate of philosophy awarded

14 1888 Board of Education sets up public lectures for working people

2 1802 First state to make use of Federal grant of 2 townships per new state for higher education. By 1860 there were 17 state universities

10 1839 First state normal school established

13 1876 Johns Hopkins. First entirely graduate college

Troy

Kinderhook

South Hadley

Boston

Litchfield

Millbury

New Haven

New York

Oberlin

OHIO

Baltimore

Lexington

NORTH CAROLINA
1795

SOUTH CAROLINA
1801

GEORGIA
1801

The Decline of Illiteracy

	White	Negro
1880	11·5%	12%
1930	2·7%	9·9%

Early State Universities 1789-1801

0   200
Miles

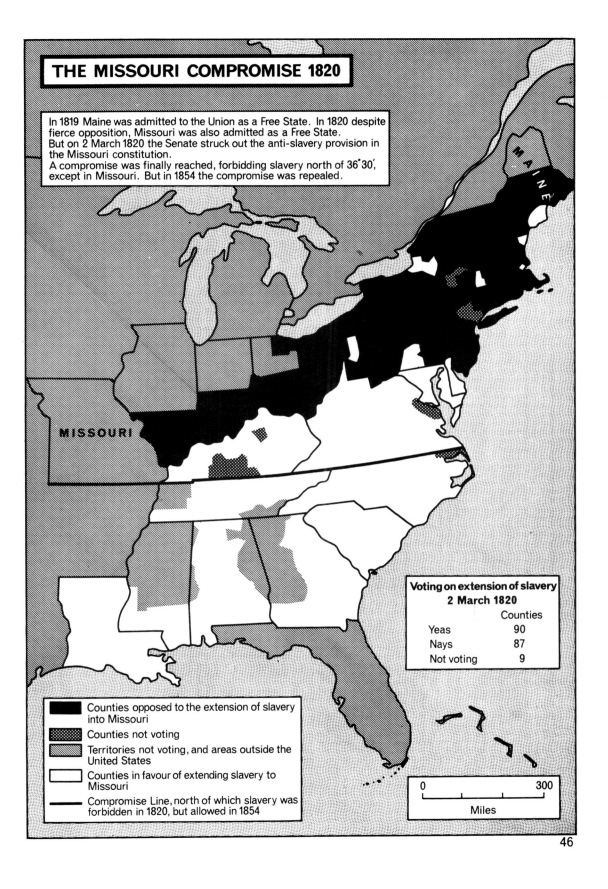

THE MISSOURI COMPROMISE 1820

In 1819 Maine was admitted to the Union as a Free State. In 1820 despite
fierce opposition, Missouri was also admitted as a Free State.
But on 2 March 1820 the Senate struck out the anti-slavery provision in
the Missouri constitution.
A compromise was finally reached, forbidding slavery north of 36°30′,
except in Missouri. But in 1854 the compromise was repealed.

MAINE

MISSOURI

**Voting on extension of slavery
2 March 1820**

	Counties
Yeas	90
Nays	87
Not voting	9

Counties opposed to the extension of slavery
into Missouri

Counties not voting

Territories not voting, and areas outside the
United States

Counties in favour of extending slavery to
Missouri

Compromise Line, north of which slavery was
forbidden in 1820, but allowed in 1854

0   300

Miles

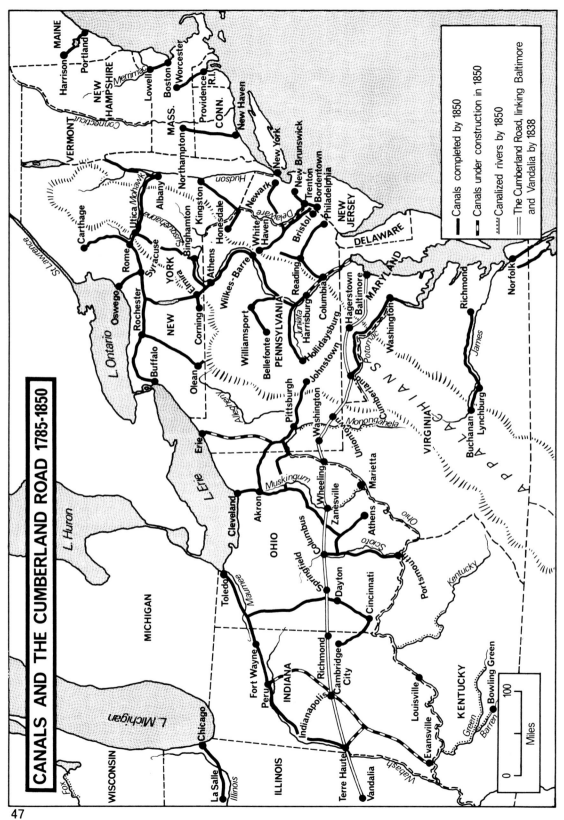

CANALS AND THE CUMBERLAND ROAD 1785-1850

Legend:
- Canals completed by 1850
- Canals under construction in 1850
- Canalized rivers by 1850
- The Cumberland Road, linking Baltimore and Vandalia by 1838

MAINE
NEW HAMPSHIRE
VERMONT
MASS.
R.I.
CONN.
NEW YORK
NEW JERSEY
DELAWARE
PENNSYLVANIA
MARYLAND
VIRGINIA
OHIO
INDIANA
ILLINOIS
KENTUCKY
MICHIGAN
WISCONSIN

L. Ontario
L. Huron
L. Erie
L. Michigan
St. Lawrence

APPALACHIANS

Harrison
Portland
Lowell
Merrimac
Worcester
Boston
Providence
New Haven
New York
Connecticut
Carthage
Albany
Northampton
Kingston
Honesdale
Newark
New Brunswick
Trenton
Bordentown
Philadelphia
Bristol
White Haven
Mohawk
Utica
Hudson
Susquehanna
Rome
Syracuse
Binghamton
Athens
Elmira
Wilkes-Barre
Reading
Columbia
Hagerstown
Baltimore
Washington
Rochester
Corning
Williamsport
Bellefonte
Harrisburg
Hollidaysburg
Juniata
Oswego
Buffalo
Olean
Allegheny
Johnstown
Pittsburgh
Washington
Union
Monongahela
Cumberland
Potomac
Norfolk
Richmond
James
Buchanan
Lynchburg
Erie
Cleveland
Akron
Muskingum
Wheeling
Zanesville
Marietta
Athens
Columbus
Springfield
Scioto
Ohio
Portsmouth
Kentucky
Dayton
Cincinnati
Toledo
Maumee
Fort Wayne
Peru
INDIANA
Indianapolis
Richmond
Cambridge City
Louisville
Evansville
Green
Barren
Bowling Green
KENTUCKY
Chicago
La Salle
Illinois
Fox
Terre Haute
Vandalia
Wabash

Scale: 0 — 100 Miles

47

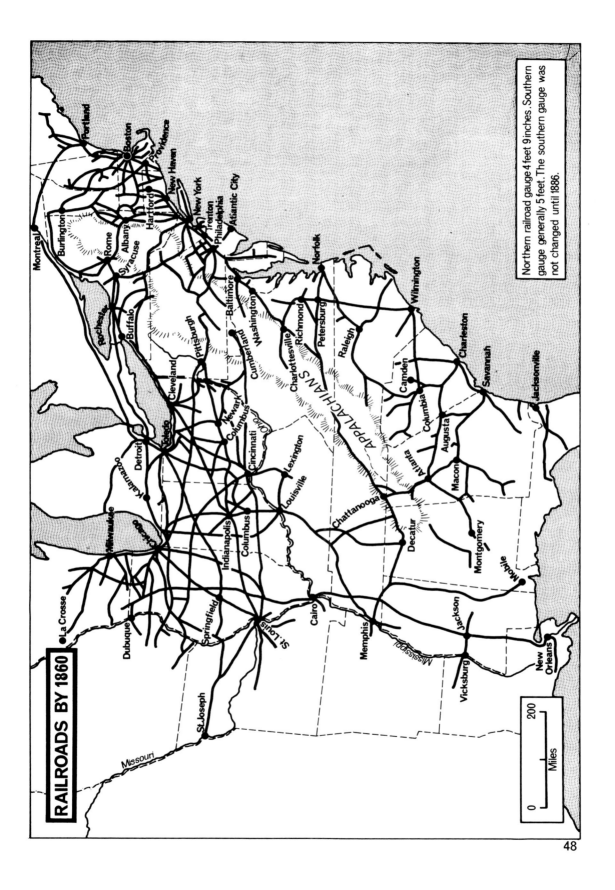

RAILROADS BY 1860

Northern railroad gauge 4 feet 9 inches. Southern gauge generally 5 feet. The southern gauge was not changed until 1886.

Montreal
Portland
Burlington
Boston
Providence
Rome
Albany
Syracuse
Hartford
New Haven
New York
Trenton
Philadelphia
Atlantic City
Rivièrederriders
Buffalo
Pittsburgh
Baltimore
Washington
Cumberland
Norfolk
Charlottesville
Richmond
Petersburg
Raleigh
Wilmington
Cleveland
Newark
Columbus
Cincinnati
Lexington
Camden
Columbia
Augusta
Charleston
Savannah
Jacksonville
Detroit
Kalamazoo
Louisville
APPALACHIANS
Atlanta
Macon
Milwaukee
Chicago
Indianapolis
Columbus
Chattanooga
Decatur
Montgomery
Mobile
La Crosse
Dubuque
Springfield
St. Louis
Cairo
Memphis
Mississippi
Jackson
Vicksburg
New Orleans
St. Joseph
Missouri

200
0
Miles

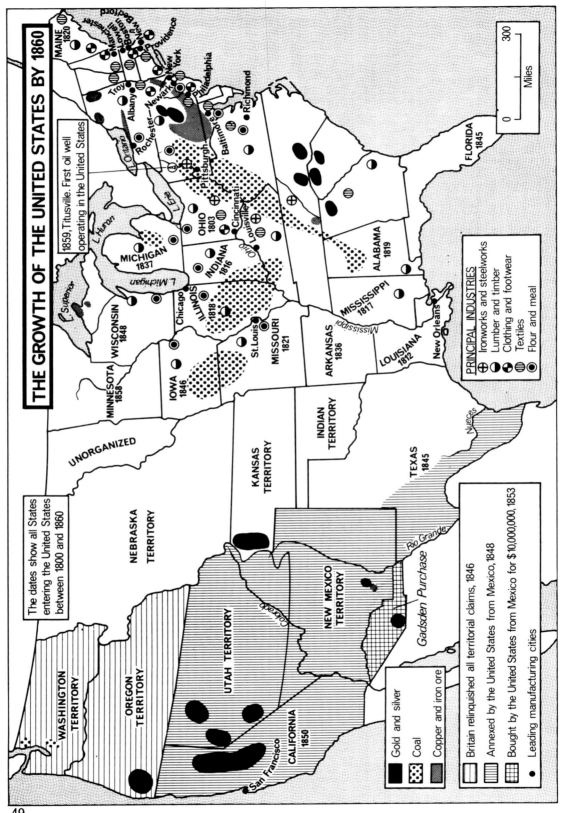

THE GROWTH OF THE UNITED STATES BY 1860

1859, Titusville. First oil well operating in the United States

The dates show all States entering the United States between 1800 and 1860

MAINE 1820

MICHIGAN 1837

WISCONSIN 1848

MINNESOTA 1858

ILLINOIS 1818

INDIANA 1816

OHIO 1803

IOWA 1846

MISSOURI 1821

ARKANSAS 1836

MISSISSIPPI 1817

ALABAMA 1819

LOUISIANA 1812

FLORIDA 1845

UNORGANIZED

NEBRASKA TERRITORY

KANSAS TERRITORY

INDIAN TERRITORY

TEXAS 1845

WASHINGTON TERRITORY

OREGON TERRITORY

UTAH TERRITORY

NEW MEXICO TERRITORY

CALIFORNIA 1850

Gadsden Purchase

Troy, Albany, Rochester, Newark, New York, Philadelphia, Baltimore, Richmond, Pittsburgh, Cincinnati, Louisville, Chicago, St. Louis, New Orleans, San Francisco

L. Superior, L. Huron, L. Michigan, L. Ontario, Erie, Ohio, Mississippi, Nueces, Rio Grande, Colorado

PRINCIPAL INDUSTRIES

⊕ Ironworks and steelworks
◑ Lumber and timber
◔ Clothing and footwear
◕ Textiles
◉ Flour and meal

Gold and silver
Coal
Copper and iron ore

Britain relinquished all territorial claims, 1846
Annexed by the United States from Mexico, 1848
Bought by the United States from Mexico for $10,000,000, 1853
• Leading manufacturing cities

0   300
Miles

49

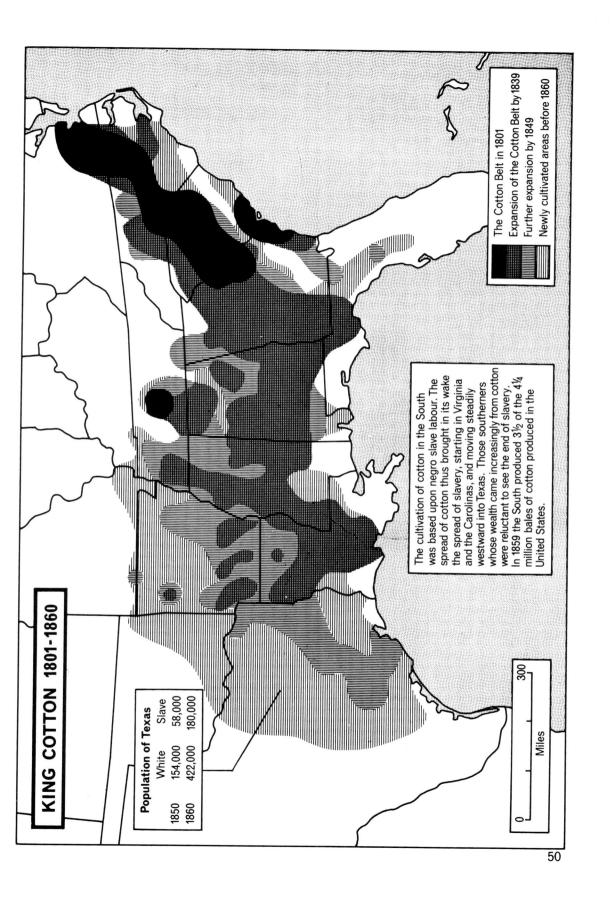

KING COTTON 1801-1860

Population of Texas

	White	Slave
1850	154,000	58,000
1860	422,000	180,000

The cultivation of cotton in the South was based upon negro slave labour. The spread of cotton thus brought in its wake the spread of slavery, starting in Virginia and the Carolinas, and moving steadily westward into Texas. Those southerners whose wealth came increasingly from cotton were reluctant to see the end of slavery. In 1859 the South produced 3½ of the 4¼ million bales of cotton produced in the United States.

The Cotton Belt in 1801

Expansion of the Cotton Belt by 1839

Further expansion by 1849

Newly cultivated areas before 1860

0   Miles   300

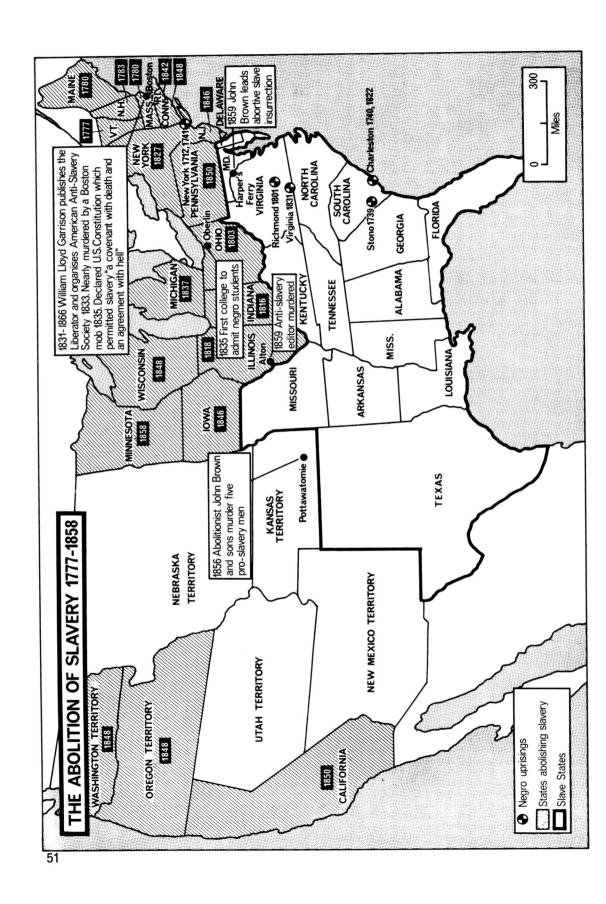

THE ABOLITION OF SLAVERY 1777-1858

1831-1866 William Lloyd Garrison publishes the Liberator and organises American Anti-Slavery Society 1833. Nearly murdered by a Boston mob 1835. Declared U.S.Constitution which permitted slavery "a covenant with death and an agreement with hell"

1835 First college to admit negro students

1859 Anti-slavery editor murdered

1856 Abolitionist John Brown and sons murder five pro-slavery men

1859 John Brown leads abortive slave insurrection

WASHINGTON TERRITORY 1848

OREGON TERRITORY 1848

CALIFORNIA 1850

NEBRASKA TERRITORY

UTAH TERRITORY

NEW MEXICO TERRITORY

KANSAS TERRITORY

Pottawatomie ●

TEXAS

MINNESOTA 1858

IOWA 1846

WISCONSIN 1848

MICHIGAN 1837

ILLINOIS 1818

INDIANA 1816

Alton

Oberlin ●

OHIO 1803

MISSOURI

ARKANSAS

LOUISIANA

MISS.

ALABAMA

TENNESSEE

KENTUCKY

Richmond 1801 ●

Harper's Ferry

Virginia 1831 ●

VIRGINIA

NORTH CAROLINA

SOUTH CAROLINA

Stono 1739 ●

GEORGIA

FLORIDA

Charleston 1740, 1822 ●

NEW YORK 1827

New York 1712, 1741

PENNSYLVANIA 1850

MD.

DELAWARE

N.J.

1846

MAINE 1780

V.T. 1777

N.H. 1783

MASS. 1780

R.I. 1842

CONN. 1848

Boston

0 — 300 Miles

● Negro uprisings

▨ States abolishing slavery

☐ Slave States

51

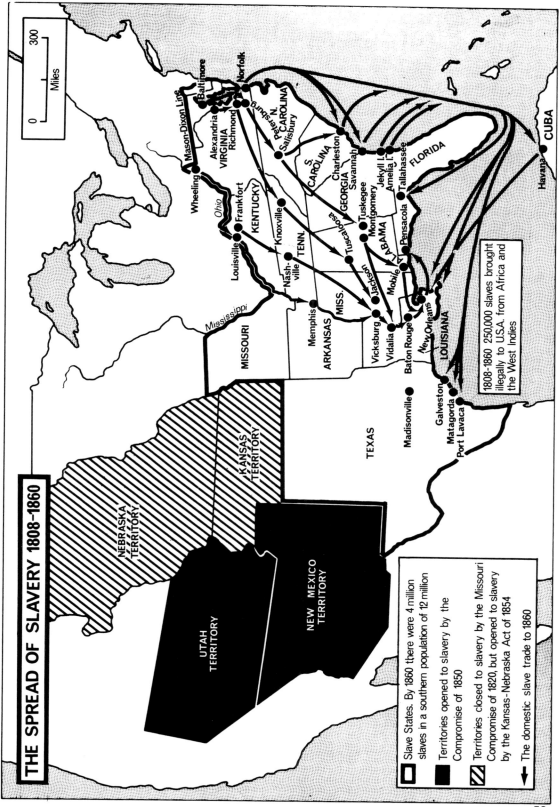

THE SPREAD OF SLAVERY 1808–1860

300

0

Miles

CUBA

Havana

FLORIDA

Tallahassee

Jekyll I.

Amelia I.

Pensacola

Mobile

New Orleans

LOUISIANA

Baton Rouge

Vidalia

Vicksburg

Galveston

Matagorda

Port Lavaca

Madisonville

TEXAS

Jackson

MISS.

ALABAMA

Montgomery

Tuskegee

Tuscaloosa

GEORGIA

Savannah

Charleston

S. CAROLINA

N. CAROLINA

Salisbury

Peters.

Norfolk

Richmond

Alexandria

VIRGINIA

Baltimore

Mason-Dixon Line

Wheeling

Ohio

Frankfort

KENTUCKY

Louisville

Knoxville

TENN.

Nash-
ville

Memphis

ARKANSAS

Mississippi

MISSOURI

NEW MEXICO TERRITORY

UTAH TERRITORY

NEBRASKA TERRITORY

KANSAS TERRITORY

1808–1860 250,000 slaves brought
illegally to U.S.A. from Africa and
the West Indies

☐ Slave States. By 1860 there were 4 million
slaves in a southern population of 12 million

■ Territories opened to slavery by the
Compromise of 1850

▨ Territories closed to slavery by the Missouri
Compromise of 1820, but opened to slavery
by the Kansas-Nebraska Act of 1854

→ The domestic slave trade to 1860

52

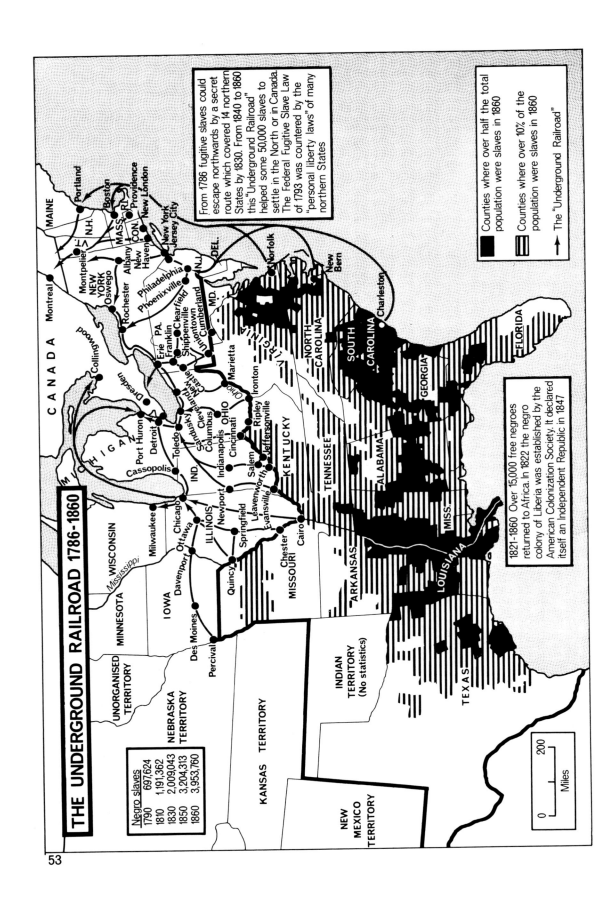

THE UNDERGROUND RAILROAD 1786-1860

Negro slaves
1790	697,624
1810	1,191,362
1830	2,009,043
1850	3,204,313
1860	3,953,760

From 1786 fugitive slaves could escape northwards by a secret route which covered 14 northern States by 1830. From 1840 to 1860 this "Underground Railroad" helped some 50,000 slaves to settle in the North or in Canada. The Federal Fugitive Slave Law of 1793 was countered by the "personal liberty laws" of many northern States

1821-1860 Over 15,000 free negroes returned to Africa. In 1822 the negro colony of Liberia was established by the American Colonization Society. It declared itself an Independent Republic in 1847

■ Counties where over half the total population were slaves in 1860

▥ Counties where over 10% of the population were slaves in 1860

→ The "Underground Railroad"

CANADA

MAINE
N.H.
MASS.
R.I.
CONN.
NEW YORK
PENNSYLVANIA
N.J.
DEL.
MD.
VIRGINIA
NORTH CAROLINA
SOUTH CAROLINA
GEORGIA
FLORIDA
ALABAMA
MISS.
TENNESSEE
KENTUCKY
OHIO
IND.
ILLINOIS
MICHIGAN
WISCONSIN
MINNESOTA
IOWA
MISSOURI
ARKANSAS
LOUISIANA
TEXAS
UNORGANISED TERRITORY
NEBRASKA TERRITORY
KANSAS TERRITORY
INDIAN TERRITORY (No statistics)
NEW MEXICO TERRITORY

Portland
Boston
Providence
New London
Montpelier
Albany
New Haven
New York
Jersey City
Norfolk
New Bern
Charleston
Rochester
Oswego
Philadelphia
Phoenixville
Clearfield
Shippenville
Uniontown
Cumberland
Erie
Franklin
Marietta
Ironton
Ripley
Jeffersonville
Cincinnati
Columbus
Indianapolis
Salem
Cleveland
Sandusky
Ottawa
Detroit
Port Huron
Toledo
Cassopolis
Chicago
Milwaukee
Newport
Leavenworth
Evansville
Springfield
Quincy
Chester
Cairo
Des Moines
Davenport
Percival
Montreal
Collingwood
Dresden

Mississippi

0   200
Miles

53

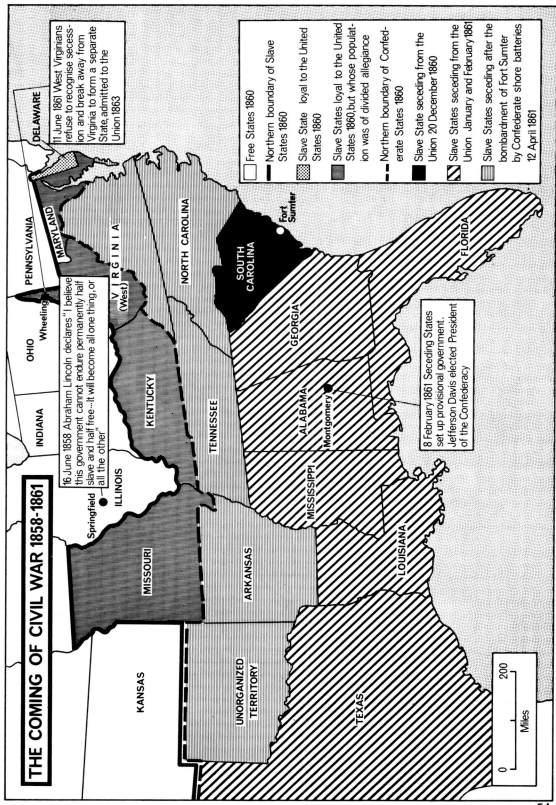

THE COMING OF CIVIL WAR 1858-1861

16 June 1858 Abraham Lincoln declares "I believe this government cannot endure permanently half slave and half free...It will become all one thing, or all the other"

11 June 1861 West Virginians refuse to recognise secession and break away from Virginia to form a separate State, admitted to the Union 1863

8 February 1861 Seceding States set up provisional government. Jefferson Davis elected President of the Confederacy

Free States 1860

Northern boundary of Slave States 1860

Slave State loyal to the United States 1860

Slave States loyal to the United States 1860, but whose population was of divided allegiance

Northern boundary of Confederate States 1860

Slave State seceding from the Union 20 December 1860

Slave States seceding from the Union January and February 1861

Slave States seceding after the bombardment of Fort Sumter by Confederate shore batteries 12 April 1861

PENNSYLVANIA

DELAWARE

MARYLAND

OHIO

Wheeling

VIRGINIA (West)

VIRGINIA

NORTH CAROLINA

Fort Sumter

SOUTH CAROLINA

FLORIDA

INDIANA

KENTUCKY

TENNESSEE

GEORGIA

ALABAMA

Montgomery

MISSISSIPPI

ILLINOIS

Springfield

MISSOURI

ARKANSAS

LOUISIANA

KANSAS

UNORGANIZED TERRITORY

TEXAS

0   200

Miles

F

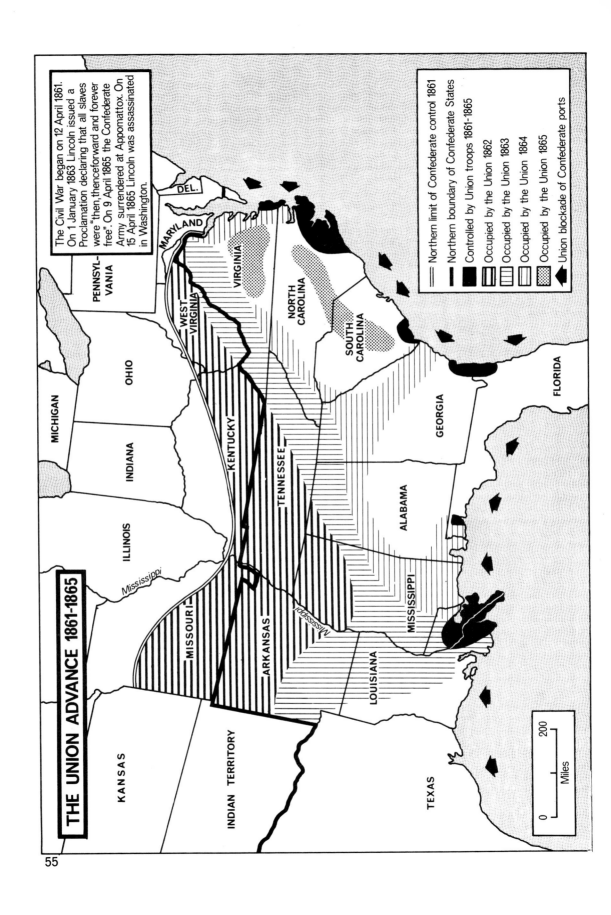

THE UNION ADVANCE 1861-1865

The Civil War began on 12 April 1861. On 1 January 1863 Lincoln issued a Proclamation declaring that all slaves were "then, thenceforward and forever free". On 9 April 1865 the Confederate Army surrendered at Appomattox. On 15 April 1865 Lincoln was assassinated in Washington.

Northern limit of Confederate control 1861
Northern boundary of Confederate States
Controlled by Union troops 1861-1865
Occupied by the Union 1862
Occupied by the Union 1863
Occupied by the Union 1864
Occupied by the Union 1865
Union blockade of Confederate ports

MICHIGAN
PENNSYL-VANIA
DEL.
MARYLAND
WEST VIRGINIA
VIRGINIA
OHIO
INDIANA
ILLINOIS
KENTUCKY
NORTH CAROLINA
TENNESSEE
SOUTH CAROLINA
GEORGIA
ALABAMA
MISSISSIPPI
FLORIDA
KANSAS
MISSOURI
ARKANSAS
LOUISIANA
INDIAN TERRITORY
TEXAS

Mississippi
Mississippi

0   200
Miles

55

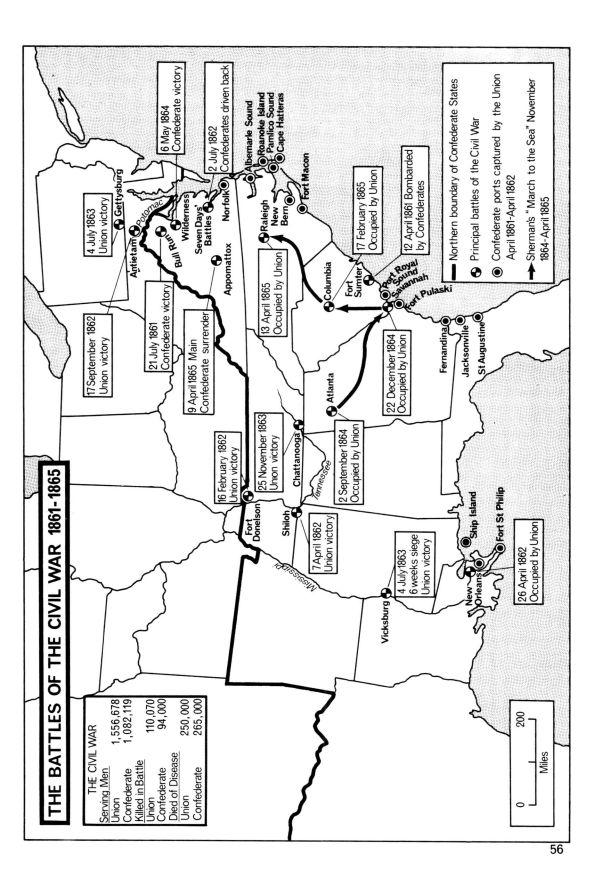

THE BATTLES OF THE CIVIL WAR 1861-1865

THE CIVIL WAR	
Serving Men	
Union	1,556,678
Confederate	1,082,119
Killed in Battle	
Union	110,070
Confederate	94,000
Died of Disease	
Union	250,000
Confederate	265,000

4 July 1863
Union victory
Gettysburg

6 May 1864
Confederate victory
Wilderness

2 July 1862
Confederates driven back

Albemarle Sound
Roanoke Island
Pamlico Sound
Cape Hatteras

Seven Days'
Battles

Bull Run
Antietam
Norfolk

Fort Macon

New
Bern

17 February 1865
Occupied by Union

12 April 1861 Bombarded
by Confederates

17 September 1862
Union victory

Appomattox

Raleigh

21 July 1861
Confederate victory

9 April 1865 Main
Confederate surrender

13 April 1865
Occupied by Union

Columbia

Fort
Sumter

Port Royal
Sound
Savannah
Fort Pulaski

Fernandina
Jacksonville
St Augustine

22 December 1864
Occupied by Union

16 February 1862
Union victory

25 November 1863
Union victory

Chattanooga

Atlanta

2 September 1864
Occupied by Union

Fort
Donelson

Shiloh

7 April 1862
Union victory

Tennessee

4 July 1863
6 weeks siege
Union victory

Ship Island
Fort St Philip

New
Orleans

26 April 1862
Occupied by Union

Vicksburg

Mississippi

Potomac

— Northern boundary of Confederate States

◑ Principal battles of the Civil War

◉ Confederate ports captured by the Union
   April 1861-April 1862

→ Sherman's "March to the Sea" November
   1864-April 1865

0   200
Miles

56

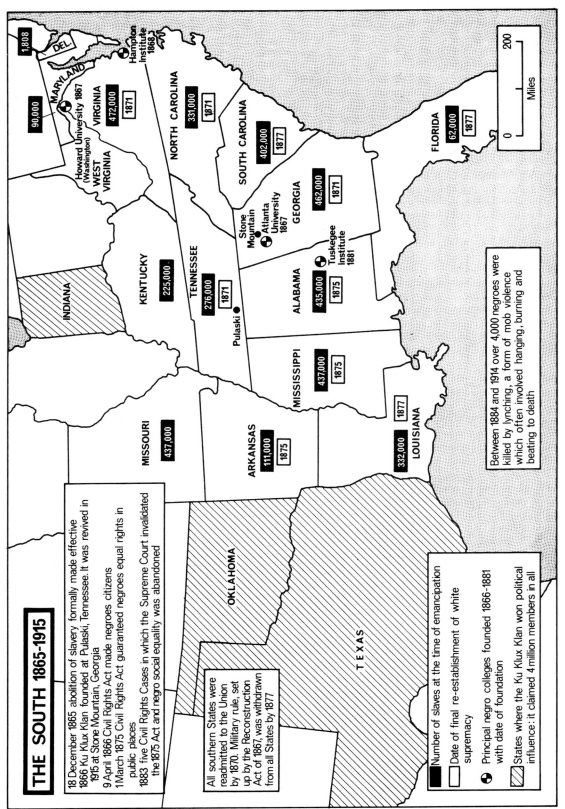

THE SOUTH 1865-1915

18 December 1865 abolition of slavery formally made effective
1866 Ku Klux Klan founded at Pulaski, Tennessee. It was revived in 1915 at Stone Mountain, Georgia
9 April 1866 Civil Rights Act made negroes citizens
1 March 1875 Civil Rights Act guaranteed negroes equal rights in public places
1883 five Civil Rights Cases in which the Supreme Court invalidated the 1875 Act and negro social equality was abandoned

All southern States were readmitted to the Union by 1870. Military rule, set up by the Reconstruction Act of 1867, was withdrawn from all States by 1877

Between 1884 and 1914 over 4,000 negroes were killed by lynching, a form of mob violence which often involved hanging, burning and beating to death

■ Number of slaves at the time of emancipation

□ Date of final re-establishment of white supremacy

◐ Principal negro colleges founded 1866-1881 with date of foundation

▨ States where the Ku Klux Klan won political influence: it claimed 4 million members in all

DEL.
MARYLAND
1,808
90,000
VIRGINIA 472,000 1871
Howard University 1867 (Washington)
WEST VIRGINIA
Hampton Institute 1868
NORTH CAROLINA 331,000 1871
SOUTH CAROLINA 402,000 1877
GEORGIA 462,000 1871
FLORIDA 62,000 1877
KENTUCKY 225,000
TENNESSEE 276,000 1871
Pulaski ●
Stone Mountain
Atlanta University 1867
ALABAMA 435,000 1875
Tuskegee Institute 1881
INDIANA
MISSISSIPPI 437,000 1875
MISSOURI 437,000
ARKANSAS 111,000 1875
LOUISIANA 332,000 1877
OKLAHOMA
TEXAS

0   200
Miles

57

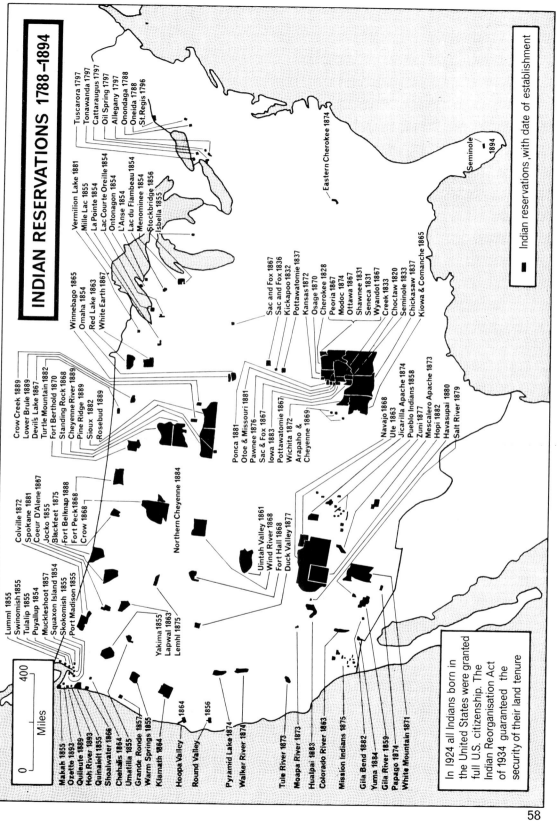

INDIAN RESERVATIONS 1788–1894

Indian reservations, with date of establishment

Tuscarora 1797
Tonawanda 1797
Cattaraugus 1797
Oil Spring 1797
Allegany 1797
Onondaga 1788
Oneida 1788
St. Regis 1796

Vermilion Lake 1881
Mille Lac 1855
La Pointe 1854
Lac Courte Oreille 1854
Ontonagon 1854
L'Anse 1854
Lac du Flambeau 1854
Menominee 1854
Stockbridge 1856
Isbella 1855

Eastern Cherokee 1874

Seminole
1894

Winnebago 1865
Omaha 1854
Red Lake 1863
White Earth 1867

Sac and Fox 1867
Sac and Fox 1836
Kickapoo 1832
Pottawatomie 1837
Kansas 1872
Osage 1870
Cherokee 1828
Peoria 1867
Modoc 1874
Ottawa 1867
Shawnee 1831
Seneca 1831
Wyandot 1867
Choctaw 1820
Seminole 1833
Chickasaw 1837
Creek 1833
Kiowa & Comanche 1865

Crow Creek 1889
Lower Brule 1889
Devils Lake 1867
Turtle Mountain 1882
Fort Berthold 1870
Standing Rock 1868
Cheyenne River 1889
Pine Ridge 1889
Sioux 1882
Rosebud 1889

Ponca 1881
Otoe & Missouri 1881
Pawnee 1876
Sac & Fox 1867
Iowa 1883
Pottawatomie 1867
Wichita 1872
Arapaho &
Cheyenne 1869

Navajo 1868
Ute 1863
Jicarilla Apache 1874
Pueblo Indians 1858
Zuni 1877
Mescalero Apache 1873
Hopi 1882
Havasupai 1880
Salt River 1879

Colville 1872
Spokane 1881
Coeur D'Alene 1867
Jocko 1855
Blackfeet 1875
Fort Belknap 1888
Fort Peck 1868
Crow 1868

Northern Cheyenne 1884

Uintah Valley 1861
Wind River 1868
Fort Hall 1868
Duck Valley 1877

Lumml 1855
Swinomish 1855
Puyallup 1854
Muckleshoot 1857
Squaxon Island 1854
Skokomish 1855
Port Madison 1855

Yakima 1855
Lapwai 1863
Lemhi 1875

Makah 1855
Ozette 1893
Quileute 1889
Hoh River 1893
Quinaiett 1855
Shoalwater 1866
Chehalis 1864
Umatilla 1855
Grande Ronde 1857
Warm Springs 1855
Klamath 1864

Hoopa Valley

Round Valley

Pyramid Lake 1874

Walker River 1874

Tule River 1873

Moapa River 1873

Hualpai 1883

Colorado River 1863

Mission Indians 1875

Gila Bend 1882

Yuma 1884

Gila River 1859

Papago 1874

White Mountain 1871

1864

1856

0   400
Miles

In 1924 all Indians born in the United States were granted full U.S. citizenship. The Indian Reorganisation Act of 1934 guaranteed the security of their land tenure

58

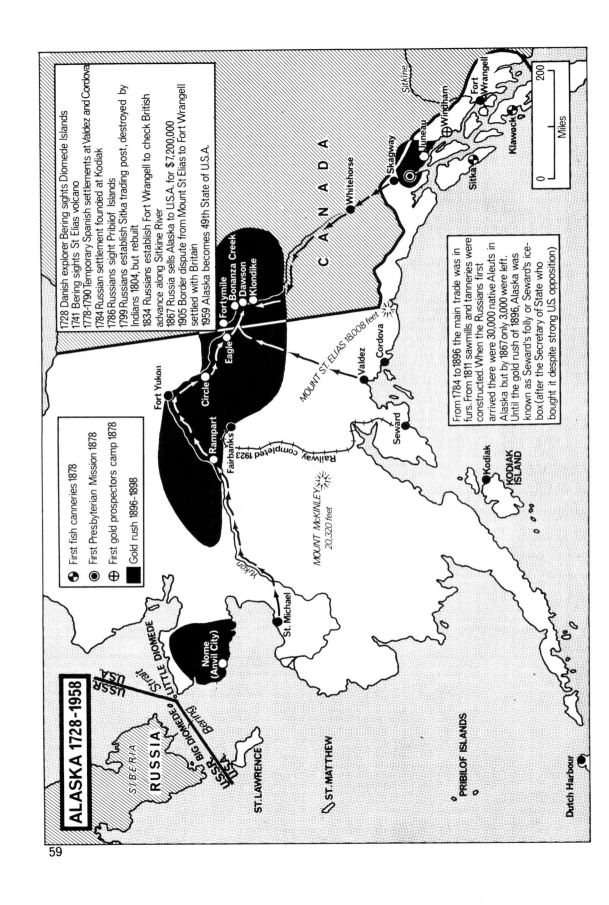

ALASKA 1728-1958

1728 Danish explorer Bering sights Diomede Islands
1741 Bering sights St Elias volcano
1778-1790 Temporary Spanish settlements at Valdez and Cordova
1784 Russian settlement founded at Kodiak
1786 Russians sight Pribilof Islands
1799 Russians establish Sitka trading post, destroyed by Indians 1804, but rebuilt
1834 Russians establish Fort Wrangell to check British advance along Sitkine River
1867 Russia sells Alaska to U.S.A. for $7,200,000
1905 Border dispute from Mount St Elias to Fort Wrangell settled with Britain
1959 Alaska becomes 49th State of U.S.A.

From 1784 to 1896 the main trade was in furs. From 1811 sawmills and tanneries were constructed. When the Russians first arrived there were 30,000 native Aleuts in Alaska but by 1867 only 3,000 were left. Until the gold rush of 1896, Alaska was known as Seward's folly or Seward's ice-box (after the Secretary of State who bought it despite strong US. opposition)

⊕ First fish canneries 1878
◉ First Presbyterian Mission 1878
⊕ First gold prospectors camp 1878
■ Gold rush 1896-1898

MOUNT McKINLEY 20,320 feet
MOUNT ST. ELIAS 18,008 feet
Railway completed 1923

CANADA

RUSSIA
SIBERIA
USSR
USA
Bering Strait
BIG DIOMEDE
LITTLE DIOMEDE

ST. LAWRENCE
ST. MATTHEW
PRIBILOF ISLANDS
KODIAK ISLAND
Dutch Harbour

Nome (Anvil City)
St. Michael
Fort Yukon
Circle
Rampart
Fairbanks
Eagle
Fortymile
Dawson
Bonanza Creek
Klondike
Yukon
Kodiak
Seward
Valdez
Cordova
Whitehorse
Skagway
Juneau
Windham
Fort Wrangell
Sitka
Sitkine
Klawock

0   200
Miles

SOCIAL DISCONTENT 1876-1932

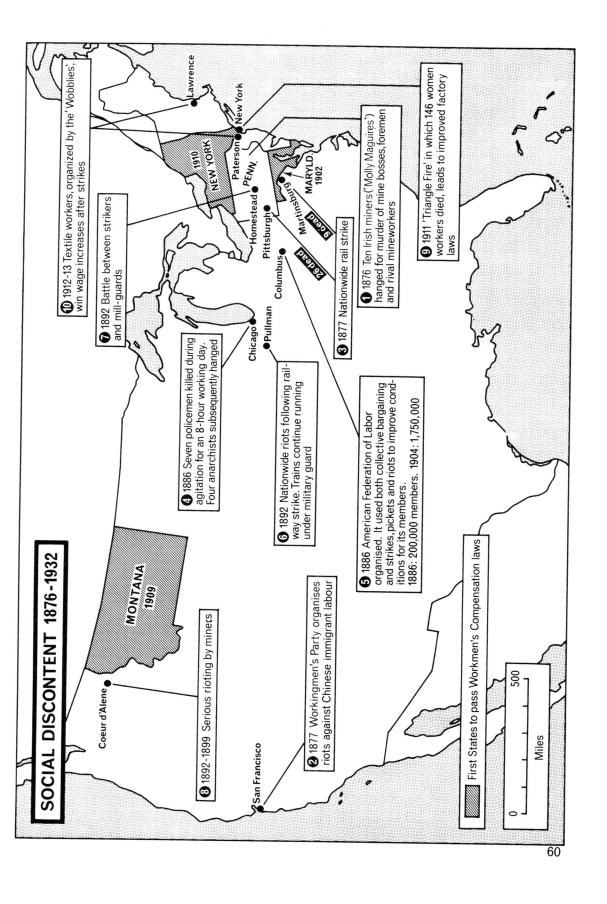

10 1912-13 Textile workers, organized by the 'Wobblies,' win wage increases after strikes

7 1892 Battle between strikers and mill-guards

4 1886 Seven policemen killed during agitation for an 8-hour working day. Four anarchists subsequently hanged

6 1892 Nationwide riots following railway strike. Trains continue running under military guard

5 1886 American Federation of Labor organised. It used both collective bargaining and strikes, pickets and riots to improve conditions for its members. 1886: 200,000 members. 1904: 1,750,000

8 1892-1899 Serious rioting by miners

2 1877 Workingmen's Party organises riots against Chinese immigrant labour

1 1876 Ten Irish miners ('Molly Maguires') hanged for murder of mine bosses, foremen and rival mineworkers

9 1911 'Triangle Fire' in which 146 women workers died, leads to improved factory laws

3 1877 Nationwide rail strike

Lawrence
New York
Paterson
PENN.
MARYLD. 1902
Martinsburg 9 dead
Homestead
Pittsburgh
Columbus 26 dead
NEW YORK 1910

Chicago
Pullman

MONTANA 1909

Coeur d'Alene

San Francisco

First States to pass Workmen's Compensation laws

Miles
0   500

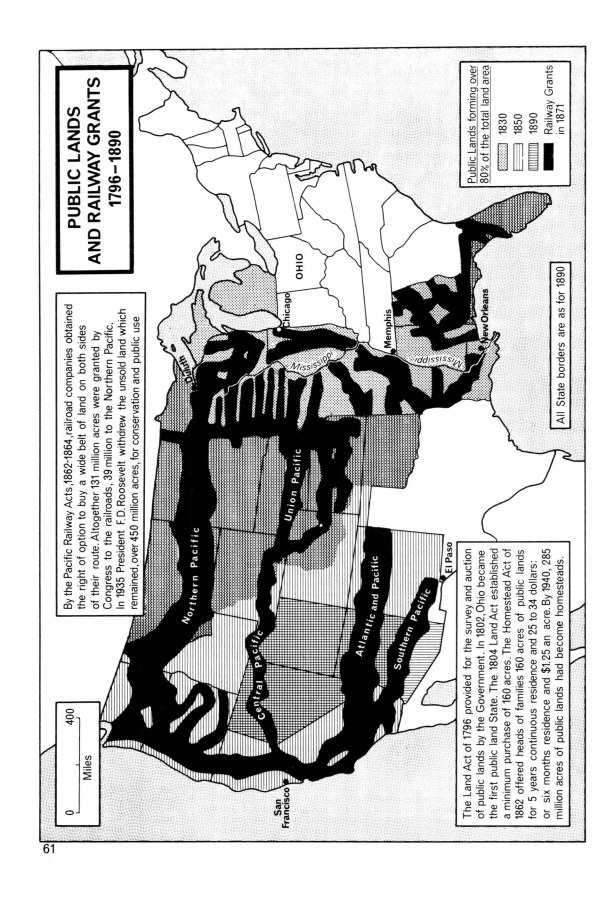

PUBLIC LANDS AND RAILWAY GRANTS 1796–1890

By the Pacific Railway Acts, 1862-1864, railroad companies obtained the right of option to buy a wide belt of land on both sides of their route. Altogether 131 million acres were granted by Congress to the railroads, 39 million to the Northern Pacific. In 1935 President F.D.Roosevelt withdrew the unsold land which remained, over 450 million acres, for conservation and public use

The Land Act of 1796 provided for the survey and auction of public lands by the Government. In 1802, Ohio became the first public land State. The 1804 Land Act established a minimum purchase of 160 acres. The Homestead Act of 1862 offered heads of families 160 acres of public lands for 5 years continuous residence and 25 to 34 dollars; or six months residence and $1.25 an acre. By 1940, 285 million acres of public lands had become homesteads.

All State borders are as for 1890

Public Lands forming over 80% of the total land area

1830

1850

1890

Railway Grants in 1871

0   400

Miles

OHIO

Chicago

Memphis

New Orleans

Mississippi

Mississippi

Duluth

Northern Pacific

Union Pacific

Central Pacific

Atlantic and Pacific

Southern Pacific

El Paso

San Francisco

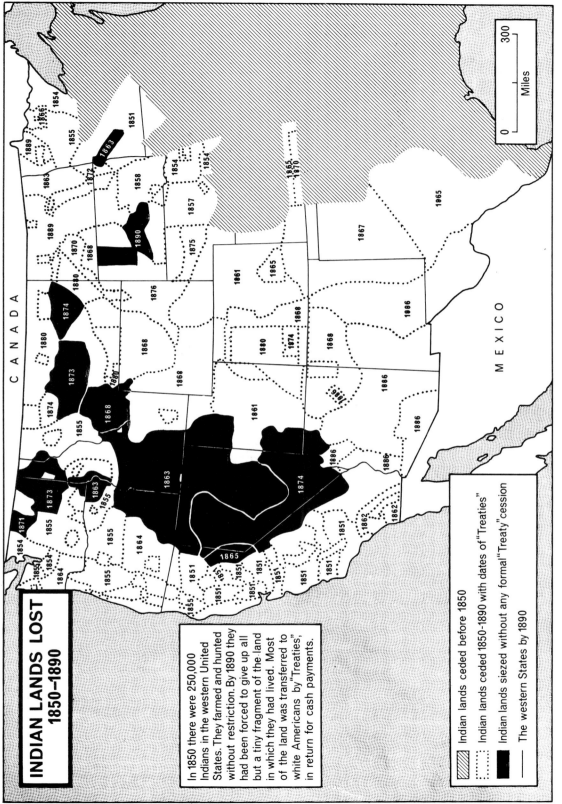

INDIAN LANDS LOST 1850–1890

In 1850 there were 250,000 Indians in the western United States. They farmed and hunted without restriction. By 1890 they had been forced to give up all but a tiny fragment of the land in which they had lived. Most of the land was transferred to white Americans by "Treaties", in return for cash payments.

Indian lands ceded before 1850

Indian lands ceded 1850-1890 with dates of "Treaties"

Indian lands siezed without any formal "Treaty" cession

The western States by 1890

CANADA

MEXICO

300

0

Miles

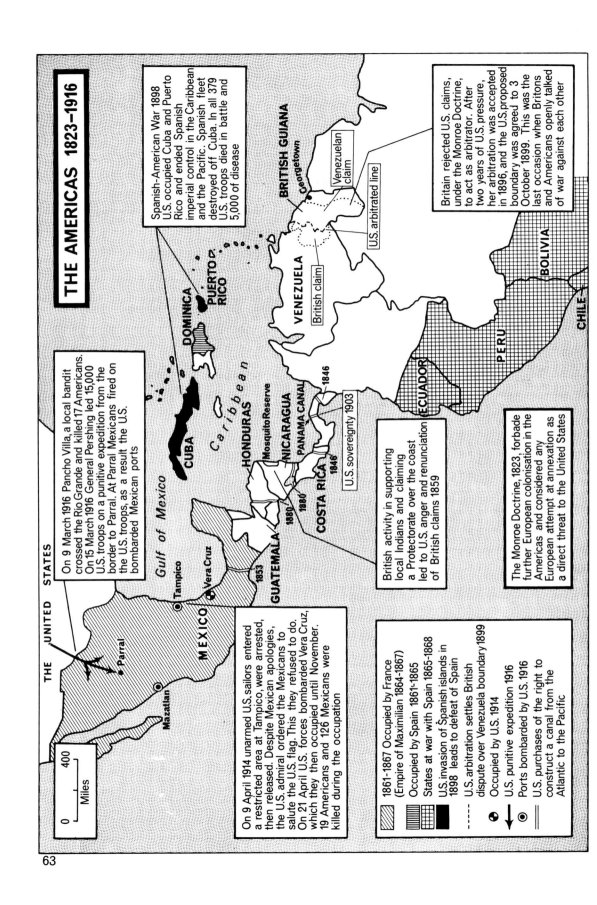

THE AMERICAS 1823–1916

Spanish-American War 1898 U.S. occupied Cuba and Puerto Rico and ended Spanish imperial control in the Caribbean and the Pacific. Spanish fleet destroyed off Cuba. In all 379 U.S. troops died in battle and 5,000 of disease

Britain rejected U.S. claims, under the Monroe Doctrine, to act as arbitrator. After two years of U.S. pressure, her arbitration was accepted in 1896, and the U.S.proposed boundary was agreed to 3 October 1899. This was the last occasion when Britons and Americans openly talked of war against each other

BRITISH GUIANA
Georgetown

Venezuelan claim

U.S. arbitrated line

VENEZUELA

British claim

On 9 March 1916 Pancho Villa, a local bandit crossed the Rio Grande and killed 17 Americans. On 15 March 1916 General Pershing led 15,000 U.S. troops on a punitive expedition from the border to Parral. At Parral Mexicans fired on the U.S. troops, as a result the U.S. bombarded Mexican ports

DOMINICA

PUERTO RICO

CUBA

Caribbean

Gulf of Mexico

Tampico
Vera Cruz

MEXICO

Mazatlán

Parral

THE UNITED STATES

0 400
Miles

HONDURAS
Mosquito Reserve

NICARAGUA
PANAMA CANAL

1846

U.S. sovereignty 1903

1853

GUATEMALA

1880
1860

COSTA RICA
1846

British activity in supporting local Indians and claiming a Protectorate over the coast led to U.S. anger and renunciation of British claims 1859

ECUADOR

PERU

BOLIVIA

CHILE

On 9 April 1914 unarmed U.S.sailors entered a restricted area at Tampico, were arrested, then released. Despite Mexican apologies, the U.S. admiral ordered the Mexicans to salute the U.S. flag. This they refused to do. On 21 April U.S. forces bombarded Vera Cruz, which they then occupied until November. 19 Americans and 126 Mexicans were killed during the occupation

The Monroe Doctrine, 1823, forbade further European colonisation in the Americas and considered any European attempt at annexation as a direct threat to the United States

1861-1867 Occupied by France (Empire of Maximilian 1864-1867)

Occupied by Spain 1861-1865

States at war with Spain 1865-1868

U.S. invasion of Spanish islands in 1898 leads to defeat of Spain

U.S. arbitration settles British dispute over Venezuela boundary 1899

Occupied by U.S. 1914

U.S. punitive expedition 1916

Ports bombarded by U.S. 1916

U.S. purchases of the right to construct a canal from the Atlantic to the Pacific

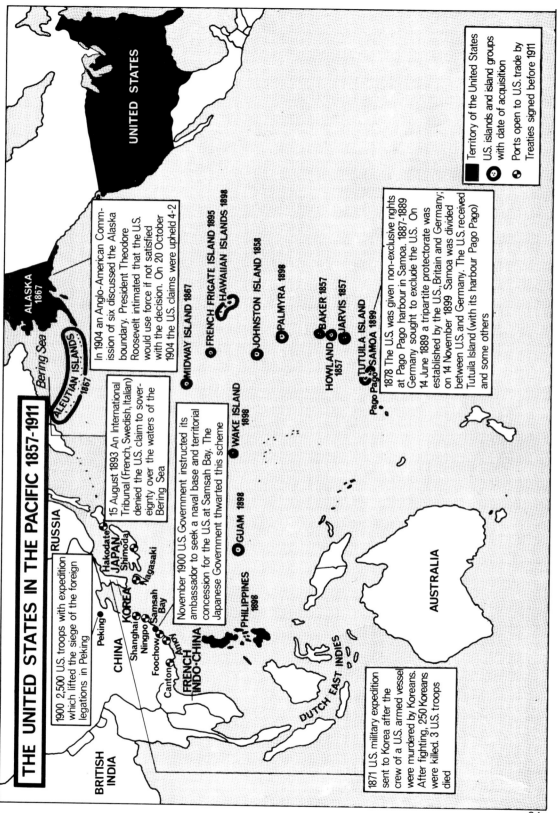

THE UNITED STATES IN THE PACIFIC 1857-1911

1900 2,500 U.S. troops with expedition which lifted the siege of the foreign legations in Peking

15 August 1893 An International Tribunal (French, Swedish, Italian) denied the U.S. claim to sovereignty over the waters of the Bering Sea

November 1900 U.S. Government instructed its ambassador to seek a naval base and territorial concession for the U.S. at Samsah Bay. The Japanese Government thwarted this scheme

In 1904 an Anglo-American Commission of six discussed the Alaska boundary. President Theodore Roosevelt intimated that the U.S. would use force if not satisfied with the decision. On 20 October 1904 the U.S. claims were upheld 4-2

1878 The U.S. was given non-exclusive rights at Pago Pago harbour in Samoa. 1887-1889 Germany sought to exclude the U.S. On 14 June 1889 a tripartite protectorate was established by the U.S., Britain and Germany; on 14 November 1899 Samoa was divided between U.S. and Germany. The U.S. received Tutuila Island (with its harbour Pago Pago) and some others

1871 U.S. military expedition sent to Korea after the crew of a U.S. armed vessel were murdered by Koreans. After fighting, 250 Koreans were killed. 3 U.S. troops died

UNITED STATES

ALASKA 1867

Bering Sea

ALEUTIAN ISLANDS 1867

RUSSIA

Peking

CHINA

Hakodate
JAPAN
Shimoda
Nagasaki

KOREA
Samsah
Bay

Shanghai
Ningpo
Foochow
Amoy
Canton

FRENCH
INDO-CHINA

PHILIPPINES
1898

GUAM 1898

WAKE ISLAND
1898

MIDWAY ISLAND 1867

FRENCH FRIGATE ISLAND 1895
HAWAIIAN ISLANDS 1898

JOHNSTON ISLAND 1858

PALMYRA 1898

HOWLAND
1857
BAKER 1857
JARVIS 1857

TUTUILA ISLAND
Pago Pago SAMOA 1899

BRITISH
INDIA

DUTCH EAST INDIES

AUSTRALIA

Territory of the United States

U.S. islands and island groups with date of acquisition

Ports open to U.S. trade by Treaties signed before 1911

64

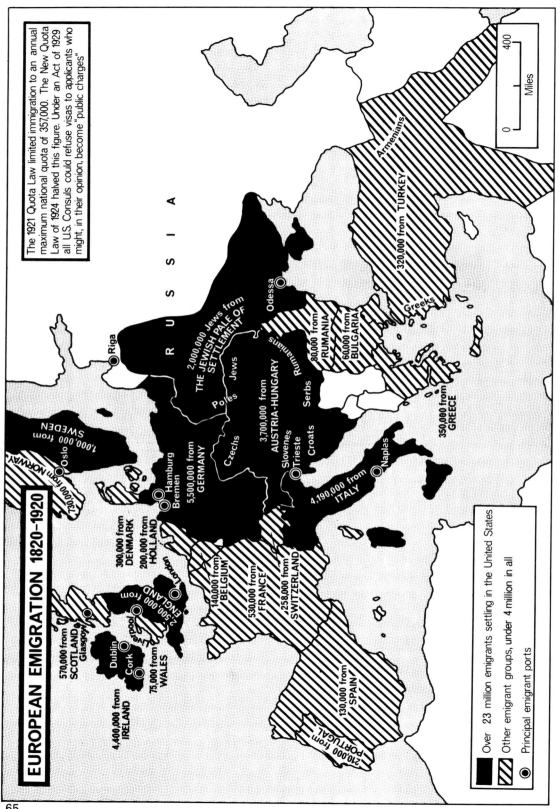

EUROPEAN EMIGRATION 1820–1920

The 1921 Quota Law limited immigration to an annual maximum national quota of 357,000. The New Quota Law of 1924 halved this figure. Under an Act of 1929 all U.S. Consuls could refuse visas to applicants who might, in their opinion, become "public charges"

400,000 from NORWAY

1,000,000 from SWEDEN

570,000 from SCOTLAND

4,400,000 from IRELAND

2,500,000 from ENGLAND

75,000 from WALES

390,000 from DENMARK

200,000 from HOLLAND

140,000 from BELGIUM

530,000 from FRANCE

258,000 from SWITZERLAND

130,000 from SPAIN

210,000 from PORTUGAL

5,500,000 from GERMANY

2,000,000 Jews from THE JEWISH PALE OF SETTLEMENT

R U S S I A

Poles   Jews   Czechs

3,700,000 from AUSTRIA-HUNGARY

Slovenes   Serbs   Croats

Rumanians

80,000 from RUMANIA

60,000 from BULGARIA

Greeks

350,000 from GREECE

4,190,000 from ITALY

320,000 from TURKEY

Armenians

Riga   Oslo   Hamburg   Bremen   London   Liverpool   Glasgow   Dublin   Cork   Trieste   Naples   Odessa

Miles

0   400

Over 23 million emigrants settling in the United States

Other emigrant groups, under 4 million in all

Principal emigrant ports

65

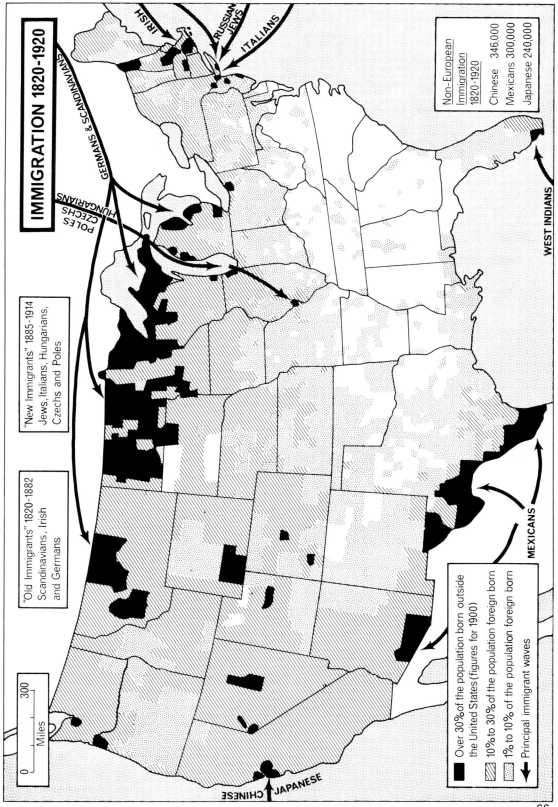

IMMIGRATION 1820-1920

IRISH

RUSSIAN JEWS

ITALIANS

GERMANS & SCANDINAVIANS

POLES
CZECHS
HUNGARIANS

Non-European
Immigration
1820-1920

Chinese 346,000
Mexicans 300,000
Japanese 240,000

WEST INDIES

"New Immigrants" 1885-1914
Jews, Italians, Hungarians,
Czechs and Poles

"Old Immigrants" 1820-1882
Scandinavians, Irish
and Germans

MEXICANS

300
Miles
0

CHINESE   JAPANESE

■ Over 30% of the population born outside
   the United States (figures for 1900)
▨ 10% to 30% of the population foreign born
⬚ 1% to 10% of the population foreign born
↓ Principal immigrant waves

66

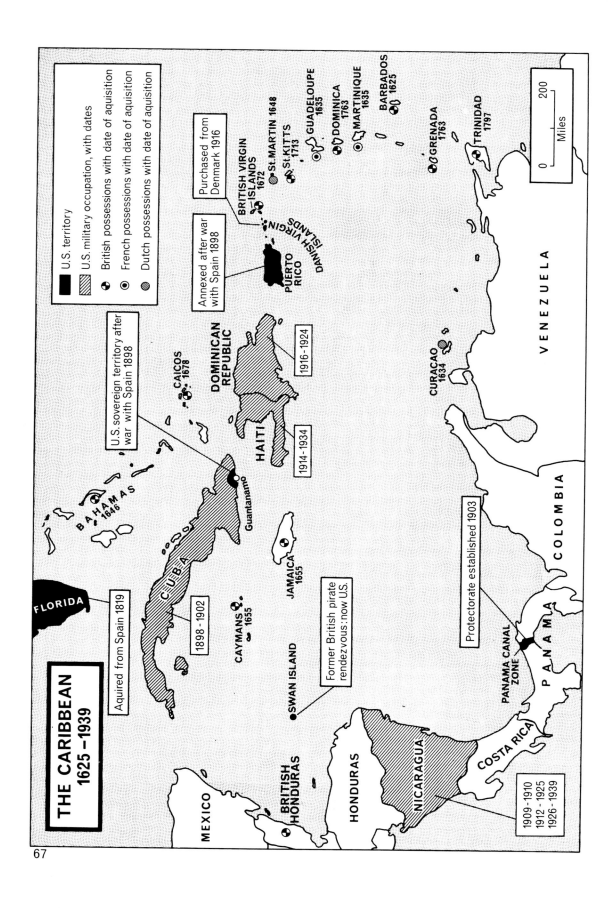

THE CARIBBEAN
1625–1939

U.S. territory
U.S. military occupation, with dates
British possessions with date of aquisition
French possessions with date of aquisition
Dutch possessions with date of aquisition

Purchased from
Denmark 1916

Annexed after war
with Spain 1898

BRITISH VIRGIN
ISLANDS
1672

St.MARTIN 1648
St.KITTS
1713
GUADELOUPE
1635
DOMINICA
1763
MARTINIQUE
1635
BARBADOS 1625
GRENADA
1763
TRINIDAD
1797

0   200
Miles

PUERTO
RICO

DANISH VIRGIN
ISLANDS

U.S. sovereign territory after
war with Spain 1898

CAICOS
1678

DOMINICAN
REPUBLIC

1916-1924

HAITI

1914-1934

BAHAMAS
1646

Guantanamo

CUBA

Aquired from Spain 1819

FLORIDA

1898 - 1902

CAYMANS
1655

JAMAICA
1655

SWAN ISLAND

Former British pirate
rendezvous : now U.S.

CURACAO
1634

VENEZUELA

COLOMBIA

Protectorate established 1903

PANAMA CANAL
ZONE

PANAMA

COSTA RICA

NICARAGUA

1909-1910
1912-1925
1926-1939

BRITISH
HONDURAS

HONDURAS

MEXICO

67

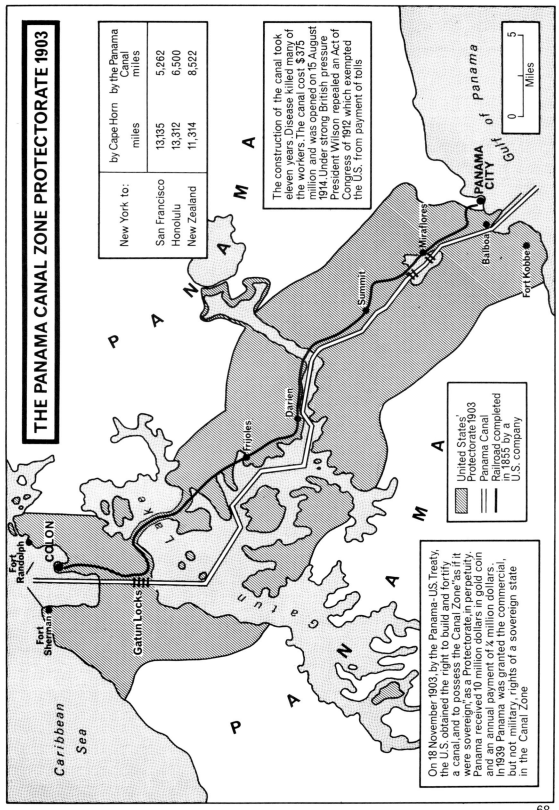

THE PANAMA CANAL ZONE PROTECTORATE 1903

New York to:	by Cape Horn miles	by the Panama Canal miles
San Francisco	13,135	5,262
Honolulu	13,312	6,500
New Zealand	11,314	8,522

The construction of the canal took eleven years. Disease killed many of the workers. The canal cost $375 million and was opened on 15 August 1914. Under strong British pressure President Wilson repealed an Act of Congress of 1912 which exempted the U.S. from payment of tolls

Caribbean Sea

Fort Sherman
Fort Randolph
COLON
Gatun Locks

Frijoles

Darien

Summit

Miraflores
PANAMA CITY
Balboa
Fort Kobbe

Gulf of Panama

P A N A M A

United States' Protectorate 1903

Panama Canal

Railroad completed in 1855 by a U.S. company

0 5
Miles

On 18 November 1903, by the Panama-U.S. Treaty, the U.S. obtained the right to build and fortify a canal, and to possess the Canal Zone "as if it were sovereign", as a Protectorate, in perpetuity. Panama received 10 million dollars in gold coin and an annual payment of ¼ million dollars. In 1939 Panama was granted the commercial, but not military, rights of a sovereign state in the Canal Zone

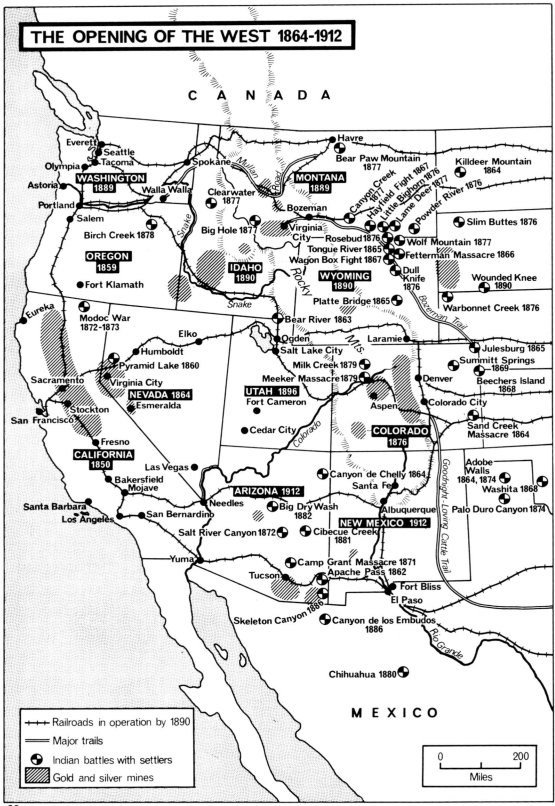

THE OPENING OF THE WEST 1864-1912

C A N A D A

Everett
Seattle
Olympia Tacoma
Astoria Spokane
Portland Walla Walla
WASHINGTON 1889
Salem
Birch Creek 1878
OREGON 1859
Fort Klamath

Havre
Bear Paw Mountain 1877
Killdeer Mountain 1864
MONTANA 1889
Clearwater 1877
Bozeman
Canyon Creek 1877
Hayfield Fight 1867
Little Bighorn 1876
Lame Deer 1877
Powder River 1876
Big Hole 1877
Virginia City
Rosebud 1876
Slim Buttes 1876
Tongue River 1865
Wolf Mountain 1877
Wagon Box Fight 1867
Fetterman Massacre 1866
IDAHO 1890
WYOMING 1890
Dull Knife 1876
Wounded Knee 1890
Platte Bridge 1865
Warbonnet Creek 1876

Eureka
Modoc War 1872-1873
Bear River 1863
Elko
Ogden
Laramie
Julesburg 1865
Humboldt
Salt Lake City
Summitt Springs 1869
Pyramid Lake 1860
Milk Creek 1879
Beechers Island 1868
Sacramento
Meeker Massacre 1879
Denver
Virginia City
NEVADA 1864
UTAH 1896
Colorado City
Stockton
Esmeralda
Fort Cameron
Aspen
Sand Creek Massacre 1864
San Francisco
Fresno
Cedar City
COLORADO 1876
CALIFORNIA 1850
Las Vegas
Adobe Walls 1864, 1874
Bakersfield
Canyon de Chelly 1864
Washita 1868
Mojave
Santa Fe
Palo Duro Canyon 1874
ARIZONA 1912
Needles
Big Dry Wash 1882
Albuquerque
Santa Barbara
San Bernardino
NEW MEXICO 1912
Los Angeles
Salt River Canyon 1872
Cibecue Creek 1881
Yuma
Camp Grant Massacre 1871
Tucson
Apache Pass 1862
Fort Bliss
Skeleton Canyon 1886
El Paso
Canyon de los Embudos 1886
Chihuahua 1880
Rio Grande

M E X I C O

Rocky Mts.
Snake
Mullan Road
Bozeman Trail
Colorado
Goodnight-Loving Cattle Trail

+++ Railroads in operation by 1890
=== Major trails
◑ Indian battles with settlers
▨ Gold and silver mines

0   200
Miles

69

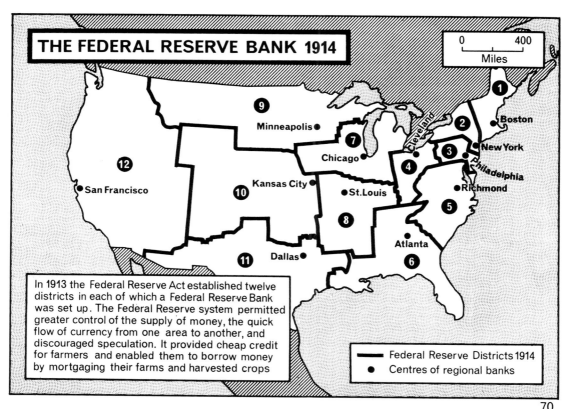

THE FEDERAL RESERVE BANK 1914

0 — 400
Miles

① Boston
② New York
③ Philadelphia
④ Cleveland
⑤ Richmond
⑥ Atlanta
⑦ Chicago
⑧ St. Louis
⑨ Minneapolis
⑩ Kansas City
⑪ Dallas
⑫ San Francisco

In 1913 the Federal Reserve Act established twelve districts in each of which a Federal Reserve Bank was set up. The Federal Reserve system permitted greater control of the supply of money, the quick flow of currency from one area to another, and discouraged speculation. It provided cheap credit for farmers and enabled them to borrow money by mortgaging their farms and harvested crops

——— Federal Reserve Districts 1914
● Centres of regional banks

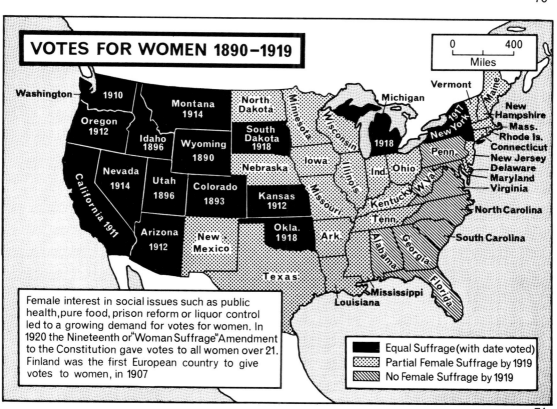

VOTES FOR WOMEN 1890-1919

0 — 400
Miles

Washington 1910
Oregon 1912
Montana 1914
North Dakota
South Dakota 1918
Minnesota
Wisconsin
Michigan
1918
New York 1917
Maine
Vermont
New Hampshire
Mass.
Rhode Is.
Connecticut
New Jersey
Delaware
Maryland
Virginia
Idaho 1896
Wyoming 1890
Nebraska
Iowa
Illinois
Ind.
Ohio
Penn.
W.Va.
Nevada 1914
Utah 1896
Colorado 1893
Kansas 1912
Missouri
Kentucky
Tenn.
North Carolina
South Carolina
California 1911
Arizona 1912
New Mexico
Okla. 1918
Ark.
Alabama
Georgia
Florida
Texas
Mississippi
Louisiana

Female interest in social issues such as public health, pure food, prison reform or liquor control led to a growing demand for votes for women. In 1920 the Nineteenth or "Woman Suffrage" Amendment to the Constitution gave votes to all women over 21. Finland was the first European country to give votes to women, in 1907

■ Equal Suffrage (with date voted)
▨ Partial Female Suffrage by 1919
▩ No Female Suffrage by 1919

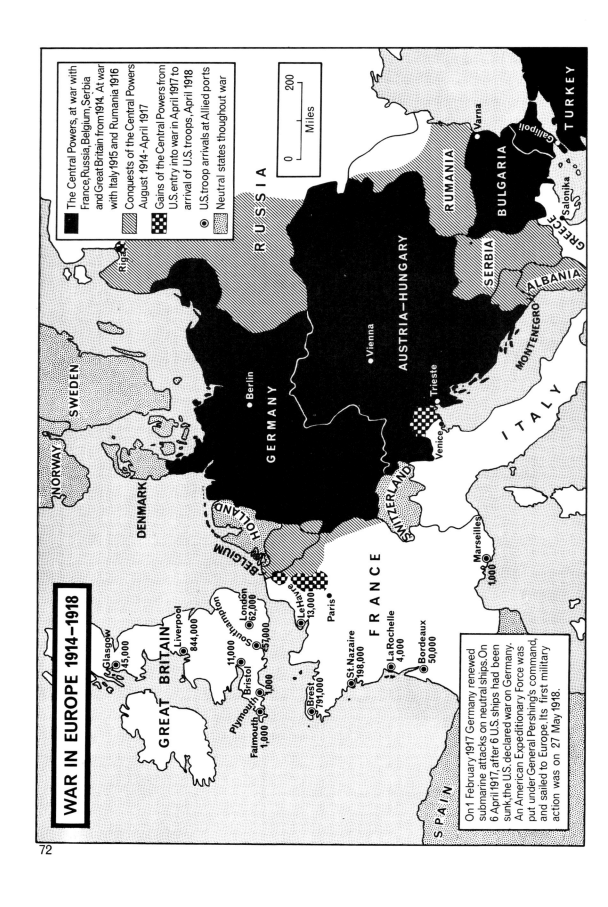

WAR IN EUROPE 1914–1918

The Central Powers, at war with France, Russia, Belgium, Serbia and Great Britain from 1914. At war with Italy 1915 and Rumania 1916

Conquests of the Central Powers August 1914 - April 1917

Gains of the Central Powers from U.S. entry into war in April 1917 to arrival of U.S. troops, April 1918

U.S. troop arrivals at Allied ports

Neutral states thoughout war

200

0

Miles

RUSSIA

Riga

SWEDEN

NORWAY

DENMARK

Berlin

GERMANY

HOLLAND

BELGIUM

Vienna

AUSTRIA–HUNGARY

SWITZERLAND

Trieste

Venice

ITALY

MONTENEGRO

ALBANIA

SERBIA

RUMANIA

Varna

BULGARIA

Gallipoli

TURKEY

Salonika

GREECE

FRANCE

Marseilles
1,000

Glasgow
15,000

GREAT BRITAIN

Liverpool
844,000

London
62,000

Southampton
57,000

11,000

Bristol
1,000

Plymouth
1,000

Falmouth
1,000

LeHavre
13,000

Paris

Brest
791,000

St. Nazaire
198,000

La Rochelle
4,000

Bordeaux
50,000

SPAIN

On 1 February 1917 Germany renewed submarine attacks on neutral ships. On 6 April 1917, after 6 U.S. ships had been sunk, the U.S. declared war on Germany. An American Expeditionary Force was put under General Pershing's command, and sailed to Europe. Its first military action was on 27 May 1918.

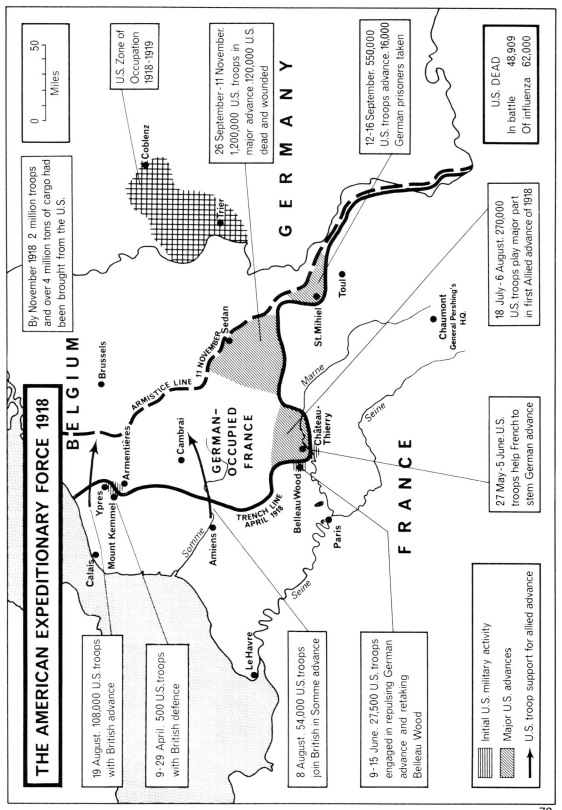

THE AMERICAN EXPEDITIONARY FORCE 1918

By November 1918 2 million troops and over 4 million tons of cargo had been brought from the U.S.

U.S. Zone of Occupation 1918-1919

26 September - 11 November. 1,200,000 U.S. troops in major advance. 120,000 U.S. dead and wounded

12-16 September. 550,000 U.S. troops advance. 16,000 German prisoners taken

U.S. DEAD
In battle 48,909
Of influenza 62,000

18 July - 6 August. 270,000 U.S. troops play major part in first Allied advance of 1918

27 May - 5 June. U.S. troops help French to stem German advance

19 August. 108,000 U.S. troops with British advance

9-29 April. 500 U.S. troops with British defence

8 August. 54,000 U.S. troops join British in Somme advance

9-15 June. 27,500 U.S. troops engaged in repulsing German advance and retaking Belleau Wood

GERMANY

BELGIUM

FRANCE

GERMAN-OCCUPIED FRANCE

Coblenz

Trier

Sedan

St. Mihiel

Toul

Chaumont
General Pershing's H.Q.

ARMISTICE LINE 11 NOVEMBER

Brussels

Armentières

Cambrai

Ypres

Mount Kemmel

Calais

Amiens

Le Havre

Paris

Belleau Wood

Château-Thierry

Marne

Seine

Seine

Somme

TRENCH LINE APRIL 1918

Scale
0 50 Miles

Initial U.S. military activity

Major U.S. advances

U.S. troop support for allied advance

73

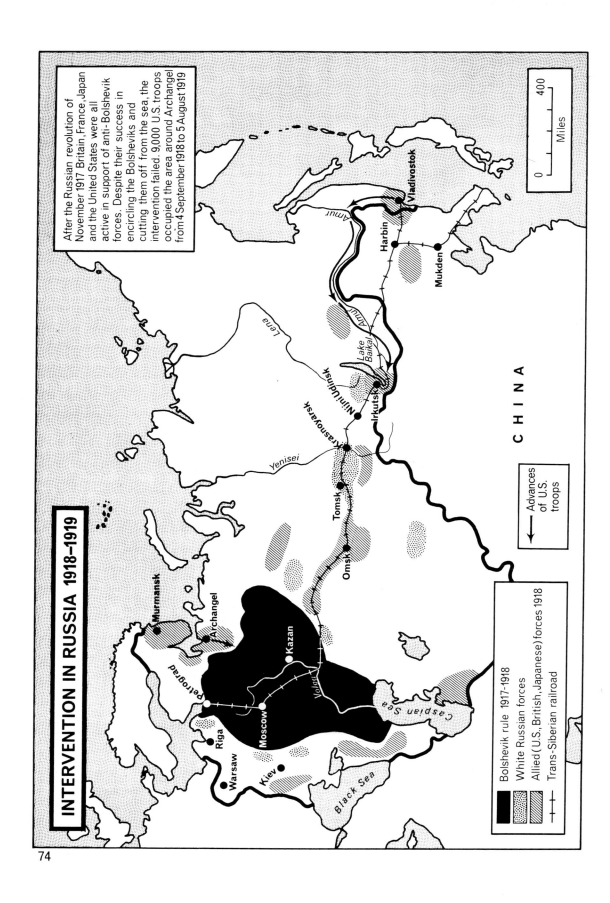

INTERVENTION IN RUSSIA 1918–1919

After the Russian revolution of November 1917 Britain, France, Japan and the United States were all active in support of anti-Bolshevik forces. Despite their success in encircling the Bolsheviks and cutting them off from the sea, the intervention failed. 9,000 U.S. troops occupied the area around Archangel from 4 September 1918 to 5 August 1919

0   400
Miles

Murmansk

Archangel

Petrograd

Riga

Warsaw

Kiev

Moscow

Kazan

Black Sea

Caspian Sea

Volga

Omsk

Tomsk

Krasnoyarsk

Yenisei

Lena

Nijni Udinsk

Irkutsk

Lake Baikal

Amur

Harbin

Mukden

Vladivostok

Amur

C H I N A

Bolshevik rule 1917-1918

White Russian forces

Allied (U.S., British, Japanese) forces 1918

Trans-Siberian railroad

Advances of U.S. troops

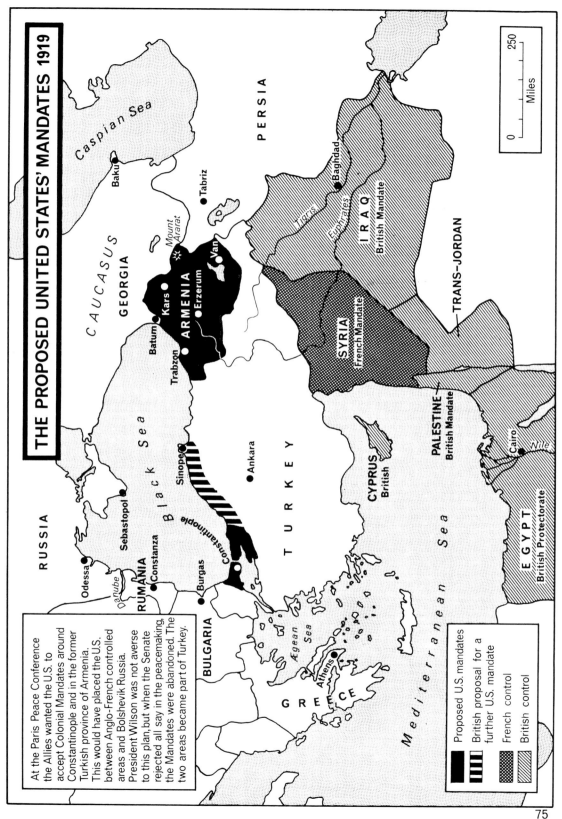

THE PROPOSED UNITED STATES' MANDATES 1919

At the Paris Peace Conference the Allies wanted the U.S. to accept Colonial Mandates around Constantinople and in the former Turkish province of Armenia. This would have placed the U.S. between Anglo-French controlled areas and Bolshevik Russia. President Wilson was not averse to this plan, but when the Senate rejected all say in the peacemaking, the Mandates were abandoned. The two areas became part of Turkey.

Key:
- Proposed U.S. mandates
- British proposal for a further U.S. mandate
- French control
- British control

250 Miles
0

Labels on map:

RUSSIA

Caspian Sea

PERSIA

Baku

Tabriz

Mount Ararat

Van

CAUCASUS

GEORGIA

ARMENIA

Kars

Erzerum

IRAQ
British Mandate

Baghdad

Tigris

Euphrates

TRANS-JORDAN

SYRIA
French Mandate

Batum

Trabzon

Black Sea

Sinope

Ankara

TURKEY

CYPRUS
British

PALESTINE
British Mandate

Cairo

Nile

EGYPT
British Protectorate

Mediterranean Sea

Odessa

Sebastopol

Constanza

RUMANIA

Danube

Burgas

BULGARIA

Constantinople

Aegean Sea

Athens

GREECE

75

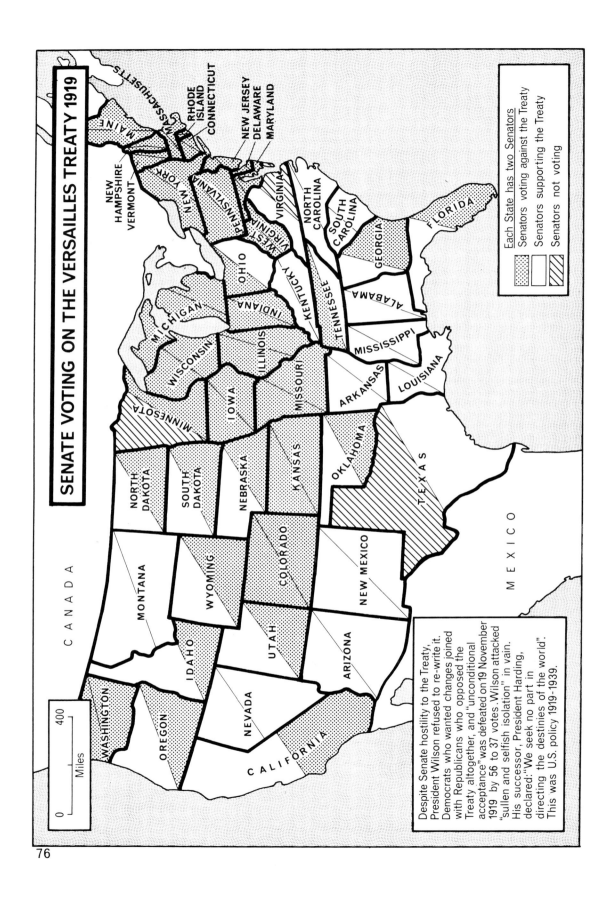

SENATE VOTING ON THE VERSAILLES TREATY 1919

CANADA

MEXICO

Each State has two Senators
- Senators voting against the Treaty
- Senators supporting the Treaty
- Senators not voting

WASHINGTON
OREGON
CALIFORNIA
NEVADA
IDAHO
MONTANA
WYOMING
UTAH
ARIZONA
NEW MEXICO
COLORADO
NORTH DAKOTA
SOUTH DAKOTA
NEBRASKA
KANSAS
OKLAHOMA
T E X A S
MINNESOTA
IOWA
MISSOURI
ARKANSAS
LOUISIANA
WISCONSIN
MICHIGAN
ILLINOIS
INDIANA
OHIO
KENTUCKY
TENNESSEE
MISSISSIPPI
ALABAMA
GEORGIA
FLORIDA
SOUTH CAROLINA
NORTH CAROLINA
VIRGINIA
WEST VIRGINIA
PENNSYLVANIA
NEW YORK
MAINE
NEW HAMPSHIRE
VERMONT
MASSACHUSETTS
RHODE ISLAND
CONNECTICUT
NEW JERSEY
DELAWARE
MARYLAND

Despite Senate hostility to the Treaty,
President Wilson refused to re-write it.
Democrats who wanted changes joined
with Republicans who opposed the
Treaty altogether, and "unconditional
acceptance" was defeated on 19 November
1919 by 56 to 37 votes. Wilson attacked
"sullen and selfish isolation" in vain.
His successor, President Harding,
declared: "We seek no part in
directing the destinies of the world".
This was U.S. policy 1919-1939.

0   400
Miles

76

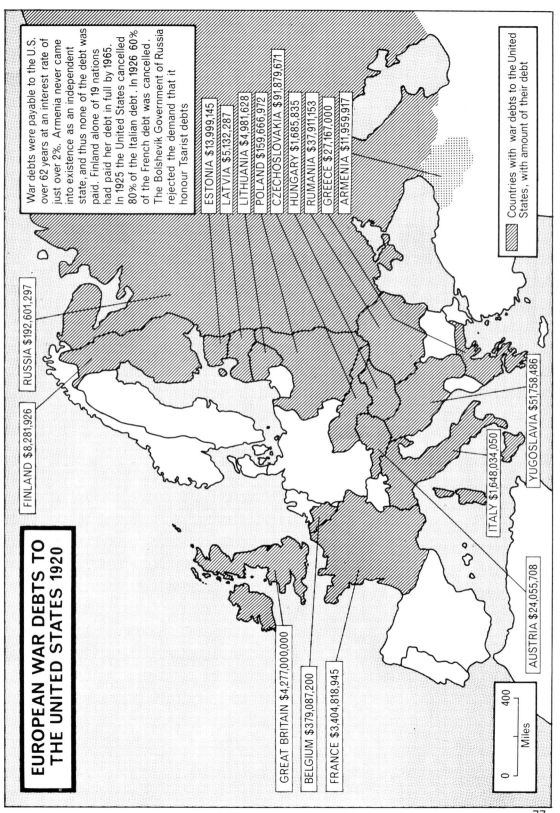

EUROPEAN WAR DEBTS TO THE UNITED STATES 1920

War debts were payable to the U.S. over 62 years at an interest rate of just over 2%. Armenia never came into existence as an independent state, and thus none of the debt was paid. Finland alone of 19 nations had paid her debt in full by 1965. In 1925 the United States cancelled 80% of the Italian debt. In 1926 60% of the French debt was cancelled. The Bolshevik Government of Russia rejected the demand that it honour Tsarist debts

ESTONIA $13,999,145
LATVIA $5,132,287
LITHUANIA $4,981,628
POLAND $159,666,972
CZECHOSLOVAKIA $91,879,671
HUNGARY $1,685,835
RUMANIA $37,911,153
GREECE $27,167,000
ARMENIA $11,959,917

Countries with war debts to the United States, with amount of their debt

RUSSIA $192,601,297

FINLAND $8,281,926

YUGOSLAVIA $51,758,486

ITALY $1,648,034,050

AUSTRIA $24,055,708

GREAT BRITAIN $4,277,000,000

BELGIUM $379,087,200

FRANCE $3,404,818,945

0   400
Miles

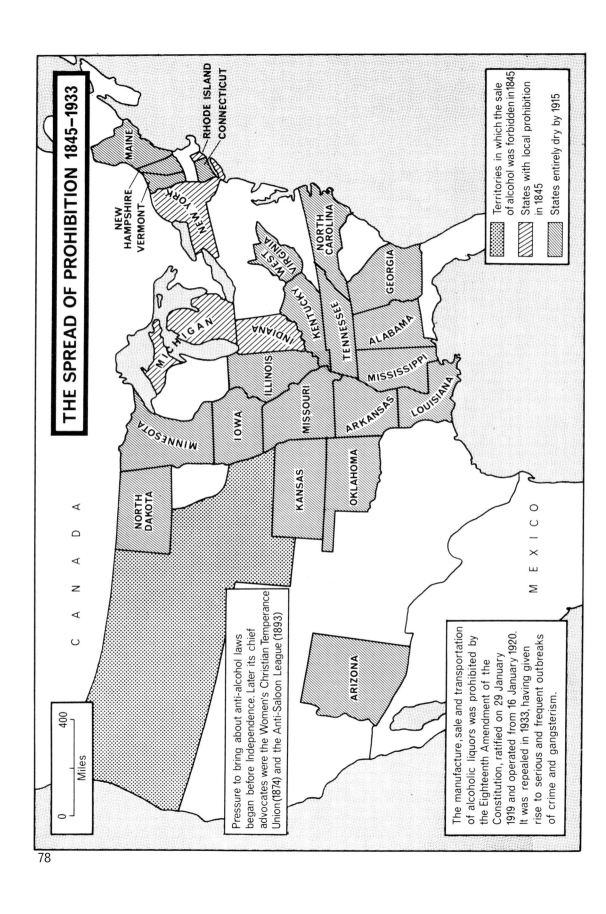

THE SPREAD OF PROHIBITION 1845–1933

CANADA

MEXICO

Legend:
- Territories in which the sale of alcohol was forbidden in 1845
- States with local prohibition in 1845
- States entirely dry by 1915

NORTH DAKOTA
MINNESOTA
MICHIGAN
IOWA
ILLINOIS
INDIANA
MISSOURI
KANSAS
OKLAHOMA
ARKANSAS
LOUISIANA
MISSISSIPPI
ALABAMA
TENNESSEE
KENTUCKY
WEST VIRGINIA
GEORGIA
NORTH CAROLINA
ARIZONA

MAINE
NEW HAMPSHIRE
VERMONT
NEW YORK
RHODE ISLAND
CONNECTICUT

Pressure to bring about anti-alcohol laws began before Independence. Later its chief advocates were the Women's Christian Temperance Union (1874) and the Anti-Saloon League (1893)

The manufacture, sale and transportation of alcoholic liquors was prohibited by the Eighteenth Amendment of the Constitution, ratified on 29 January 1919 and operated from 16 January 1920. It was repealed in 1933, having given rise to serious and frequent outbreaks of crime and gangsterism.

0   400
Miles

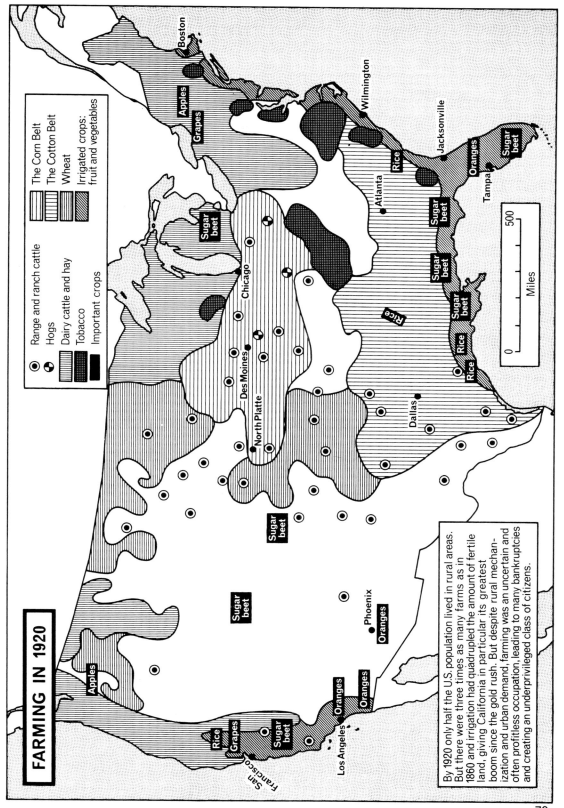

FARMING IN 1920

Legend:

- The Corn Belt
- The Cotton Belt
- Wheat
- Irrigated crops: fruit and vegetables
- ⊙ Range and ranch cattle
- ◔ Hogs
- Dairy cattle and hay
- Tobacco
- Important crops

Cities and labels: Boston, Apples, Grapes, Wilmington, Rice, Jacksonville, Oranges, Sugar beet, Atlanta, Tampa, Sugar beet, Sugar beet, Sugar beet, Rice, Rice, Rice, Chicago, Des Moines, North Platte, Dallas, Sugar beet, Phoenix, Oranges, Sugar beet, Apples, Oranges, Oranges, Los Angeles, Rice, Grapes, Sugar beet, San Francisco

Scale: 0 — 500 Miles

By 1920 only half the U.S. population lived in rural areas. But there were three times as many farms as in 1860 and irrigation had quadrupled the amount of fertile land, giving California in particular its greatest boom since the gold rush. But despite rural mechanization and urban demand, farming was an uncertain and often profitless occupation, leading to many bankruptcies and creating an underprivileged class of citizens.

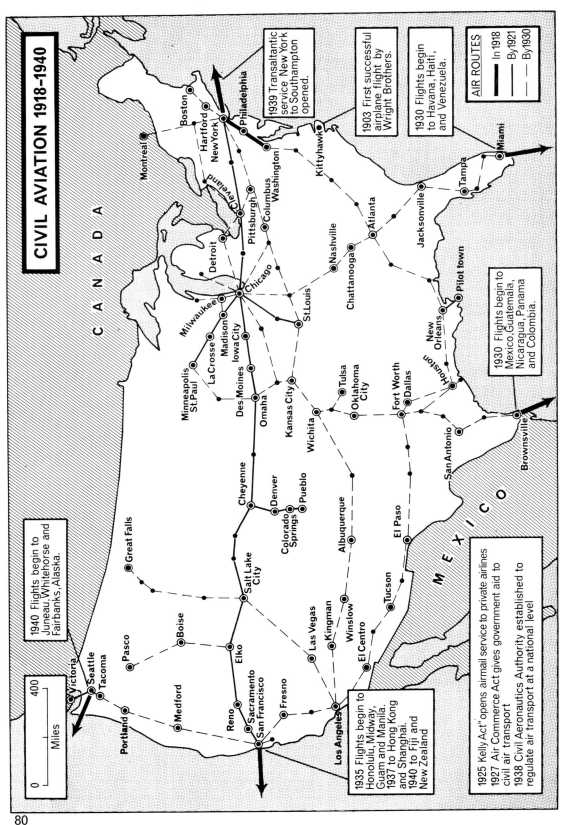

CIVIL AVIATION 1918-1940

CANADA

MEXICO

AIR ROUTES
— In 1918
— By1921
--- By1930

1939 Transaltantic service New York to Southampton opened.

1903 First successful airplane flight by Wright Brothers.

1930 Flights begin to Havana, Haiti, and Venezuela.

1930 Flights begin to Mexico, Guatemala, Nicaragua, Panama and Colombia.

1940 Flights begin to Juneau, Whitehorse and Fairbanks, Alaska.

1935 Flights begin to Honolulu, Midway, Guam and Manila. 1937 to Hong Kong and Shanghai. 1940 to Fiji and New Zealand

1925 Kelly Act" opens airmail service to private airlines
1927 Air Commerce Act gives government aid to civil air transport
1938 Civil Aeronautics Authority established to regulate air transport at a national level

0   400
Miles

Victoria
Seattle
Tacoma
Portland
Pasco
Medford
Boise
Great Falls
Reno
Sacramento
San Francisco
Fresno
Elko
Salt Lake City
Las Vegas
Kingman
Winslow
El Centro
Tucson
Los Angeles
El Paso
Albuquerque
Cheyenne
Denver
Colorado Springs
Pueblo
Minneapolis St.Paul
La Crosse
Madison
Iowa City
Des Moines
Omaha
Milwaukee
Chicago
Kansas City
Wichita
Tulsa
Oklahoma City
Fort Worth
Dallas
San Antonio
Brownsville
Houston
New Orleans
Pilot town
Nashville
Chattanooga
Atlanta
St.Louis
Jacksonville
Tampa
Miami
Columbus
Washington
Pittsburgh
Cleveland
Detroit
Kittyhawk
Boston
Hartford
New York
Philadelphia
Montreal

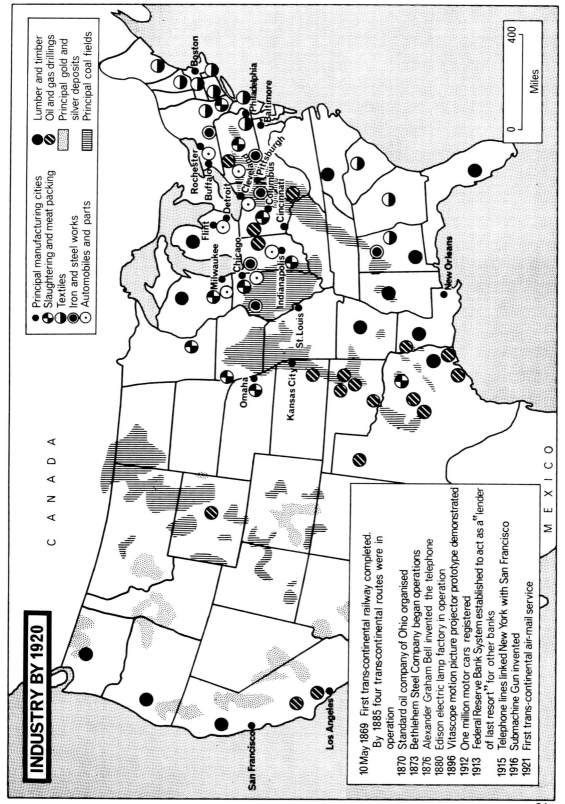

INDUSTRY BY 1920

Legend:

- Principal manufacturing cities
- Slaughtering and meat packing
- Textiles
- Iron and steel works
- Automobiles and parts
- Lumber and timber
- Oil and gas drillings
- Principal gold and silver deposits
- Principal coal fields

CANADA

MEXICO

Cities labelled: Boston, Philadelphia, Baltimore, Pittsburgh, Rochester, Buffalo, Cleveland, Detroit, Columbus, Cincinnati, Flint, Milwaukee, Chicago, Indianapolis, St. Louis, Omaha, Kansas City, New Orleans, Los Angeles, San Francisco

0   400
Miles

10 May 1869 First trans-continental railway completed. By 1885 four trans-continental routes were in operation
1870 Standard oil company of Ohio organised
1873 Bethlehem Steel Company began operations
1876 Alexander Graham Bell invented the telephone
1880 Edison electric lamp factory in operation
1896 Vitascope motion picture projector prototype demonstrated
1912 One million motor cars registered
1913 Federal Reserve Bank System established to act as a "lender of last resort" for other banks
1915 Telephone lines linked New York with San Francisco
1916 Submachine Gun invented
1921 First trans-continental air-mail service

81

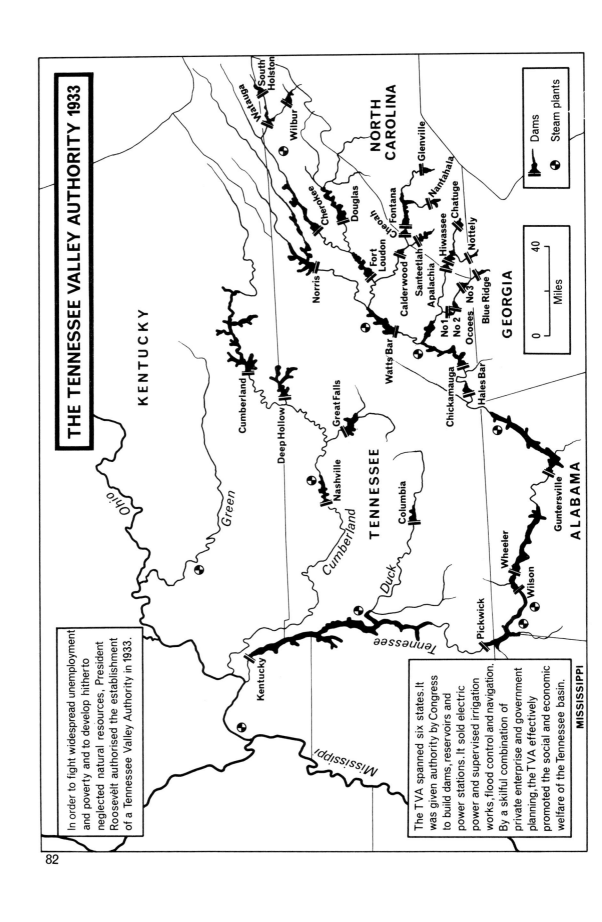

THE TENNESSEE VALLEY AUTHORITY 1933

In order to fight widespread unemployment and poverty and to develop hitherto neglected natural resources, President Roosevelt authorised the establishment of a Tennessee Valley Authority in 1933.

The TVA spanned six states. It was given authority by Congress to build dams, reservoirs and power stations. It sold electric power and supervised irrigation works, flood control and navigation. By a skilful combination of private enterprise and government planning, the TVA effectively promoted the social and economic welfare of the Tennessee basin.

Dams

Steam plants

40

0   Miles

KENTUCKY

TENNESSEE

NORTH CAROLINA

GEORGIA

ALABAMA

MISSISSIPPI

Ohio

Green

Cumberland

Duck

Tennessee

Mississippi

Watauga

South Holston

Wilbur

Cherokee

Douglas

Cheoah

Fontana

Glenville

Nantahala

Chatuge

Hiwassee

Nottely

Norris

Fort Loudon

Calderwood

Santeetlah

Apalachia

No 1

No 2

Ocoees   No 3

Blue Ridge

Watts Bar

Chickamauga

Hales Bar

Cumberland

Deep Hollow

Great Falls

Nashville

Columbia

Wheeler

Guntersville

Wilson

Pickwick

Kentucky

82

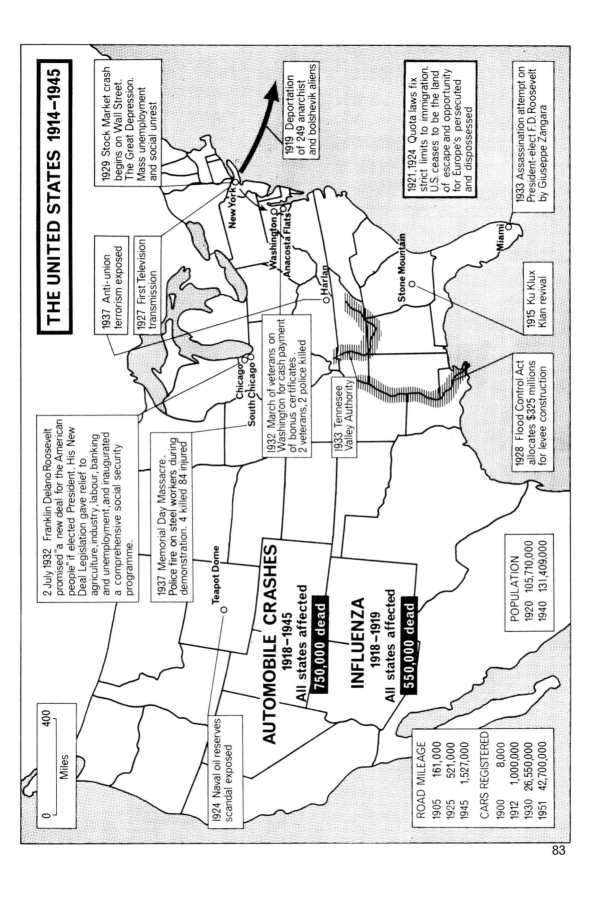

THE UNITED STATES 1914–1945

1929 Stock Market crash begins on Wall Street. The Great Depression. Mass unemployment and social unrest

1919 Deportation of 249 anarchist and bolshevik aliens

1921,1924 Quota laws fix strict limits to immigration. U.S. ceases to be the land of escape and opportunity for Europe's persecuted and dispossessed

1933 Assassination attempt on President-elect F.D.Roosevelt by Giuseppe Zangara

1937 Anti-union terrorism exposed

1927 First Television transmission

1915 Ku Klux Klan revival

New York

Washington
Anacostá Flats

Harlan

Stone Mountain

Miami

2 July 1932 Franklin Delano Roosevelt promised "a new deal for the American people" if elected President. His New Deal Legislation gave relief to agriculture, industry, labour, banking and unemployment, and inaugurated a comprehensive social security programme.

1937 Memorial Day Massacre. Police fire on steel workers during demonstration. 4 killed 84 injured

Chicago
South Chicago

1932 March of veterans on Washington for cash payment of bonus certificates. 2 veterans, 2 police killed

1933 Tennesee Valley Authority

1928 Flood Control Act allocates $325 millions for levee construction

Teapot Dome

AUTOMOBILE CRASHES
1918–1945
All states affected
750,000 dead

INFLUENZA
1918–1919
All states affected
550,000 dead

1924 Naval oil reserves scandal exposed

POPULATION	
1920	105,710,000
1940	131,409,000

ROAD MILEAGE	
1905	161,000
1925	521,000
1945	1,527,000

CARS REGISTERED	
1900	8,000
1912	1,000,000
1930	26,550,000
1951	42,700,000

0 — 400
Miles

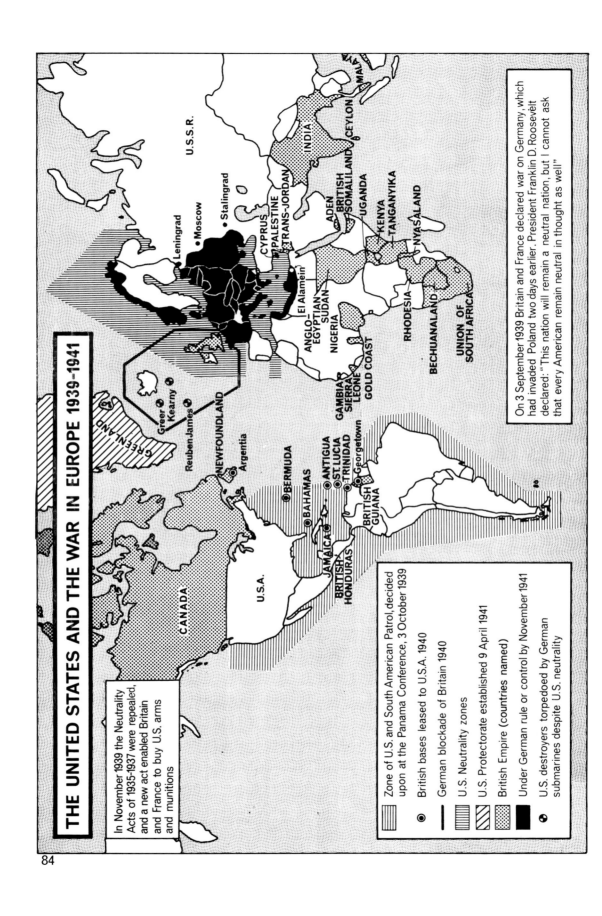

THE UNITED STATES AND THE WAR IN EUROPE 1939–1941

In November 1939 the Neutrality Acts of 1935-1937 were repealed, and a new act enabled Britain and France to buy U.S. arms and munitions

On 3 September 1939 Britain and France declared war on Germany, which had invaded Poland two days earlier. President Franklin D. Roosevelt declared: "This nation will remain a neutral nation, but I cannot ask that every American remain neutral in thought as well"

Zone of U.S. and South American Patrol, decided upon at the Panama Conference, 3 October 1939

⊙ British bases leased to U.S.A. 1940

— German blockade of Britain 1940

U.S. Neutrality zones

U.S. Protectorate established 9 April 1941

British Empire (countries named)

Under German rule or control by November 1941

⊙ U.S. destroyers torpedoed by German submarines despite U.S. neutrality

U.S.S.R.

Leningrad
• Moscow
• Stalingrad

CYPRUS
PALESTINE
TRANS-JORDAN
ADEN
BRITISH SOMALILAND
CEYLON
INDIA
MALA
UGANDA
KENYA
TANGANYIKA
NYASALAND
RHODESIA
BECHUANALAND
UNION OF SOUTH AFRICA

El Alamein
ANGLO-EGYPTIAN SUDAN
NIGERIA
GOLD COAST
GAMBIA
SIERRA LEONE

GREENLAND

Greer ⊙   ⊙ Kearny

Reuben James ⊙

NEWFOUNDLAND
Argentia

⊙ BERMUDA

⊙ BAHAMAS
ANTIGUA
JAMAICA ⊙ ST LUCIA
TRINIDAD
BRITISH HONDURAS
BRITISH GUIANA
Georgetown

CANADA

U.S.A.

84

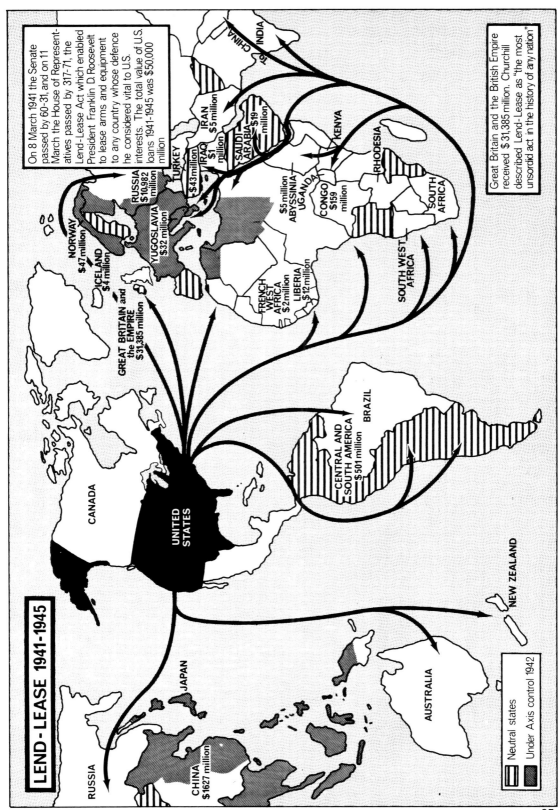

LEND-LEASE 1941-1945

On 8 March 1941 the Senate passed by 60-31, and on 11 March the House of Representatives passed by 317-71, the Lend-Lease Act which enabled President Franklin D. Roosevelt to lease arms and equipment to any country whose defence he considered vital to U.S. interests. The total value of U.S. loans 1941-1945 was $50,000 million

Great Britain and the British Empire received $31,385 million. Churchill described Lend-Lease as "the most unsordid act in the history of any nation"

CANADA

UNITED STATES

RUSSIA

JAPAN

CHINA
$1627 million

AUSTRALIA

NEW ZEALAND

CENTRAL AND SOUTH AMERICA $501 million

BRAZIL

GREAT BRITAIN and the EMPIRE $31,385 million

NORWAY $47 million

ICELAND $4 million

RUSSIA $10,982 million

YUGOSLAVIA $32 million

TURKEY $43 million

IRAQ $1 million

IRAN $5 million

SAUDI ARABIA $19 million

To CHINA

INDIA

KENYA

UGANDA

ABYSSINIA $5 million

CONGO $159 million

RHODESIA

SOUTH AFRICA

FRENCH WEST AFRICA $2 million

LIBERIA $12 million

SOUTH WEST AFRICA

Neutral states

Under Axis control 1942

85

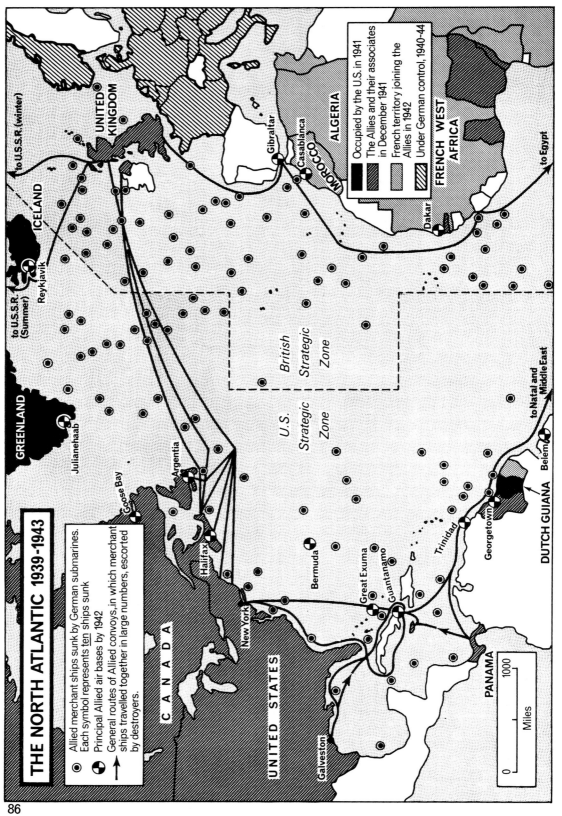

THE NORTH ATLANTIC 1939-1943

Allied merchant ships sunk by German submarines. Each symbol represents ten ships sunk

Principal Allied air bases by 1942

General routes of Allied convoys, in which merchant ships travelled together in large numbers, escorted by destroyers.

Occupied by the U.S. in 1941

The Allies and their associates in December 1941

French territory joining the Allies in 1942

Under German control, 1940-44

GREENLAND

ICELAND

Reykjavik

Julianehaab

to U.S.S.R. (winter)

to U.S.S.R. (Summer)

UNITED KINGDOM

Gibraltar

Casablanca

MOROCCO

ALGERIA

FRENCH WEST AFRICA

Dakar

to Egypt

CANADA

Goose Bay

Argentia

Halifax

New York

Galveston

UNITED STATES

U.S. Strategic Zone

British Strategic Zone

Bermuda

Great Exuma

Guantanamo

Trinidad

Georgetown

DUTCH GUIANA

Belem

to Natal and Middle East

PANAMA

1000

Miles

0

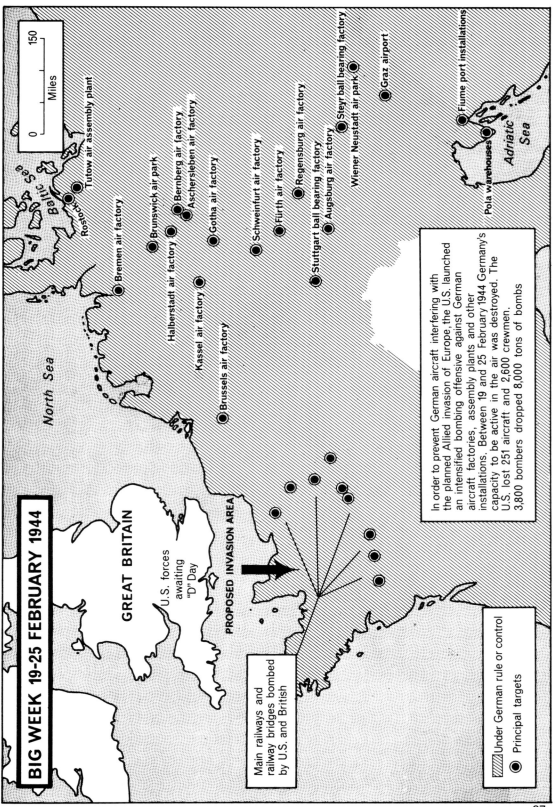

BIG WEEK 19-25 FEBRUARY 1944

150

Miles

0

GREAT BRITAIN

U.S. forces
awaiting
"D" Day

PROPOSED INVASION AREA

North Sea

Baltic Sea

Rostock

Tutow air assembly plant

Bremen air factory

Brunswick air park

Brunswick air factory

Bernberg air factory

Aschersleben air factory

Halberstadt air factory

Gotha air factory

Kassel air factory

Brussels air factory

Schweinfurt air factory

Fürth air factory

Regensburg air factory

Stuttgart ball bearing factory

Augsburg air factory

Wiener Neustadt air park

Steyr ball bearing factory

Graz airport

Fiume port installations

Pola warehouses

Adriatic Sea

In order to prevent German aircraft interfering with the planned Allied invasion of Europe, the U.S. launched an intensified bombing offensive against German aircraft factories, assembly plants and other installations. Between 19 and 25 February 1944 Germany's capacity to be active in the air was destroyed. The U.S. lost 251 aircraft and 2,600 crewmen. The 3,800 bombers dropped 8,000 tons of bombs

Main railways and
railway bridges bombed
by U.S. and British

Under German rule or control

Principal targets

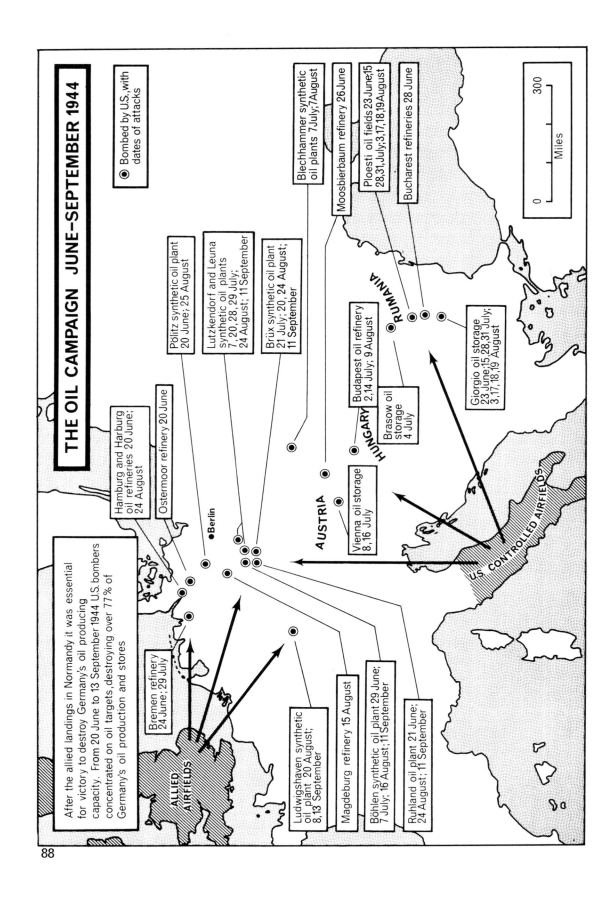

THE OIL CAMPAIGN JUNE–SEPTEMBER 1944

⦿ Bombed by U.S, with dates of attacks

After the allied landings in Normandy it was essential for victory to destroy Germany's oil producing capacity. From 20 June to 13 September 1944 U.S. bombers concentrated on oil targets, destroying over 77% of Germany's oil production and stores

Blechhammer synthetic oil plants 7July; 7August

Moosbierbaum refinery 26 June

Ploesti oil fields 23 June;15 28,31,July; 3,17,18,19August

Bucharest refineries 28 June

0 300

Miles

Pölitz synthetic oil plant 20 June; 25 August

Lutzkendorf and Leuna synthetic oil plants 7, 20, 28, 29 July; 24 August; 11 September

Brüx synthetic oil plant 21 July; 20, 24 August; 11 September

Hamburg and Harburg oil refineries 20 June; 24 August

Ostermoor refinery 20 June

RUMANIA

Budapest oil refinery 2,14 July; 9 August

Giorgio oil storage 23 June;15, 28,31 July; 3,17,18,19 August

Brasow oil storage 4 July

•Berlin

HUNGARY

AUSTRIA

Vienna oil storage 8, 16 July

US CONTROLLED AIRFIELDS

Bremen refinery 24 June; 29 July

ALLIED AIRFIELDS

Ludwigshaven synthetic oil plant 20 August; 8,13 September

Magdeburg refinery 15 August

Böhlen synthetic oil plant 29 June; 7 July; 16 August;11September

Ruhland oil plant 21 June; 24 August; 11 September

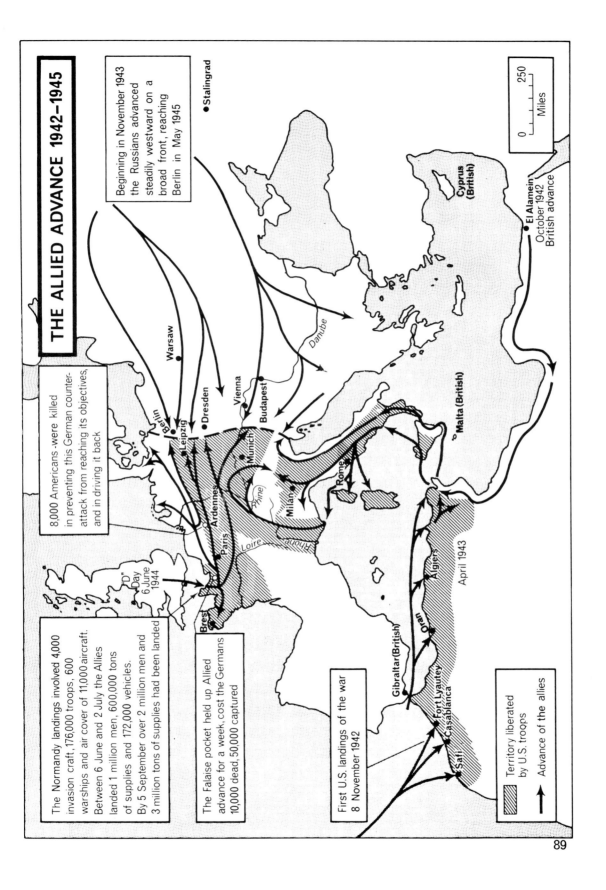

THE ALLIED ADVANCE 1942–1945

Beginning in November 1943 the Russians advanced steadily westward on a broad front, reaching Berlin in May 1945

8,000 Americans were killed in preventing this German counter-attack from reaching its objectives, and in driving it back

The Normandy landings involved 4,000 invasion craft, 176,000 troops, 600 warships and air cover of 11,000 aircraft. Between 6 June and 2 July the Allies landed 1 million men, 600,000 tons of supplies and 172,000 vehicles. By 5 September over 2 million men and 3 million tons of supplies had been landed

The Falaise pocket held up Allied advance for a week, cost the Germans 10,000 dead, 50,000 captured

First U.S. landings of the war 8 November 1942

El Alamein
October 1942
British advance

•Stalingrad

Warsaw

Vienna
Dresden
Budapest

Danube

Berlin
Leipzig
Munich

Ardennes
Paris
Rhine
Loire
Rhône
Milan
Rome

April 1943

Cyprus
(British)

Malta (British)

Gibraltar (British)
Oran
Algiers

Fort Lyautey
Casablanca
Safi

"D" Day
6 June 1944
Brest

Territory liberated by U.S. troops

Advance of the allies

0   250
Miles

89

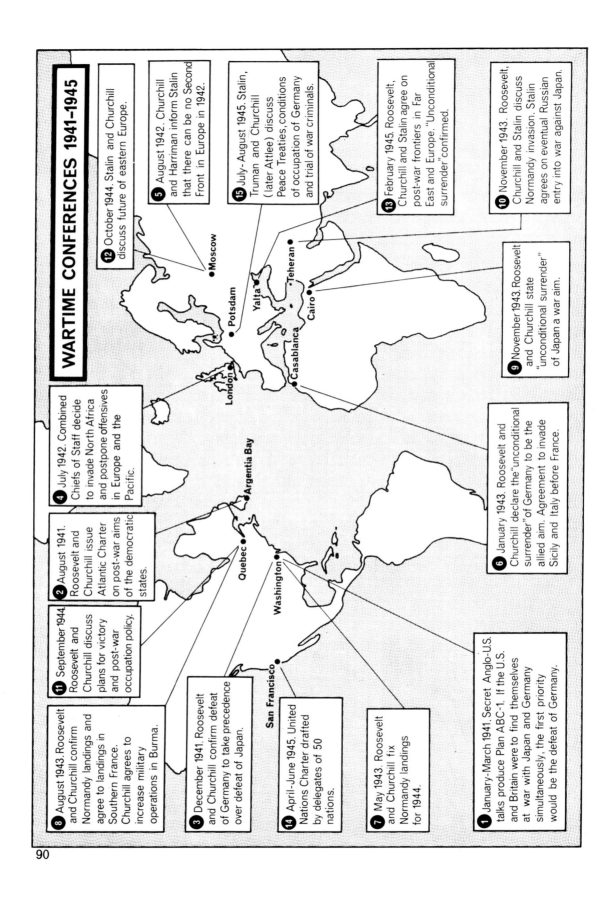

WARTIME CONFERENCES 1941–1945

12 October 1944. Stalin and Churchill discuss future of eastern Europe.

5 August 1942. Churchill and Harriman inform Stalin that there can be no Second Front in Europe in 1942.

15 July–August 1945. Stalin, Truman and Churchill (later Attlee) discuss Peace Treaties, conditions of occupation of Germany and trial of war criminals.

13 February 1945. Roosevelt, Churchill and Stalin agree on post-war frontiers in Far East and Europe. "Unconditional surrender" confirmed.

10 November 1943. Roosevelt, Churchill and Stalin discuss Normandy invasion. Stalin agrees on eventual Russian entry into war against Japan.

9 November 1943. Roosevelt and Churchill state "unconditional surrender" of Japan a war aim.

4 July 1942. Combined Chiefs of Staff decide to invade North Africa and postpone offensives in Europe and the Pacific.

2 August 1941. Roosevelt and Churchill issue Atlantic Charter on post-war aims of the democratic states.

11 September 1944. Roosevelt and Churchill discuss plans for victory and post-war occupation policy.

8 August 1943. Roosevelt and Churchill confirm Normandy landings and agree to landings in Southern France. Churchill agrees to increase military operations in Burma.

3 December 1941. Roosevelt and Churchill confirm defeat of Germany to take precedence over defeat of Japan.

14 April–June 1945. United Nations Charter drafted by delegates of 50 nations.

7 May 1943. Roosevelt and Churchill fix Normandy landings for 1944.

6 January 1943. Roosevelt and Churchill declare the "unconditional surrender" of Germany to be the allied aim. Agreement to invade Sicily and Italy before France.

1 January–March 1941. Secret Anglo-U.S. talks produce Plan ABC-1. If the U.S. and Britain were to find themselves at war with Japan and Germany simultaneously, the first priority would be the defeat of Germany.

● Moscow
● Potsdam
Yalta ●
● Teheran
Casablanca ●
Cairo ●
London ●
● Argentia Bay
Quebec ●
Washington ●
San Francisco ●

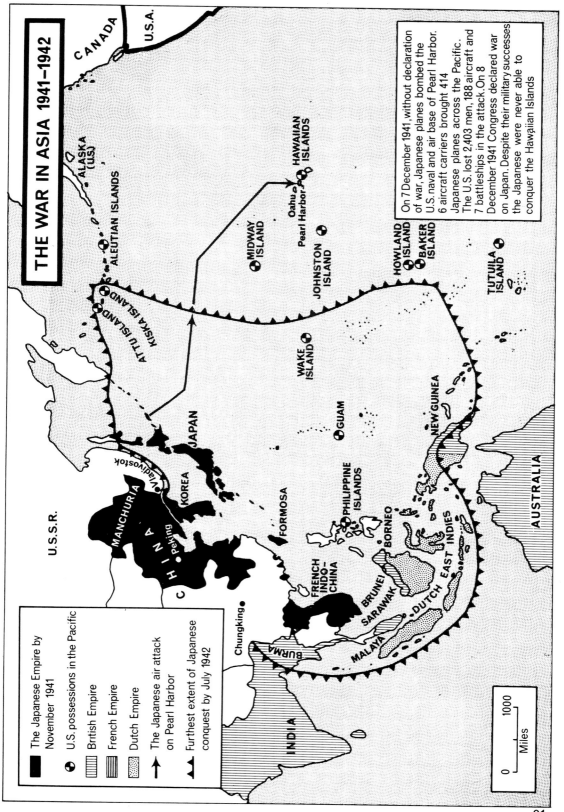

THE WAR IN ASIA 1941–1942

On 7 December 1941, without declaration of war, Japanese planes bombed the U.S. naval and air base of Pearl Harbor. 6 aircraft carriers brought 414 Japanese planes across the Pacific. The U.S. lost 2,403 men, 188 aircraft and 7 battleships in the attack. On 8 December 1941 Congress declared war on Japan. Despite their military successes the Japanese were never able to conquer the Hawaiian Islands

CANADA

U.S.A.

ALASKA (U.S.)

ALEUTIAN ISLANDS

ATTU ISLAND

KISKA ISLAND

MIDWAY ISLAND

Oahu

Pearl Harbor

HAWAIIAN ISLANDS

JOHNSTON ISLAND

HOWLAND ISLAND

BAKER ISLAND

WAKE ISLAND

TUTUILA ISLAND

U.S.S.R.

Vladivostok

MANCHURIA

KOREA

JAPAN

Peking

C H I N A

FORMOSA

GUAM

NEW GUINEA

PHILIPPINE ISLANDS

AUSTRALIA

Chungking

FRENCH INDO–CHINA

BORNEO

BRUNEI

SARAWAK

DUTCH EAST INDIES

MALAYA

BURMA

INDIA

The Japanese Empire by November 1941

U.S. possessions in the Pacific

British Empire

French Empire

Dutch Empire

The Japanese air attack on Pearl Harbor

Furthest extent of Japanese conquest by July 1942

0   1000

Miles

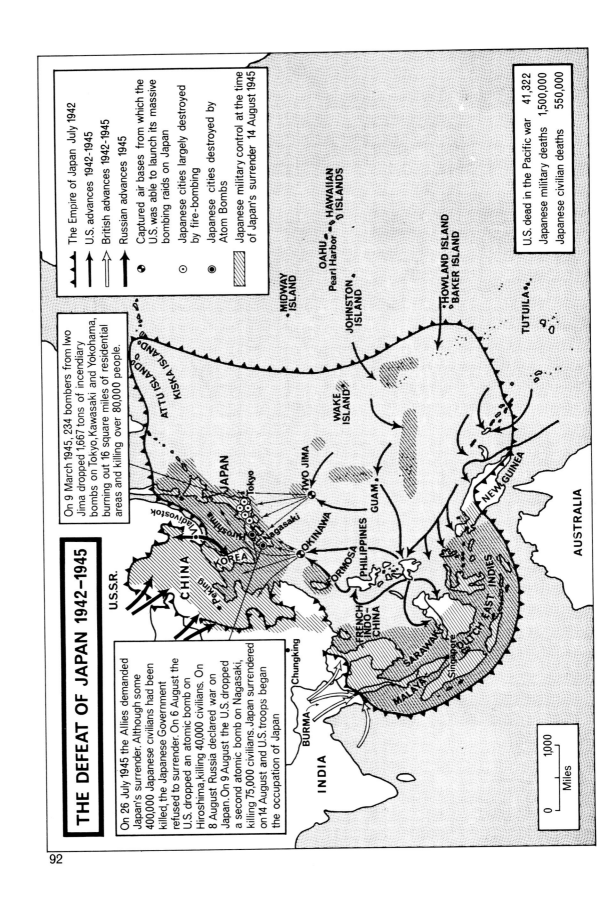

THE DEFEAT OF JAPAN 1942-1945

On 26 July 1945 the Allies demanded Japan's surrender. Although some 400,000 Japanese civilians had been killed, the Japanese Government refused to surrender. On 6 August the U.S. dropped an atomic bomb on Hiroshima, killing 40,000 civilians. On 8 August Russia declared war on Japan. On 9 August the U.S. dropped a second atomic bomb on Nagasaki, killing 75,000 civilians. Japan surrendered on 14 August and U.S. troops began the occupation of Japan

On 9 March 1945, 234 bombers from Iwo Jima dropped 1,667 tons of incendiary bombs on Tokyo, Kawasaki and Yokohama, burning out 16 square miles of residential areas and killing over 80,000 people.

Legend:

- The Empire of Japan July 1942
- U.S. advances 1942-1945
- British advances 1942-1945
- Russian advances 1945
- Captured air bases from which the U.S. was able to launch its massive bombing raids on Japan
- ⊙ Japanese cities largely destroyed by fire-bombing
- ◉ Japanese cities destroyed by Atom Bombs
- Japanese military control at the time of Japan's surrender 14 August 1945

U.S. dead in the Pacific war	41,322
Japanese military deaths	1,500,000
Japanese civilian deaths	550,000

INDIA

BURMA

Chungking

CHINA

Peking

U.S.S.R.

Vladivostok

KOREA

JAPAN

Tokyo

Hiroshima

Nagasaki

OKINAWA

FORMOSA

PHILIPPINES

FRENCH INDO-CHINA

MALAYA

Singapore

SARAWAK

DUTCH EAST INDIES

NEW GUINEA

AUSTRALIA

IWO JIMA

GUAM

WAKE ISLAND

MIDWAY ISLAND

OAHU HAWAIIAN ISLANDS

Pearl Harbor

JOHNSTON ISLAND

HOWLAND ISLAND

BAKER ISLAND

TUTUILA

ATTU ISLAND

KISKA ISLAND

0   1,000
Miles

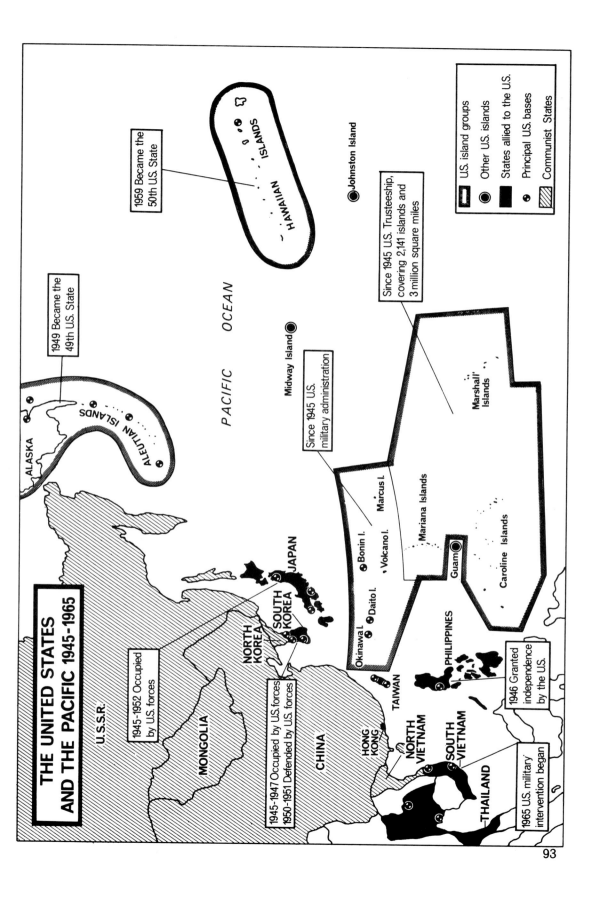

THE UNITED STATES
AND THE PACIFIC 1945-1965

U.S.S.R.

MONGOLIA

CHINA

ALASKA

ALEUTIAN ISLANDS

PACIFIC OCEAN

HAWAIIAN ISLANDS

1949 Became the 49th U.S. State

1959 Became the 50th U.S. State

Johnston Island

Midway Island

Since 1945 U.S. Trusteeship, covering 2,141 islands and 3 million square miles

Since 1945 U.S. military administration

Marshall Islands

Marcus I.

Mariana Islands

Bonin I.

Volcano I.

Okinawa I.

Daito I.

Caroline Islands

Guam

JAPAN

SOUTH KOREA

NORTH KOREA

1945-1952 Occupied by U.S. forces

1945-1947 Occupied by U.S. forces
1950-1951 Defended by U.S. forces

TAIWAN

HONG KONG

NORTH VIETNAM

SOUTH VIETNAM

THAILAND

PHILIPPINES

1946 Granted independence by the U.S.

1965 U.S. military intervention began

U.S. island groups

Other U.S. islands

States allied to the U.S.

Principal U.S. bases

Communist States

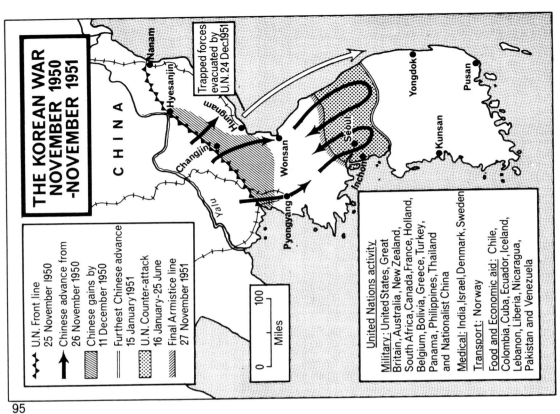

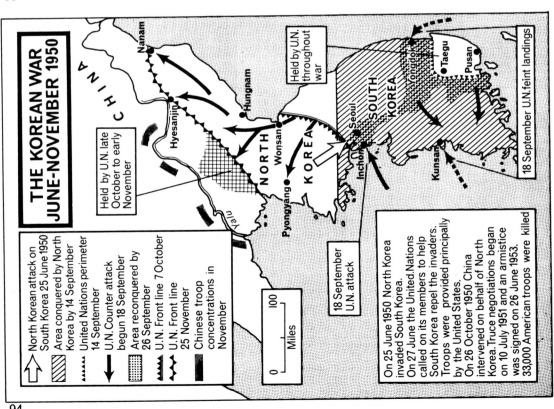

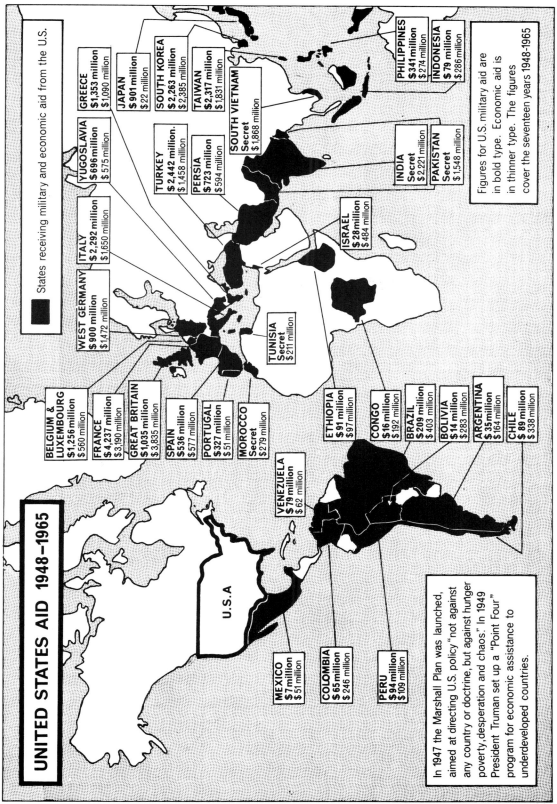

UNITED STATES AID 1948–1965

States receiving military and economic aid from the U.S.

U.S.A

MEXICO
$7million
$51 million

COLOMBIA
$65million
$246 million

PERU
$94million
$109 million

VENEZUELA
$79 million
$62 million

ETHIOPIA
$91 million
$97 million

CONGO
$16 million
$192 million

BRAZIL
$209 million
$403 million

BOLIVIA
$14 million
$283 million

ARGENTINA
$35million
$164 million

CHILE
$89 million
$338million

BELGIUM &
LUXEMBOURG
$1,256million
$560 million

FRANCE
$4,237 million
$3,190 million

GREAT BRITAIN
$1,035million
$3,835 million

SPAIN
$536 million
$577 million

PORTUGAL
$327 million
$51 million

MOROCCO
Secret
$279 million

WEST GERMANY
$900 million
$1,472 million

ITALY
$2,292 million
$1,650 million

YUGOSLAVIA
$696million
$575 million

GREECE
$1,353 million
$1,090 million

JAPAN
$901million
$22 million

SOUTH KOREA
$2,263 million
$2,385 million

TAIWAN
$2,317 million
$1,831 million

TURKEY
$2,442 million.
$1,458 million

PERSIA
$723 million
$594 million

SOUTH VIETNAM
Secret
$1,868 million

TUNISIA
Secret
$211 million

ISRAEL
$28million
$484 million

INDIA
Secret
$2,221 million

PAKISTAN
Secret
$1,548 million

PHILIPPINES
$341million
$274 million

INDONESIA
$79 million
$286 million

Figures for U.S. military aid are
in bold type. Economic aid is
in thinner type. The figures
cover the seventeen years 1948-1965

In 1947 the Marshall Plan was launched,
aimed at directing U.S. policy "not against
any country or doctrine, but against hunger
poverty, desperation and chaos." In 1949
President Truman set up a "Point Four"
program for economic assistance to
underdeveloped countries.

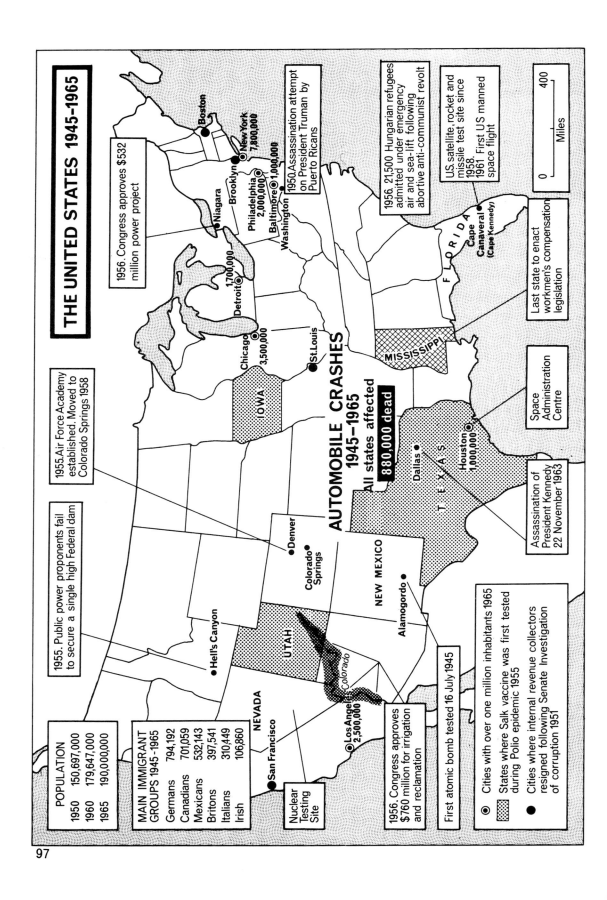

THE UNITED STATES 1945–1965

1956. Congress approves $532 million power project

1950 Assassination attempt on President Truman by Puerto Ricans

1956. 21,500 Hungarian refugees admitted under emergency air and sea-lift following abortive anti-communist revolt

U.S. satellite, rocket and missile test site since 1958.
1961 First US manned space flight

Boston

New York 7,800,000

Brooklyn

Niagara

Philadelphia 2,000,000

Baltimore 1,000,000

Washington

Detroit 1,700,000

Chicago 3,500,000

St.Louis

IOWA

F L O R I D A

Cape Canaveral (Cape Kennedy)

Last state to enact workmen's compensation legislation

MISSISSIPPI

0   400

Miles

1955.Air Force Academy established. Moved to Colorado Springs 1958

Space Administration Centre

AUTOMOBILE CRASHES
1945–1965
All states affected
880,000 dead

Dallas

Houston 1,000,000

T E X A S

Assassination of President Kennedy 22 November 1963

1955. Public power proponents fail to secure a single high Federal dam

Denver

Colorado Springs

NEW MEXICO

Alamogordo

Hell's Canyon

UTAH

Colorado

NEVADA

San Francisco

Los Angeles 2,500,000

Nuclear Testing Site

1956. Congress approves $760 million for irrigation and reclamation

POPULATION

1950	150,697,000
1960	179,647,000
1965	190,000,000

MAIN IMMIGRANT
GROUPS 1945-1965

Germans	794,192
Canadians	701,059
Mexicans	532,143
Britons	397,541
Italians	310,449
Irish	106,860

First atomic bomb tested 16 July 1945

◉ Cities with over one million inhabitants 1965

States where Salk vaccine was first tested during Polio epidemic 1955

● Cities where internal revenue collectors resigned following Senate Investigation of corruption 1951

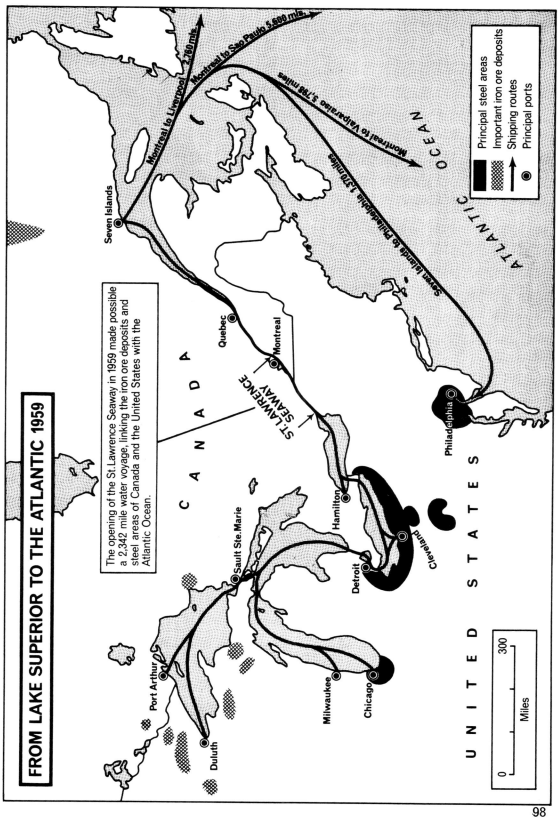

FROM LAKE SUPERIOR TO THE ATLANTIC 1959

The opening of the St. Lawrence Seaway in 1959 made possible a 2,342 mile water voyage, linking the iron ore deposits and steel areas of Canada and the United States with the Atlantic Ocean.

ST. LAWRENCE SEAWAY

CANADA

UNITED STATES

ATLANTIC OCEAN

Montreal to Liverpool 2,760 mls.
Montreal to Sao Paulo 5,800 mls.
Montreal to Valparaiso 1,798 miles
Seven Islands to Philadelphia 1,370 miles

Duluth
Port Arthur
Sault Ste. Marie
Milwaukee
Chicago
Detroit
Hamilton
Cleveland
Philadelphia
Quebec
Montreal
Seven Islands

Legend:
- Principal steel areas
- Important iron ore deposits
- Shipping routes
- Principal ports

Miles
0   300

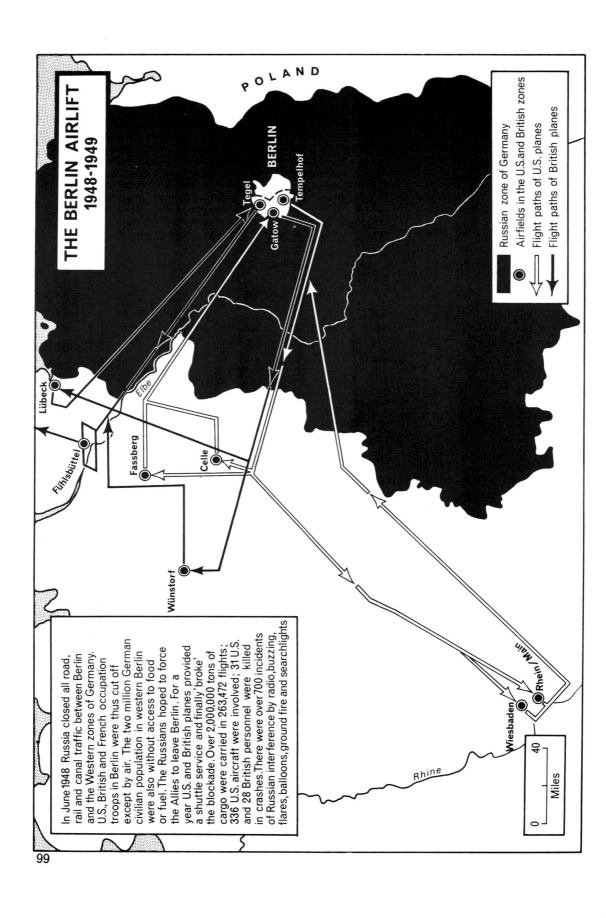

POLAND

THE BERLIN AIRLIFT 1948-1949

BERLIN

Tegel
Gatow
Tempelhof

Russian zone of Germany
Airfields in the U.S.and British zones
Flight paths of U.S. planes
Flight paths of British planes

Lübeck

Elbe

Fühlsbüttel

Fassberg

Celle

Wünstorf

Main

Rhein

Wiesbaden

Rhine

In June 1948 Russia closed all road, rail and canal traffic between Berlin and the Western zones of Germany. U.S., British and French occupation troops in Berlin were thus cut off except by air. The two million German civilian population in western Berlin were also without access to food or fuel. The Russians hoped to force the Allies to leave Berlin. For a year U.S. and British planes provided a shuttle service and finally 'broke' the blockade. Over 2,000,000 tons of cargo were carried in 263,472 flights; 336 U.S. aircraft were involved; 31 U.S. and 28 British personnel were killed in crashes.There were over 700 incidents of Russian interference by radio,buzzing, flares,balloons,ground fire and searchlights

0   40

Miles

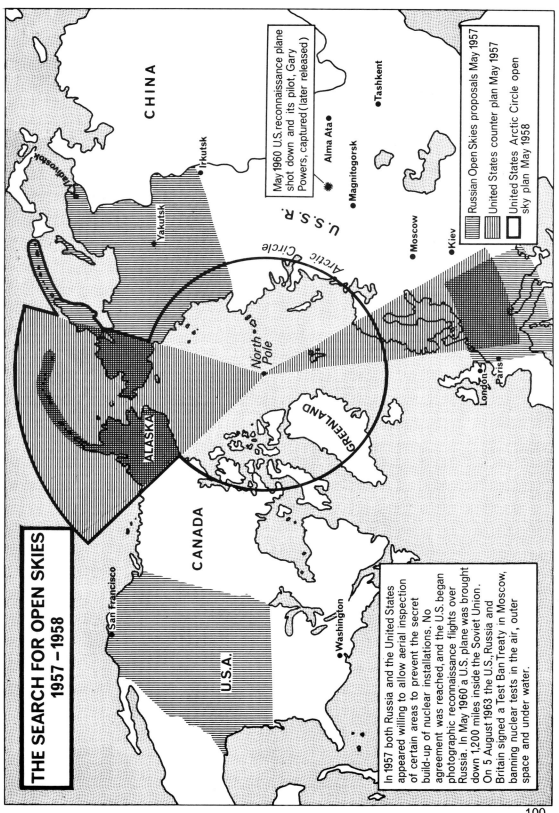

THE SEARCH FOR OPEN SKIES 1957 – 1958

CHINA

U.S.S.R.

Vladivostok

Irkutsk

Yakutsk

●Tashkent

Alma Ata●

●Magnitogorsk

●Moscow

●Kiev

Arctic Circle

North Pole

GREENLAND

ALASKA

CANADA

U.S.A.

San Francisco

Washington

London●
Paris●

May 1960 U.S. reconnaissance plane shot down and its pilot, Gary Powers, captured (later released)

Russian Open Skies proposals May 1957

United States counter plan May 1957

United States Arctic Circle open sky plan May 1958

In 1957 both Russia and the United States appeared willing to allow aerial inspection of certain areas to prevent the secret build-up of nuclear installations. No agreement was reached, and the U.S. began photographic reconnaissance flights over Russia. In May 1960 a U.S. plane was brought down 1,200 miles inside the Soviet Union. On 5 August 1963 the U.S., Russia and Britain signed a Test Ban Treaty in Moscow, banning nuclear tests in the air, outer space and under water.

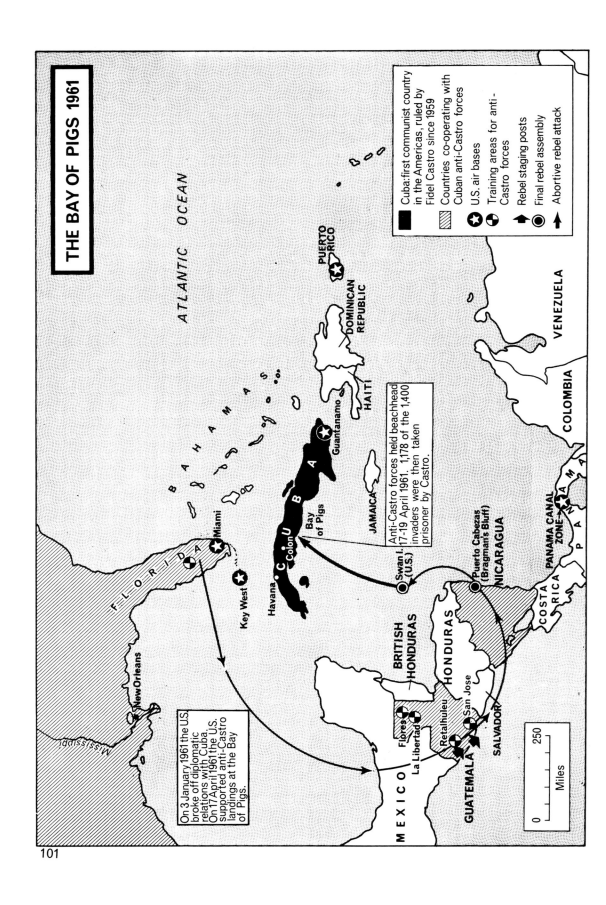

THE BAY OF PIGS 1961

ATLANTIC OCEAN

Cuba: first communist country in the Americas, ruled by Fidel Castro since 1959

Countries co-operating with Cuban anti-Castro forces

⭐ U.S. air bases

◑ Training areas for anti-Castro forces

◆ Rebel staging posts

◉ Final rebel assembly

↑ Abortive rebel attack

PUERTO RICO

DOMINICAN REPUBLIC

HAITI

Guantanamo

JAMAICA

BAHAMAS

Miami

Key West

Havana • Colón • C U B A

Bay of Pigs

New Orleans

Mississippi

FLORIDA

Swan I. (U.S.)

Anti-Castro forces held beachhead 17-19 April 1961. 1,178 of the 1,400 invaders were then taken prisoner by Castro.

On 3 January 1961 the U.S. broke off diplomatic relations with Cuba. On 17 April 1961 the U.S. supported anti-Castro landings at the Bay of Pigs.

MEXICO

BRITISH HONDURAS

HONDURAS

GUATEMALA

Flores

La Libertad

Retalhuleu

San José

SALVADOR

Puerto Cabezas (Bragman's Bluff)

NICARAGUA

COSTA RICA

PANAMA CANAL ZONE

PANAMA

COLOMBIA

VENEZUELA

0 250

Miles

101

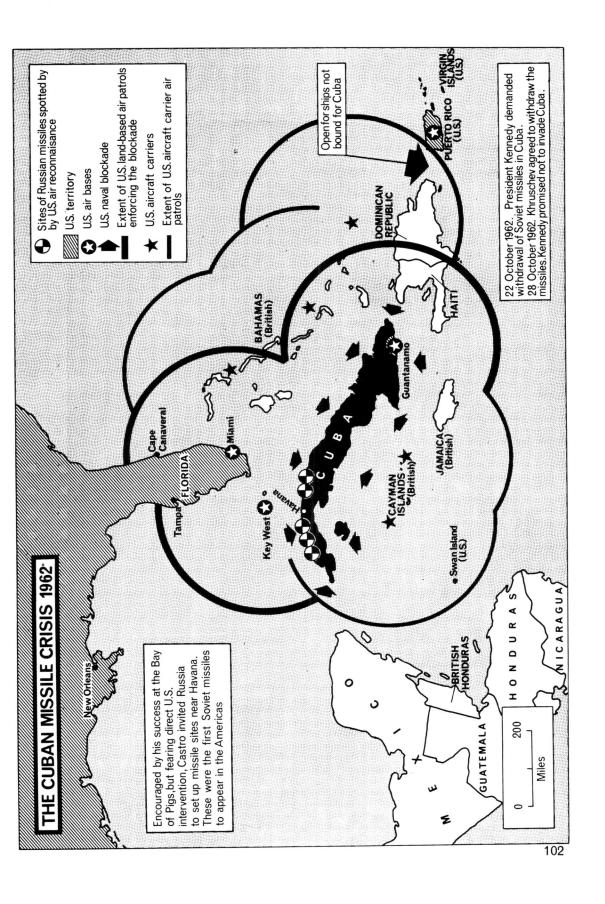

THE CUBAN MISSILE CRISIS 1962

Encouraged by his success at the Bay of Pigs, but fearing direct U.S. intervention, Castro invited Russia to set up missile sites near Havana. These were the first Soviet missiles to appear in the Americas

Open for ships not bound for Cuba

22 October 1962. President Kennedy demanded withdrawal of Soviet missiles in Cuba.
28 October 1962. Khruschev agreed to withdraw the missiles. Kennedy promised not to invade Cuba.

Sites of Russian missiles spotted by U.S. air reconnaissance
U.S. territory
U.S. air bases
U.S. naval blockade
Extent of U.S. land-based air patrols enforcing the blockade
U.S. aircraft carriers
Extent of U.S. aircraft carrier air patrols

New Orleans

FLORIDA
Cape Canaveral
Miami
Tampa
Key West
Havana
C U B A
Guantanamo
BAHAMAS (British)
CAYMAN ISLANDS (British)
JAMAICA (British)
Swan Island (U.S.)
HAITI
DOMINICAN REPUBLIC
PUERTO RICO (U.S.)
VIRGIN ISLANDS (U.S.)

M E X I C O
GUATEMALA
BRITISH HONDURAS
H O N D U R A S
NICARAGUA

0   200
Miles

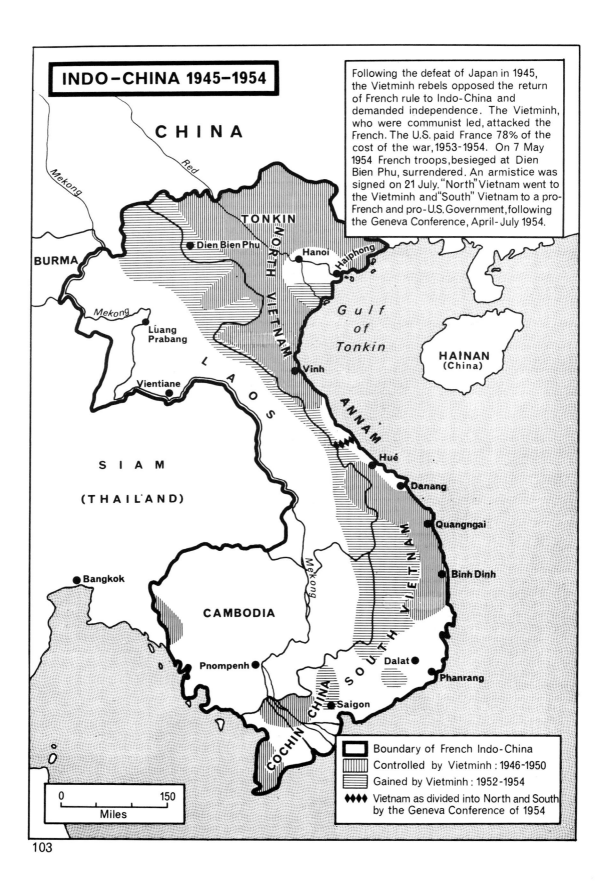

INDO-CHINA 1945-1954

CHINA

Following the defeat of Japan in 1945, the Vietminh rebels opposed the return of French rule to Indo-China and demanded independence. The Vietminh, who were communist led, attacked the French. The U.S. paid France 78% of the cost of the war, 1953-1954. On 7 May 1954 French troops, besieged at Dien Bien Phu, surrendered. An armistice was signed on 21 July. "North" Vietnam went to the Vietminh and "South" Vietnam to a pro-French and pro-U.S. Government, following the Geneva Conference, April-July 1954.

BURMA

Mekong

Red

TONKIN

NORTH VIETNAM

● Dien Bien Phu

● Hanoi

Haiphong

Gulf of Tonkin

HAINAN (China)

Mekong

● Lüang Prabang

LAOS

● Vientiane

● Vinh

ANNAM

● Hué

● Danang

SIAM

(THAILAND)

● Quangngai

SOUTH VIETNAM

● Bangkok

CAMBODIA

Mekong

● Binh Dinh

● Dalat

COCHIN CHINA

● Pnompenh

● Phanrang

● Saigon

	Boundary of French Indo-China
	Controlled by Vietminh : 1946-1950
	Gained by Vietminh : 1952-1954
◆◆◆◆	Vietnam as divided into North and South by the Geneva Conference of 1954

0 — 150 Miles

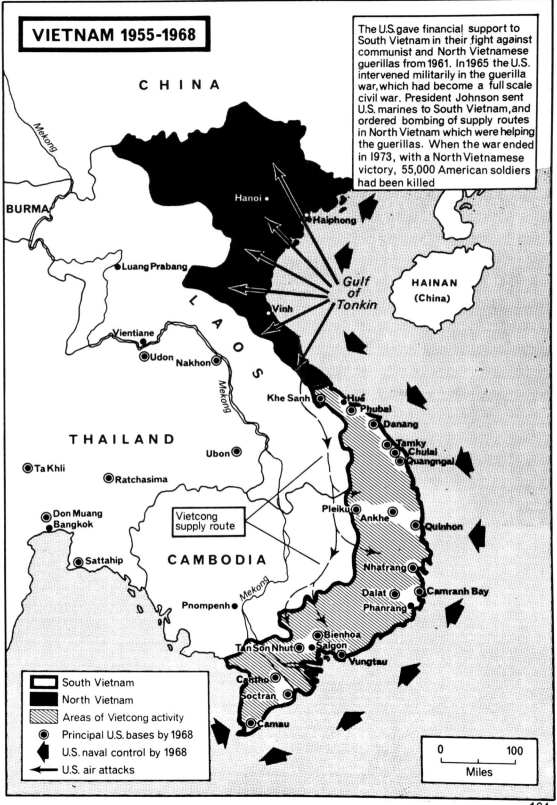

VIETNAM 1955-1968

CHINA

BURMA

Mekong

Hanoi •

● Haiphong

Luang Prabang •

L A O S

Vinh •

Gulf
of
Tonkin

HAINAN
(China)

Vientiane •

● Udon Nakhon ●

Mekong

Khe Sanh ●

Hué ●
● Phubai
● Danang

THAILAND

Ubon ●

● Tamky
● Chulai
● Quangngai

● Ta Khli

● Ratchasima

Pleiku ●
Ankhe ●

Quinhon ●

● Don Muang
Bangkok ●

Vietcong
supply route

C A M B O D I A

● Sattahip

Mekong

Nhatrang ●

Dalat ●
Phanrang

● Camranh Bay

Pnompenh ●

● Bienhoa
Tan Son Nhut ● ● Saigon
● Vungtau

Cantho ●
Soctran ●

● Camau

The U.S. gave financial support to
South Vietnam in their fight against
communist and North Vietnamese
guerillas from 1961. In 1965 the U.S.
intervened militarily in the guerilla
war, which had become a full scale
civil war. President Johnson sent
U.S. marines to South Vietnam, and
ordered bombing of supply routes
in North Vietnam which were helping
the guerillas. When the war ended
in 1973, with a North Vietnamese
victory, 55,000 American soldiers
had been killed

☐	South Vietnam
■	North Vietnam
▨	Areas of Vietcong activity
◉	Principal U.S. bases by 1968
◄	U.S. naval control by 1968
←	U.S. air attacks

0   100

Miles

104

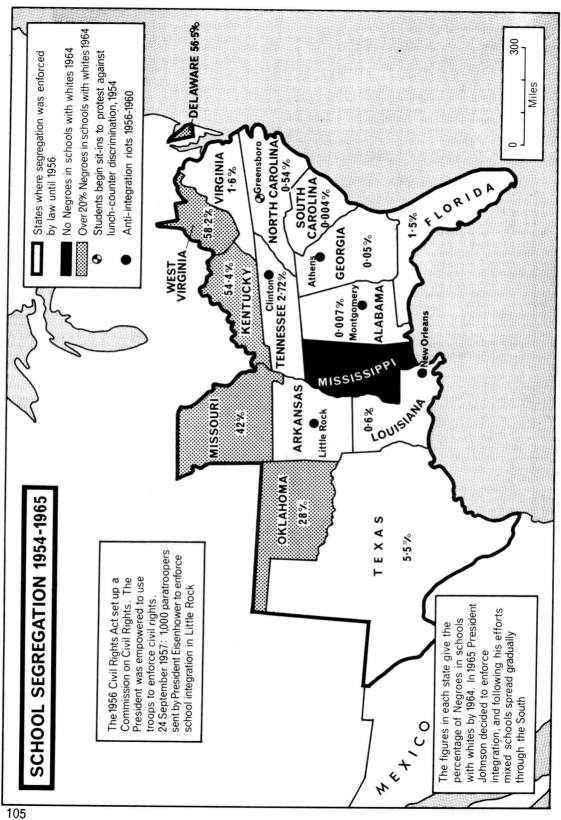

SCHOOL SEGREGATION 1954-1965

States where segregation was enforced by law until 1956

No Negroes in schools with whites 1964

Over 20% Negroes in schools with whites 1964

Students begin sit-ins to protest against lunch-counter discrimination, 1954

Anti-integration riots 1956-1960

The 1956 Civil Rights Act set up a Commission on Civil Rights. The President was empowered to use troops to enforce civil rights.
24 September 1957: 1,000 paratroopers sent by President Eisenhower to enforce school integration in Little Rock

The figures in each state give the percentage of Negroes in schools with whites by 1964. In 1965 President Johnson decided to enforce integration, and following his efforts mixed schools spread gradually through the South

DELAWARE 56·5%

VIRGINIA 1·6%

Greensboro

NORTH CAROLINA 0·54%

SOUTH CAROLINA 0·004%

GEORGIA 0·05%

FLORIDA 1·5%

Athens

WEST VIRGINIA 58·2%

KENTUCKY 54·4%

Clinton

TENNESSEE 2·72%

Montgomery

ALABAMA 0·007%

MISSISSIPPI

New Orleans

MISSOURI 42%

ARKANSAS

Little Rock

LOUISIANA 0·6%

OKLAHOMA 28%

TEXAS 5·5%

MEXICO

0 300

Miles

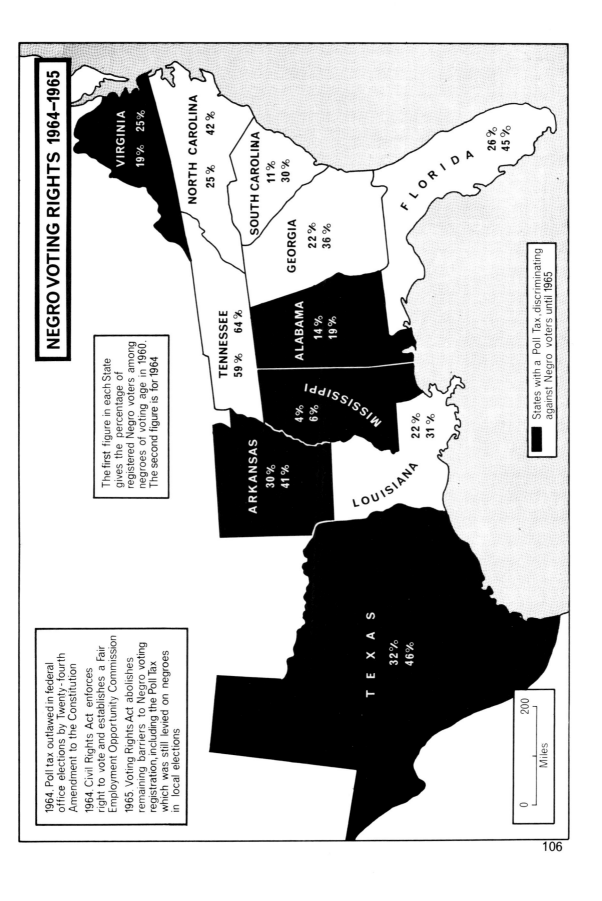

NEGRO VOTING RIGHTS 1964–1965

The first figure in each State gives the percentage of registered Negro voters among negroes of voting age in 1960. The second figure is for 1964

1964. Poll tax outlawed in federal office elections by Twenty-fourth Amendment to the Constitution

1964. Civil Rights Act enforces right to vote and establishes a Fair Employment Opportunity Commission

1965. Voting Rights Act abolishes remaining barriers to Negro voting registration, including the Poll Tax which was still levied on negroes in local elections

States with a Poll Tax, discriminating against Negro voters until 1965

VIRGINIA
19 % 25 %

NORTH CAROLINA
25 % 42 %

SOUTH CAROLINA
11 % 30 %

GEORGIA
22 % 36 %

FLORIDA
26 % 45 %

TENNESSEE
59 % 64 %

ALABAMA
14 % 19 %

MISSISSIPPI
4 % 6 %

ARKANSAS
30 % 41 %

LOUISIANA
22 % 31 %

TEXAS
32 % 46 %

0   200
Miles

106

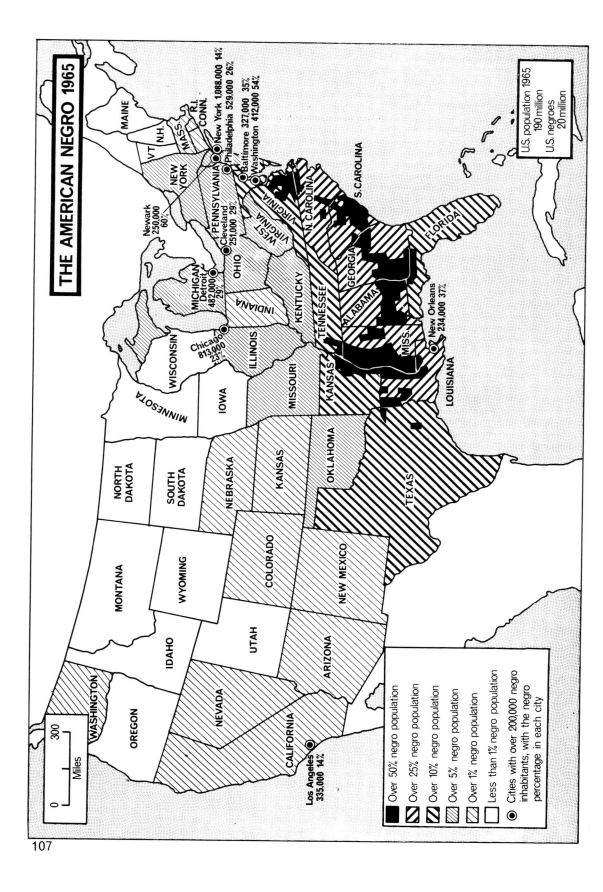

THE AMERICAN NEGRO 1965

U.S. population 1965
190 million
U.S. negroes
20 million

New York 1,088,000 14%
Philadelphia 529,000 26%
Baltimore 327,000 35%
Washington 412,000 54%

Newark 250,000 60%
Cleveland 251,000 29%
Detroit 482,000 29%
Chicago 813,000 23%

New Orleans 234,000 37%

Los Angeles 335,000 14%

MAINE
R.I.
CONN.
MASS.
N.H.
VT
NEW YORK
PENNSYLVANIA
WEST VIRGINIA
VIRGINIA
N. CAROLINA
S. CAROLINA
FLORIDA
GEORGIA
ALABAMA
TENNESSEE
KENTUCKY
MISS.
LOUISIANA
OHIO
INDIANA
MICHIGAN
WISCONSIN
ILLINOIS
MISSOURI
MINNESOTA
IOWA
KANSAS
NEBRASKA
OKLAHOMA
TEXAS
NORTH DAKOTA
SOUTH DAKOTA
COLORADO
NEW MEXICO
WYOMING
MONTANA
UTAH
ARIZONA
IDAHO
NEVADA
CALIFORNIA
WASHINGTON
OREGON

0   300
Miles

- Over 50% negro population
- Over 25% negro population
- Over 10% negro population
- Over 5% negro population
- Over 1% negro population
- Less than 1% negro population
- ◉ Cities with over 200,000 negro inhabitants, with the negro percentage in each city

107

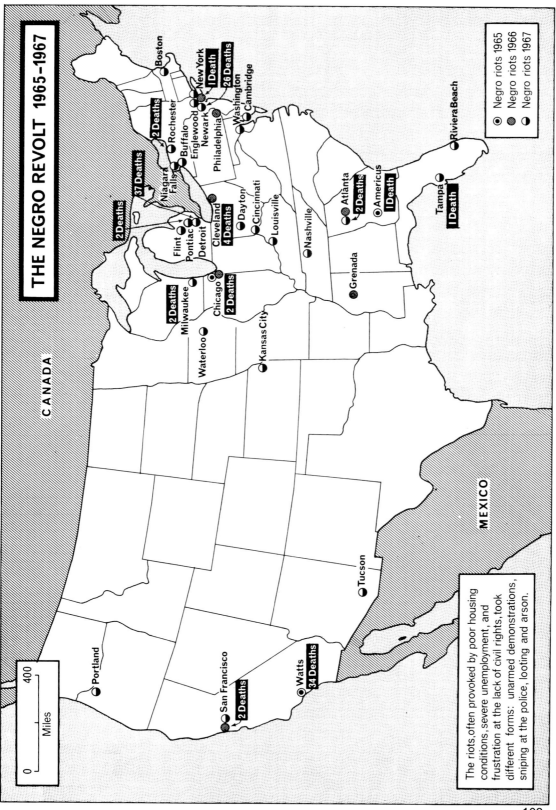

THE NEGRO REVOLT 1965-1967

CANADA

MEXICO

Portland

San Francisco **2 Deaths**

Watts **34 Deaths**

Tucson

Waterloo

Milwaukee **2 Deaths**

Chicago **2 Deaths**

Kansas City

Flint **2 Deaths**
Pontiac
Detroit **37 Deaths**
Cleveland **4 Deaths**

Dayton
Cincinnati
Louisville

Nashville

Grenada

Niagara Falls
Buffalo **2 Deaths**
Rochester
Englewood
Newark **26 Deaths**
Philadelphia

Boston

New York **1 Death**

Washington
Cambridge

Atlanta **2 Deaths**
Americus **1 Death**

Riviera Beach

Tampa **1 Death**

- ◉ Negro riots 1965
- ◓ Negro riots 1966
- ◑ Negro riots 1967

0 — 400
Miles

The riots, often provoked by poor housing conditions, severe unemployment, and frustration at the lack of civil rights, took different forms: unarmed demonstrations, sniping at the police, looting and arson.

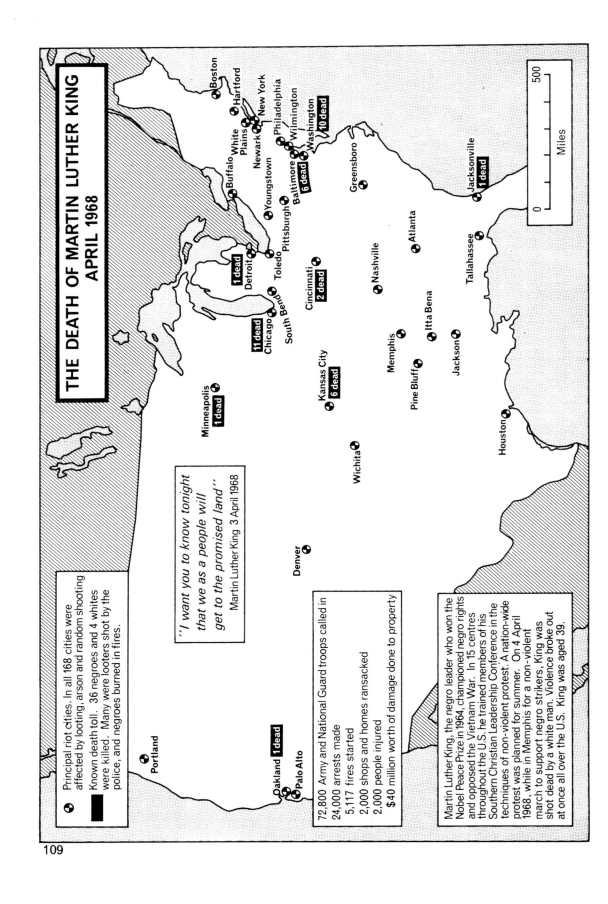

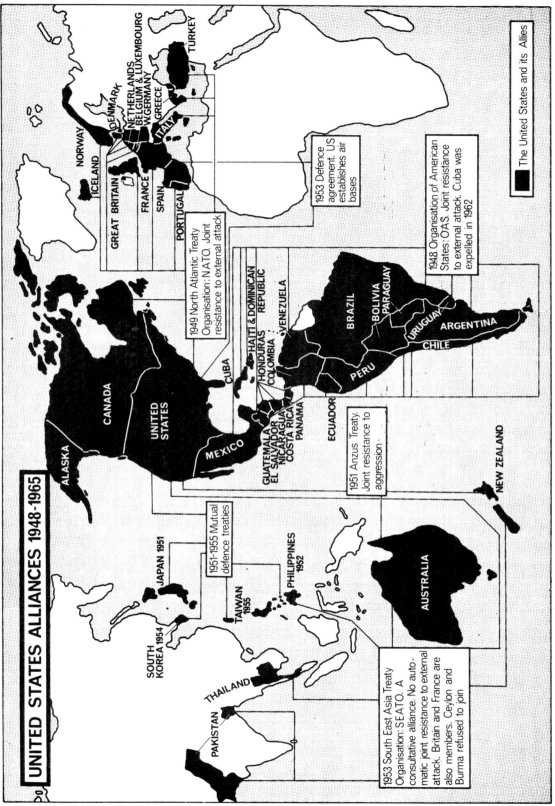

UNITED STATES ALLIANCES 1948-1965

The United States and its Allies

ALASKA

CANADA

UNITED STATES

MEXICO

GUATEMALA
EL SALVADOR
NICARAGUA
COSTA RICA
PANAMA

CUBA

HAITI & DOMINICAN REPUBLIC
HONDURAS
COLOMBIA
VENEZUELA

ECUADOR

PERU

BRAZIL

BOLIVIA
PARAGUAY

CHILE

URUGUAY

ARGENTINA

NORWAY
ICELAND
GREAT BRITAIN
FRANCE
SPAIN
PORTUGAL
DENMARK
NETHERLANDS
BELGIUM & LUXEMBOURG
W.GERMANY
GREECE
ITALY
TURKEY

JAPAN 1951

SOUTH KOREA 1954

TAIWAN 1955

PHILIPPINES 1952

THAILAND

PAKISTAN

AUSTRALIA

NEW ZEALAND

1949 North Atlantic Treaty Organisation: NATO. Joint resistance to external attack

1953 Defence agreement. US establishes air bases

1948 Organisation of American States: OAS. Joint resistance to external attack. Cuba was expelled in 1962

1951 Anzus Treaty. Joint resistance to aggression

1951-1955 Mutual defence treaties

1953 South East Asia Treaty Organisation: SEATO. A consultative alliance. No automatic joint resistance to external attack. Britain and France are also members. Ceylon and Burma refused to join

110

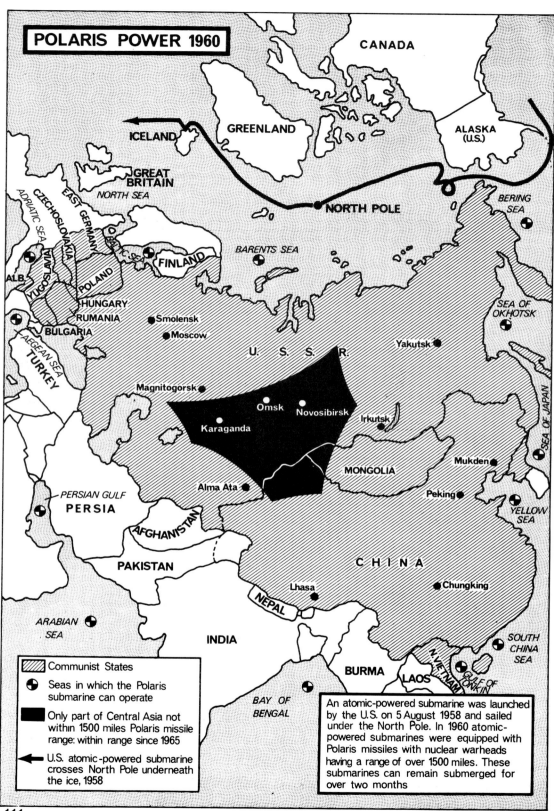

POLARIS POWER 1960

CANADA

GREENLAND

ICELAND

ALASKA (U.S.)

BERING SEA

GREAT BRITAIN

NORTH SEA

NORTH POLE

EAST GERMANY

CZECHOSLOVAKIA

ADRIATIC SEA

BALTIC SEA

YUGOSLAVIA

ALB.

POLAND

FINLAND

BARENTS SEA

SEA OF OKHOTSK

HUNGARY

RUMANIA

BULGARIA

AEGEAN SEA

TURKEY

U. S. S. R.

Yakutsk

● Smolensk
● Moscow

Magnitogorsk ●

○ Omsk   ○ Novosibirsk

Irkutsk

Mukden ●

PERSIAN GULF
PERSIA

● Karaganda

Alma Ata ●

MONGOLIA

Peking ●

YELLOW SEA

SEA OF JAPAN

AFGHANISTAN

PAKISTAN

C H I N A

Chungking ●

NEPAL

Lhasa ●

ARABIAN SEA

INDIA

BURMA

LAOS

N.VIETNAM

GULF OF TONKIN

SOUTH CHINA SEA

BAY OF BENGAL

Communist States

⊕ Seas in which the Polaris submarine can operate

■ Only part of Central Asia not within 1500 miles Polaris missile range: within range since 1965

← U.S. atomic-powered submarine crosses North Pole underneath the ice, 1958

An atomic-powered submarine was launched by the U.S. on 5 August 1958 and sailed under the North Pole. In 1960 atomic-powered submarines were equipped with Polaris missiles with nuclear warheads having a range of over 1500 miles. These submarines can remain submerged for over two months

111

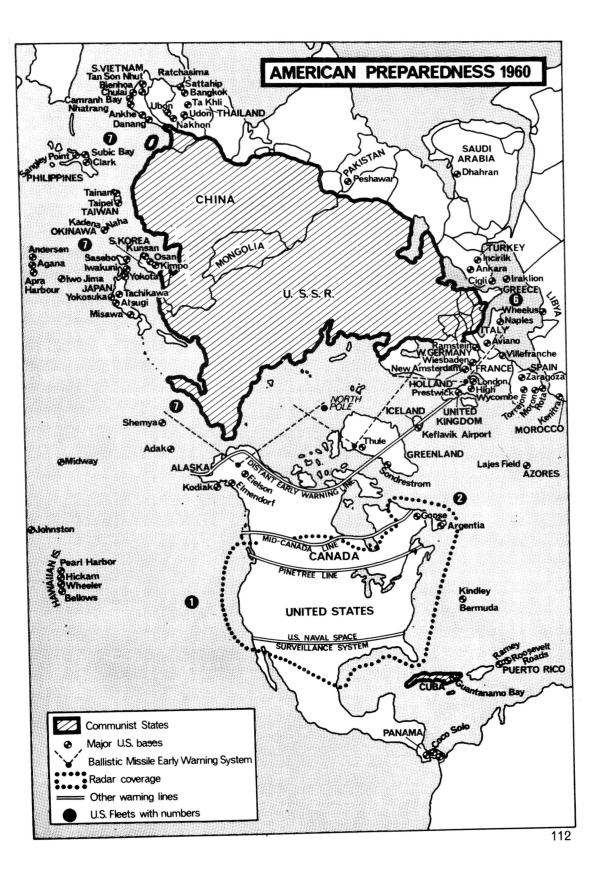

AMERICAN PREPAREDNESS 1960

S.VIETNAM
Tan Son Nhut
Bienhoa   Ratchasima
Chulai   Sattahip
Camranh Bay   Bangkok
Nhatrang   Ubon Ta Khli
Ankhe   Udon THAILAND
Danang   Nakhon

①

Sangley Point **⑦** Subic Bay
PHILIPPINES   Clark

Tainan
Taipei
TAIWAN
Kadena Naha
OKINAWA

Andersen **⑦** S.KOREA
Agana   Kunsan
Sasebo   Osan
Iwakuni   Kimpo
Apra   Iwo Jima Yokota
Harbour Yokosuka Tachikawa
Yokosuka   Atsugi
Misawa

CHINA

MONGOLIA

U.S.S.R.

PAKISTAN
Peshawar

SAUDI
ARABIA
Dhahran

TURKEY
Incirlik
Ankara
Cigli   Iraklion
GREECE
⑥ Wheelus
Naples
ITALY Aviano
Ramstein Villefranche
W.GERMANY SPAIN
Wiesbaden Zaragoza
New Amsterdam FRANCE
HOLLAND London
Prestwick High
Wycombe

LIBYA

Torrejon Moron Rota
MOROCCO
Kenitra

Shemya **⑦**

Adak

Midway

ALASKA
Kodiak Eielson
Elmendorf

DISTANT EARLY WARNING LINE

NORTH
POLE

Thule

ICELAND

Keflavik Airport

GREENLAND

Sondrestrom

UNITED
KINGDOM

Lajes Field
AZORES

Johnston

HAWAIIAN IS.
Pearl Harbor
Hickam
Wheeler
Bellows

①

MID-CANADA LINE
CANADA
PINETREE LINE

Goose
Argentia **②**

Kindley
Bermuda

UNITED STATES

U.S. NAVAL SPACE
SURVEILLANCE SYSTEM

Ramey Roosevelt
Roads
PUERTO RICO

CUBA Guantanamo Bay

PANAMA Coco Solo

▨	Communist States
✪	Major U.S. bases
✈	Ballistic Missile Early Warning System
••••	Radar coverage
═══	Other warning lines
●	U.S. Fleets with numbers

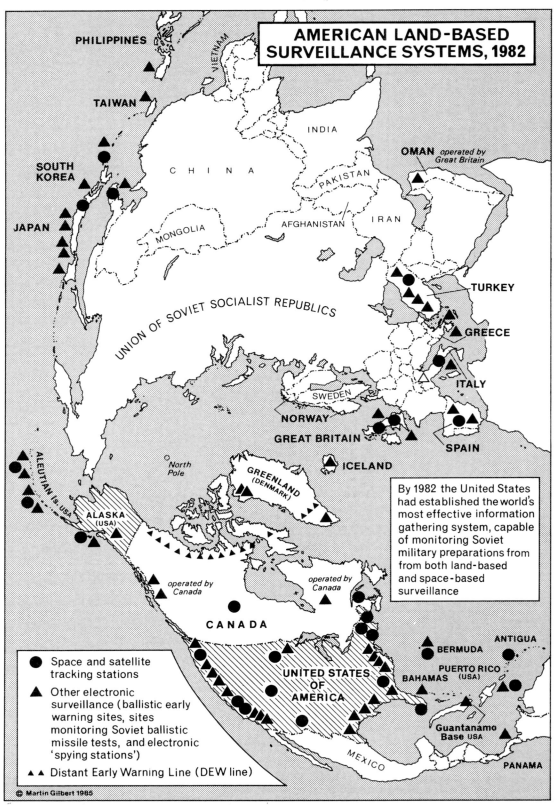

AMERICAN LAND-BASED SURVEILLANCE SYSTEMS, 1982

PHILIPPINES

TAIWAN

SOUTH KOREA

JAPAN

CHINA

MONGOLIA

INDIA

PAKISTAN

AFGHANISTAN

IRAN

OMAN *operated by Great Britain*

UNION OF SOVIET SOCIALIST REPUBLICS

TURKEY

GREECE

SWEDEN

ITALY

NORWAY

GREAT BRITAIN

SPAIN

ALEUTIAN Is. USA

North Pole

ICELAND

GREENLAND (DENMARK)

ALASKA (USA)

operated by Canada

operated by Canada

CANADA

BERMUDA

ANTIGUA

PUERTO RICO (USA)

BAHAMAS

UNITED STATES OF AMERICA

Guantanamo Base USA

MEXICO

PANAMA

By 1982 the United States had established the world's most effective information gathering system, capable of monitoring Soviet military preparations from from both land-based and space-based surveillance

● Space and satellite tracking stations

▲ Other electronic surveillance (ballistic early warning sites, sites monitoring Soviet ballistic missile tests, and electronic 'spying stations')

▲▲ Distant Early Warning Line (DEW line)

© Martin Gilbert 1985

THE UNITED STATES AND THE SOVIET UNION IN OUTER SPACE

Between 1957 and 1981 a total of 2,725 satellites were launched, most of them by the United States and the Soviet Union. Some of the principal satellites in orbit in 1981 are shown here. In March 1981 the US National Aeronautics and Space Administration (NASA) launched its Columbia Orbiter, the first re-usable space vehicle (44 missions planned by the end of 1985, nine of them military)

SATELLITES

Early Warning
USA   22
USSR 25

Communications
USA   118
USSR   366
NATO   5
UK   4
France   2

Photographic reconnaisance
USA   235
USSR   538
China   3

Electronic reconnaisance
USA   790
USSR   125

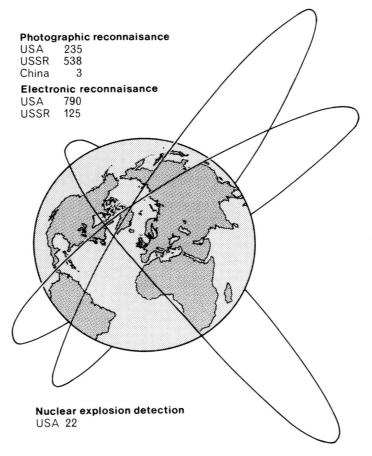

Navigation
USA   39
USSR 25

Nuclear explosion detection
USA 22

Ocean surveillance
USA   18
USSR 32

Interception- destruction
USSR 33

In January 1985, at Geneva, the United States and the Soviet Union agreed to begin talks aimed at an agreement over the restriction of warfare in outer space. The United States was involved in the development of anti-satellite missiles and anti-missile lasers, and the Soviet Union in anti-satellite satellites

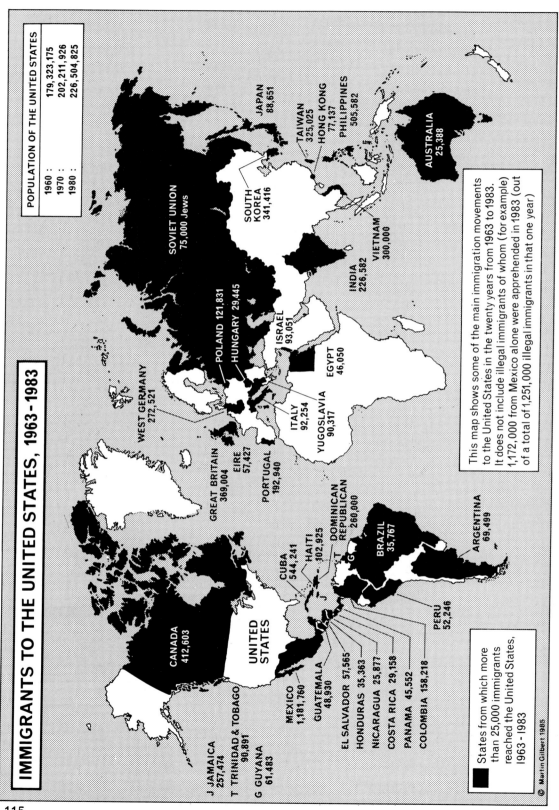

IMMIGRANTS TO THE UNITED STATES, 1963-1983

POPULATION OF THE UNITED STATES

1960	:	179,323,175
1970	:	202,211,926
1980	:	226,504,825

SOVIET UNION 75,000 Jews

JAPAN 88,651

TAIWAN 325,025

HONG KONG 77,137

PHILIPPINES 505,582

AUSTRALIA 25,388

SOUTH KOREA 341,416

VIETNAM 360,000

INDIA 226,582

POLAND 121,831

HUNGARY 29,445

ISRAEL 93,051

EGYPT 46,050

WEST GERMANY 272,521

ITALY 92,254

YUGOSLAVIA 90,317

GREAT BRITAIN 369,004

EIRE 57,427

PORTUGAL 192,940

ARGENTINA 69,499

DOMINICAN REPUBLIC 260,000

HAITI 102,925

CUBA 544,241

BRAZIL 35,767

PERU 52,246

CANADA 412,603

UNITED STATES

MEXICO 1,181,760

GUATEMALA 48,930

EL SALVADOR 57,565

HONDURAS 35,363

NICARAGUA 25,877

COSTA RICA 29,158

PANAMA 45,552

COLOMBIA 158,218

J JAMAICA 257,474

T TRINIDAD & TOBAGO 90,891

G GUYANA 61,483

This map shows some of the main immigration movements to the United States in the twenty years from 1963 to 1983. It does not include illegal immigrants of whom (for example) 1,172,000 from Mexico alone were apprehended in 1983 (out of a total of 1,251,000 illegal immigrants in that one year)

■ States from which more than 25,000 immigrants reached the United States, 1963-1983

© Martin Gilbert 1985

115

THE UNITED STATES IN THE PACIFIC, 1823-1993

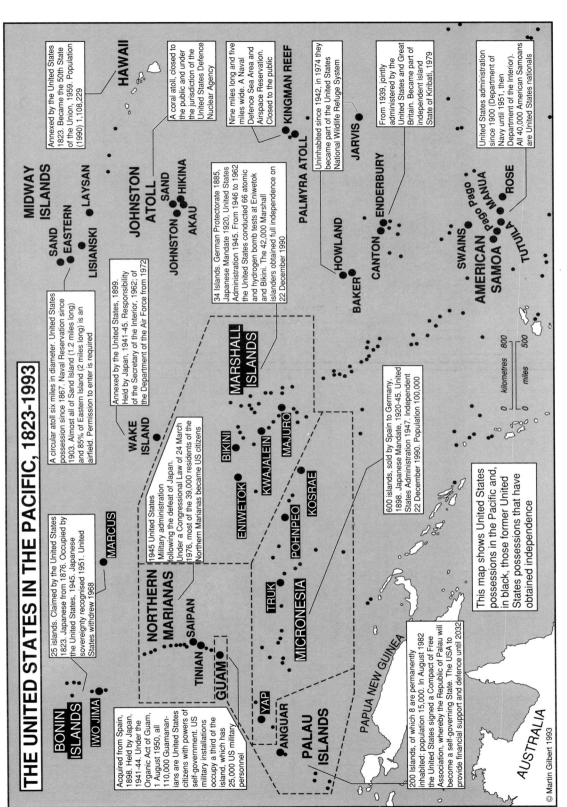

HAWAII
Annexed by the United States 1823. Became the 50th State of the Union, 1959. Population (1990) 1,108,229

MIDWAY ISLANDS

SAND
EASTERN
LAYSAN
LISIANSKI

JOHNSTON ATOLL
SAND
HIKINA
JOHNSTON
AKAU
A circular atoll six miles in diameter. United States possession since 1867. Naval Reservation since 1903. Almost all of Sand Island (1.2 miles long) and 85% of Eastern Island (2 miles long) is an airfield. Permission to enter is required

KINGMAN REEF
A coral atoll, closed to the public and under the jurisdiction of the United States Defence Nuclear Agency

Nine miles long and five miles wide. A Naval Defence Sea Area and Airspace Reservation. Closed to the public

PALMYRA ATOLL

JARVIS
Uninhabited since 1942, in 1974 they became part of the United States National Wildlife Refuge System

HOWLAND

BAKER

CANTON
ENDERBURY
From 1939, jointly administered by the United States and Great Britain. Became part of independent island State of Kiribati, 1979

AMERICAN SAMOA
pago pago
MANUA
ROSE
SWAINS
TUTUILA
United States administration since 1900 (Department of Navy until 1951, then Department of the Interior). All 40,000 American Samoans are United States nationals

BONIN ISLANDS
IWO JIMA
25 islands. Claimed by the United States 1823. Japanese from 1876. Occupied by the United States, 1945. Japanese sovereignty recognised 1951. United States withdrew 1968

MARCUS
Acquired from Spain, 1898. Held by Japan, 1941-44. Under the Organic Act of Guam, 1 August 1950, all 110,000 Guamananians are United States citizens with powers of self-government. US military installations occupy a third of the island, which has 25,000 US military personnel

WAKE ISLAND
Annexed by the United States, 1899. Held by Japan, 1941-45. Responsibility of the Secretary of the Interior, 1962; of the Department of the Air Force from 1972

1945 United States Military administration following the defeat of Japan. Under a Congressional Law of 24 March 1976, most of the 39,000 residents of the Northern Marianas became US citizens

NORTHERN MARIANAS
SAIPAN
TINIAN
GUAM

MARSHALL ISLANDS
BIKINI
ENIWETOK
KWAJALEIN
MAJURO
34 Islands. German Protectorate 1885, Japanese Mandate 1920, United States Administration 1945. From 1946 to 1962 the United States conducted 66 atomic and hydrogen bomb tests at Eniwetok and Bikini. The 42,000 Marshall islanders obtained full independence on 22 December 1990

MICRONESIA
TRUK
POHNPEO
KOSRAE
600 islands, sold by Spain to Germany, 1898. Japanese Mandate, 1920-45. United States Administration 1947. Independent 22 December 1990. Population 100,000

YAP
PALAU ISLANDS
ANGUAR
200 Islands, of which 8 are permanently inhabited: population 15,000. In August 1982 the United States signed a Compact of Free Association, whereby the Republic of Palau will become a self-governing State. The USA to provide financial support and defence until 2032

PAPUA NEW GUINEA

This map shows United States possessions in the Pacific and, in black, those former United States possessions that have obtained independence

kilometres   0   800
miles   0   500

AUSTRALIA

© Martin Gilbert 1993

GREAT POWER CONFRONTATION AND CONCILIATION, 1972-1986

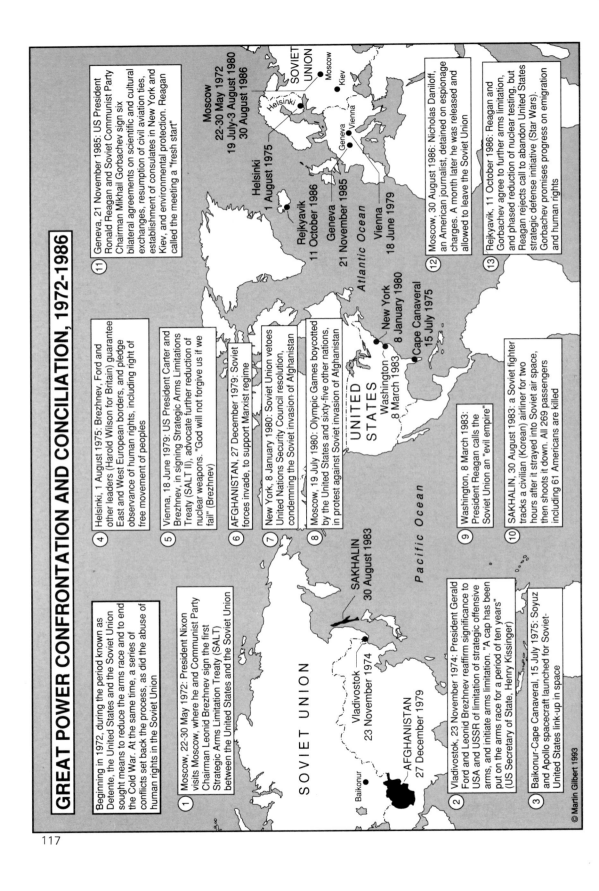

Beginning in 1972, during the period known as Detente, the United States and the Soviet Union sought means to reduce the arms race and to end the Cold War. At the same time, a series of conflicts set back the process, as did the abuse of human rights in the Soviet Union

1. Moscow, 22-30 May 1972: President Nixon visits Moscow, where he and Communist Party Chairman Leonid Brezhnev sign the first Strategic Arms Limitation Treaty (SALT) between the United States and the Soviet Union

2. Vladivostok, 23 November 1974: President Gerald Ford and Leonid Brezhnev reaffirm significance to USA and USSR of limitation of strategic offensive arms, and initiate arms limitation. "A cap has been put on the arms race for a period of ten years" (US Secretary of State, Henry Kissinger)

3. Baikonur-Cape Canaveral, 15 July 1975: Soyuz and Apollo spacecraft launched for Soviet-United States link-up in space

4. Helsinki, 1 August 1975: Brezhnev, Ford and other leaders (Harold Wilson for Britain) guarantee East and West European borders, and pledge observance of human rights, including right of free movement of peoples

5. Vienna, 18 June 1979: US President Carter and Brezhnev, in signing Strategic Arms Limitations Treaty (SALT II), advocate further reduction of nuclear weapons. "God will not forgive us if we fail" (Brezhnev)

6. AFGHANISTAN, 27 December 1979: Soviet forces invade, to support Marxist regime

7. New York, 8 January 1980: Soviet Union vetoes United Nations Security Council resolution, condemning the Soviet invasion of Afghanistan

8. Moscow, 19 July 1980: Olympic Games boycotted by the United States and sixty-five other nations, in protest against Soviet invasion of Afghanistan

9. Washington, 8 March 1983: President Reagan calls the Soviet Union an "evil empire"

10. SAKHALIN, 30 August 1983: a Soviet fighter tracks a civilian (Korean) airliner for two hours after it strayed into Soviet air space, then shoots it down. All 269 passengers including 61 Americans are killed

11. Geneva, 21 November 1985: US President Ronald Reagan and Soviet Communist Party Chairman Mikhail Gorbachev sign six bilateral agreements on scientific and cultural exchanges, resumption of civil aviation ties, establishment of consulates in New York and Kiev, and environmental protection. Reagan called the meeting a "fresh start"

12. Moscow, 30 August 1986: Nicholas Daniloff, an American journalist, detained on espionage charges. A month later he was released and allowed to leave the Soviet Union

13. Rejkyavik, 11 October 1986: Reagan and Gorbachev agree to further arms limitation, and phased reduction of nuclear testing, but Reagan rejects call to abandon United States strategic defense initiative (Star Wars). Gorbachev promises progress on emigration and human rights

Moscow 22-30 May 1972
19 July-3 August 1980
30 August 1986

SOVIET UNION

Moscow
Kiev

Helsinki

Helsinki 1 August 1975

Rejkyavik 11 October 1986

Geneva 21 November 1985

Geneva
Vienna

Vienna 18 June 1979

Atlantic Ocean

New York 8 January 1980

Washington 8 March 1983

Cape Canaveral 15 July 1975

UNITED STATES

Pacific Ocean

SAKHALIN 30 August 1983

SOVIET UNION

Vladivostok 23 November 1974

Baikonur

AFGHANISTAN 27 December 1979

© Martin Gilbert 1993

117

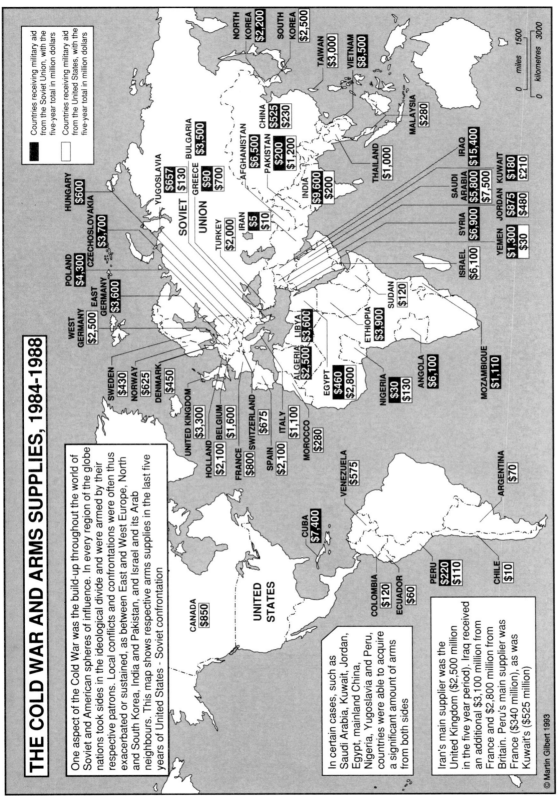

THE COLD WAR AND ARMS SUPPLIES, 1984-1988

One aspect of the Cold War was the build-up throughout the world of Soviet and American spheres of influence. In every region of the globe nations took sides in the ideological divide and were armed by their respective patrons. Local conflicts and confrontations were often thus exacerbated or sustained, as between East and West Europe, North and South Korea, India and Pakistan, and Israel and its Arab neighbours. This map shows respective arms supplies in the last five years of United States - Soviet confrontation

In certain cases, such as Saudi Arabia, Kuwait, Jordan, Egypt, mainland China, Nigeria, Yugoslavia and Peru, countries were able to acquire a significant amount of arms from both sides

Iran's main supplier was the United Kingdom ($2,500 million in the five year period). Iraq received an additional $3,100 million from France and $2,800 million from Britain. Peru's main supplier was France ($340 million), as was Kuwait's ($525 million)

Countries receiving military aid from the Soviet Union, with the five-year total in million dollars

Countries receiving military aid from the United States, with the five-year total in million dollars

NORTH KOREA	$2,200
SOUTH KOREA	$2,500
TAIWAN	$3,000
VIETNAM	$8,500
MALAYSIA	$280
CHINA	$525 / $230
AFGHANISTAN	$6,500
PAKISTAN	$200 / $1,200
INDIA	$9,600 / $200
THAILAND	$1,000
IRAQ	$15,400
KUWAIT	$180 / $210
SAUDI ARABIA	$5,800 / $7,500
JORDAN	$875 / $480
SYRIA	$6,900
YEMEN	$1,300 / $30
ISRAEL	$6,100
SUDAN	$120
ETHIOPIA	$3,900
ANGOLA	$6,100
MOZAMBIQUE	$1,110
BULGARIA	$3,500
YUGOSLAVIA	$657 / $130
GREECE	$90 / $700
SOVIET UNION	
TURKEY	$2,000
IRAN	$5 / $10
HUNGARY	$600
POLAND	$4,300
CZECHOSLOVAKIA	$3,700
EAST GERMANY	$3,600
WEST GERMANY	$2,500
LIBYA	$3,600
ALGERIA	$2,500
EGYPT	$460 / $2,800
NIGERIA	$30 / $130
SWEDEN	$430
NORWAY	$625
DENMARK	$450
UNITED KINGDOM	$3,300
HOLLAND	$2,100
BELGIUM	$1,600
FRANCE	$800
SWITZERLAND	$675
ITALY	$2,100
SPAIN	$1,100
MOROCCO	$280
VENEZUELA	$575
ARGENTINA	$70
CUBA	$7,400
CANADA	$850
UNITED STATES	
COLOMBIA	$120
ECUADOR	$60
PERU	$220 / $110
CHILE	$10

miles 0 / 1500
kilometres 0 / 3000

© Martin Gilbert 1993

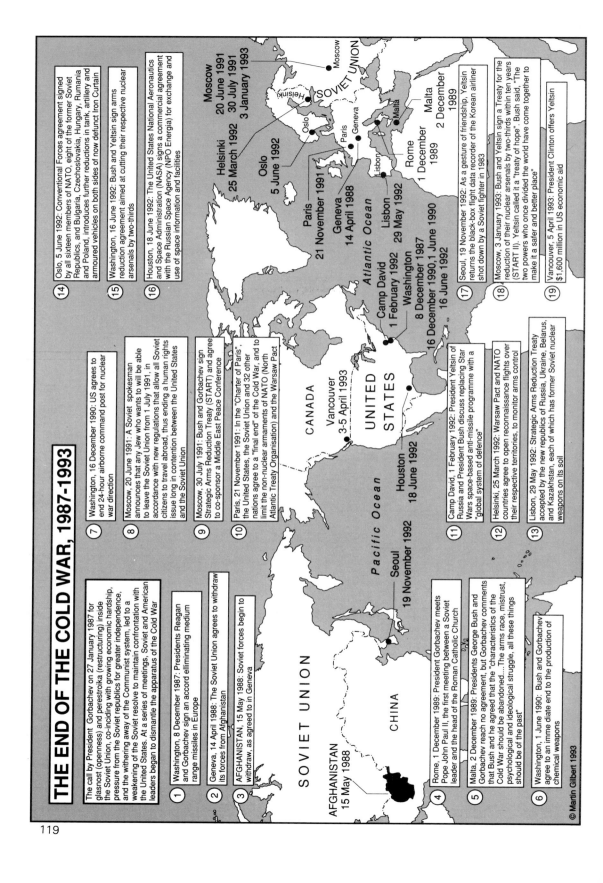

MILITARY, ECONOMIC AND HUMANITARIAN MISSIONS, 1975-1993

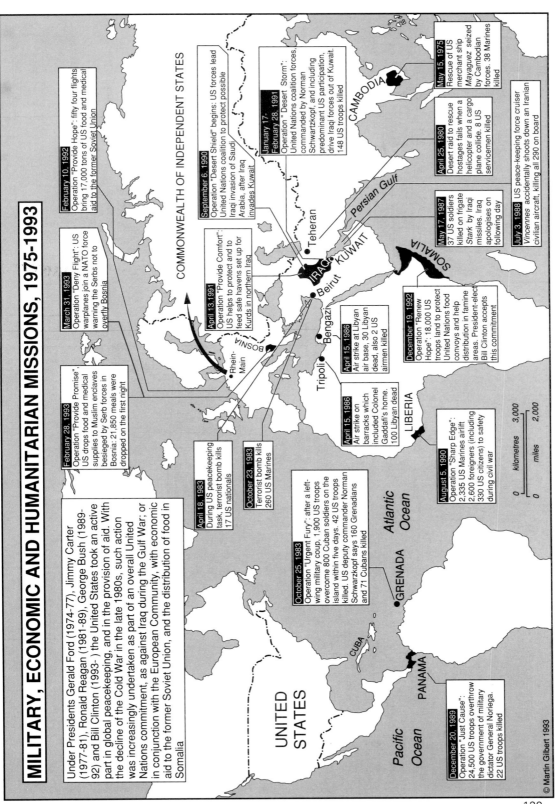

Under Presidents Gerald Ford (1974-77), Jimmy Carter (1977-81), Ronald Reagan (1981-89), George Bush (1989-92) and Bill Clinton (1993-) the United States took an active part in global peacekeeping, and in the provision of aid. With the decline of the Cold War in the late 1980s, such action was increasingly undertaken as part of an overall United Nations commitment, as against Iraq during the Gulf War; or in conjunction with the European Community, with economic aid to the former Soviet Union, and the distribution of food in Somalia

COMMONWEALTH OF INDEPENDENT STATES

February 10, 1992 Operation "Provide Hope": fifty four flights bring 17,000 tons of US food and medical aid to the former Soviet Union

March 31, 1993 Operation "Deny Flight": US warplanes join a NATO force warning the Serbs not to overfly Bosnia

September 6, 1990 Operation "Desert Shield" begins: US forces lead United Nations coalition to protect Saudi Arabia, after Iraq invades Kuwait

January 17-February 28, 1991 Operation "Desert Storm": United Nations coalition forces, commanded by Norman Schwartzkopf, and including predominant US participation, drive Iraqi forces out of Kuwait. 148 US troops killed

May 15, 1975 Rescue of US merchant ship *Mayaguez* seized by Cambodian forces. 38 Marines killed

April 25, 1980 Desert raid to rescue hostages fails when a helicopter and a cargo plane collide. 8 US servicemen killed

April 13,1991 Operation "Provide Comfort": US helps to protect and to feed safe havens set up for Kurds in northern Iraq

May 17, 1987 37 US soldiers killed on frigate *Stark* by Iraqi missiles. Iraq apologises on following day

July 3, 1988 US peace-keeping force cruiser *Vincennes* accidentally shoots down an Iranian civilian aircraft, killing all 290 on board

December 19, 1992 Operation "Renew Hope": 18,000 US troops land to protect United Nations food convoys and help distribution in famine areas. President-elect Bill Clinton accepts this commitment

April 15, 1986 Air strike at Libyan air base, 30 Libyan dead, also 2 US airmen killed

April 15, 1986 Air strike on barracks which included Colonel Gaddafi's home. 100 Libyan dead

February 28, 1993 Operation "Provide Promise": US drops food and medical supplies to Muslim enclaves besieged by Serb forces in Bosnia. 21,850 meals were dropped on the first night

April 18, 1983 During US peacekeeping task, terrorist bomb kills 17 US nationals

October 23, 1983 Terrorist bomb kills 260 US Marines

August 5, 1990 Operation "Sharp Edge": 2,335 US Marines airlift 2,600 foreigners (including 330 US citizens) to safety during civil war

October 25, 1983 Operation "Urgent Fury": after a left-wing military coup, 1,900 US troops overcome 800 Cuban soldiers on the island within five days. 42 US troops killed. US deputy commander Norman Schwarzkopf says 160 Grenadians and 71 Cubans killed

December 20, 1989 Operation "Just Cause": 24,500 US troops overthrow the government of military dictator General Noriega. 22 US troops killed

Teheran

Persian Gulf

IRAQ KUWAIT

Beirut

SOMALIA

Bengazi

BOSNIA

Rhein-Main

Tripoli

LIBERIA

Atlantic Ocean

GRENADA

CUBA

UNITED STATES

Pacific Ocean

PANAMA

CAMBODIA

kilometres 0 — 3,000
miles 0 — 2,000

© Martin Gilbert 1993

120

MAJOR NATURAL AND ACCIDENTAL DISASTERS, 1972-1993

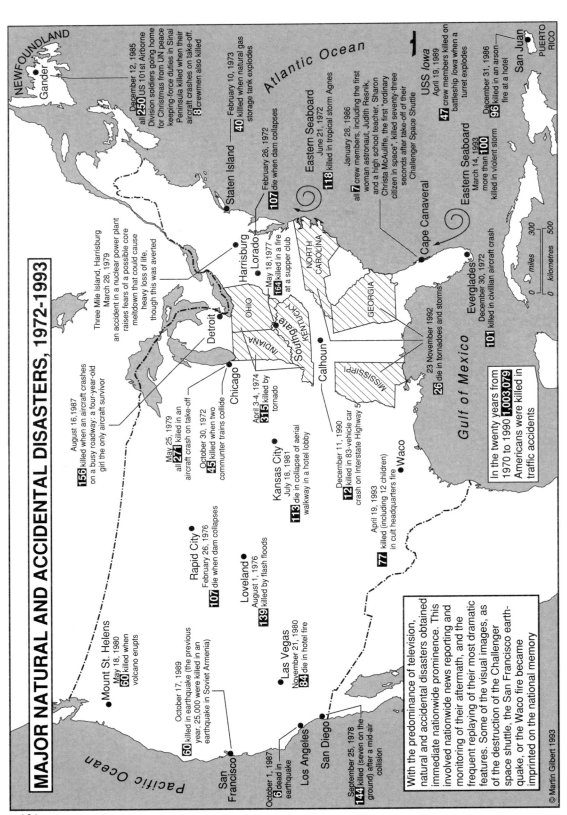

Atlantic Ocean

NEWFOUNDLAND

Gander

PUERTO RICO

San Juan

December 12, 1985 **250** US 101st Airborne Division soldiers going home for Christmas from UN peace keeping-force duties in Sinai Peninsula killed when their aircraft crashes on take-off. **8** crewmen also killed

February 10, 1973 **40** killed when natural gas storage tank explodes

April 19, 1989 USS *Iowa* **47** crew members killed on battleship *Iowa* when a turret explodes

Staten Island

February 26, 1972 **107** die when dam collapses

December 31, 1986 **96** killed in an arson fire at a hotel

Eastern Seaboard

June 21, 1972 **118** killed in tropical storm Agnes

Three Mile Island, Harrisburg March 28, 1979 an accident in a nuclear power plant raises fears of a possible core meltdown that could cause heavy loss of life, though this was averted

January 28, 1986 all **7** crew members, including the first woman astronaut, Judith Resnik, and a high school teacher, Sharon Christa McAuliffe, the first "ordinary citizen in space" killed seventy-three seconds after take-off of their Challenger Space Shuttle

Harrisburg
Lorado

May 18, 1977 **164** killed in a fire at a supper club

Cape Canaveral

Eastern Seaboard

March 14, 1993 more than **100** killed in violent storm

Detroit

NORTH CAROLINA

August 16, 1987 **156** killed when an aircraft crashes on a busy roadway: a four-year-old girl the only aircraft survivor

OHIO

KENTUCKY

Southgate

GEORGIA

May 25, 1979 all **271** killed in an aircraft crash on take-off

October 30, 1972 **45** killed when two commuter trains collide

Chicago

INDIANA

Calhoun

MISSISSIPPI

23 November 1992 **26** die in tornadoes and storms

April 3-4, 1974 **315** killed by tornado

Gulf of Mexico

Everglades

December 30, 1972 **101** killed in civillian aircraft crash

Kansas City

July 18, 1981 **113** die in collapse of aerial walkway in a hotel lobby

December 11, 1990 **12** killed in 83-vehicle car crash on Interstate Highway 5

Waco

April 19, 1993 **77** killed (including 12 children) in cult headquarters fire

0   miles   300
0   kilometres   500

In the twenty years from 1970 to 1990 **1,003,079** Americans were killed in traffic accidents

Rapid City
February 26, 1976 **107** die when dam collapses

Loveland
August 1, 1976 **139** killed by flash floods

Mount St. Helens
May 18, 1980 **60** killed when volcano erupts

October 17, 1989 **60** killed in earthquake (the previous year, 25,000 were killed in an earthquake in Soviet Armenia)

Las Vegas
November 21, 1980 **84** die in hotel fire

San Francisco

October 1, 1987 **6** dead in earthquake

Los Angeles

San Diego

September 25, 1978 **144** killed (seven on the ground) after a mid-air collision

Pacific Ocean

With the predominance of television, natural and accidental disasters obtained immediate nationwide prominence. This involved nationwide news reporting and monitoring of their aftermath, and the frequent replaying of their most dramatic features. Some of the visual images, as of the destruction of the Challenger space shuttle, the San Francisco earth-quake, or the Waco fire became imprinted on the national memory

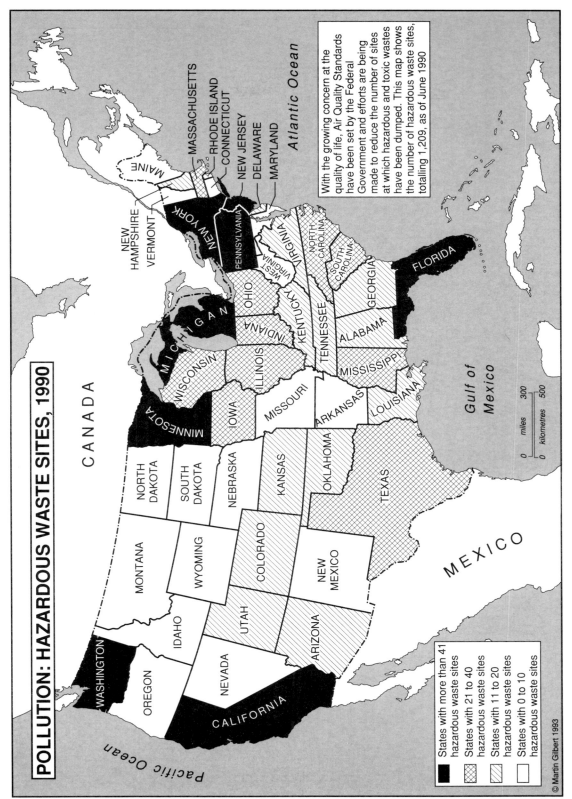

POLLUTION: HAZARDOUS WASTE SITES, 1990

With the growing concern at the quality of life, Air Quality Standards have been set by the Federal Government and efforts are being made to reduce the number of sites at which hazardous and toxic wastes have been dumped. This map shows the number of hazardous waste sites, totalling 1,209, as of June 1990

CANADA

Atlantic Ocean

Gulf of Mexico

MEXICO

Pacific Ocean

States with more than 41 hazardous waste sites

States with 21 to 40 hazardous waste sites

States with 11 to 20 hazardous waste sites

States with 0 to 10 hazardous waste sites

© Martin Gilbert 1993

MASSACHUSETTS
RHODE ISLAND
CONNECTICUT
NEW JERSEY
DELAWARE
MARYLAND

NEW HAMPSHIRE
VERMONT
MAINE
NEW YORK
PENNSYLVANIA
WEST VIRGINIA
VIRGINIA
NORTH CAROLINA
SOUTH CAROLINA
GEORGIA
FLORIDA
ALABAMA
MISSISSIPPI
TENNESSEE
KENTUCKY
OHIO
INDIANA
ILLINOIS
MICHIGAN
WISCONSIN
IOWA
MISSOURI
ARKANSAS
LOUISIANA
MINNESOTA
NORTH DAKOTA
SOUTH DAKOTA
NEBRASKA
KANSAS
OKLAHOMA
TEXAS
COLORADO
NEW MEXICO
MONTANA
WYOMING
UTAH
ARIZONA
IDAHO
NEVADA
CALIFORNIA
OREGON
WASHINGTON

miles 300
kilometres 500
0 0

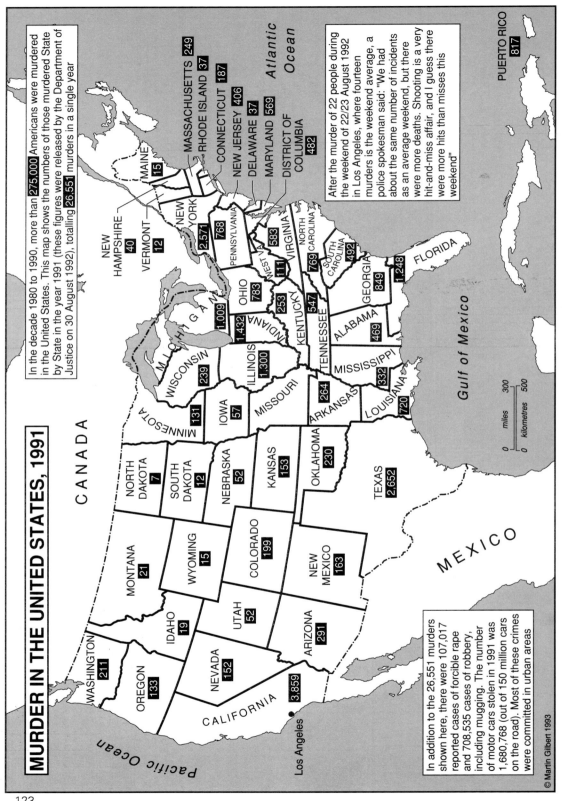

MURDER IN THE UNITED STATES, 1991

In the decade 1980 to 1990, more than 275,000 Americans were murdered in the United States. This map shows the numbers of those murdered State by State in the year 1991 (these figures were released by the Department of Justice on 30 August 1992), totalling 26,551 murders in a single year

After the murder of 22 people during the weekend of 22/23 August 1992 in Los Angeles, where fourteen murders is the weekend average, a police spokesman said: "We had about the same number of incidents as an average weekend, but there were more deaths. Shooting is a very hit-and-miss affair, and I guess there were more hits than misses this weekend"

In addition to the 26,551 murders shown here, there were 107,017 reported cases of forcible rape and 708,535 cases of robbery, including mugging. The number of motor cars stolen in 1991 was 1,680,768 (out of 150 million cars on the road). Most of these crimes were committed in urban areas

© Martin Gilbert 1993

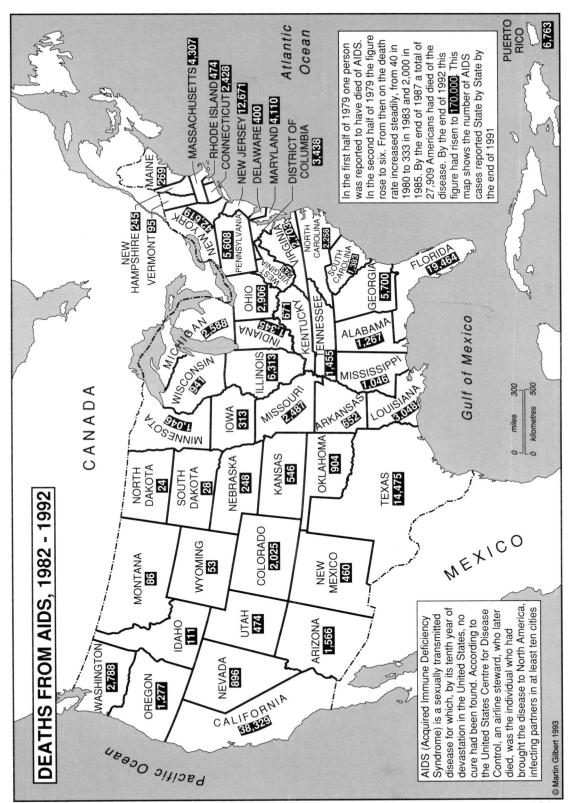

DEATHS FROM AIDS, 1982 - 1992

Atlantic Ocean

Pacific Ocean

CANADA

MEXICO

Gulf of Mexico

PUERTO RICO 6,763

In the first half of 1979 one person was reported to have died of AIDS. In the second half of 1979 the figure rose to six. From then on the death rate increased steadily, from 40 in 1980 to 333 in 1983 and 2,000 in 1985. By the end of 1987 a total of 27,909 Americans had died of the disease. By the end of 1992 this figure had risen to 170,000. This map shows the number of AIDS cases reported State by State by the end of 1991

AIDS (Acquired Immune Deficiency Syndrome) is a sexually transmitted disease for which, by its tenth year of devastation in the United States, no cure had been found. According to the United States Centre for Disease Control, an airline steward, who later died, was the individual who had brought the disease to North America, infecting partners in at least ten cities

MASSACHUSETTS 4,307
RHODE ISLAND 474
CONNECTICUT 2,428
NEW JERSEY 12,671
DELAWARE 400
MARYLAND 4,110
DISTRICT OF COLUMBIA 3,438

MAINE 269
NEW HAMPSHIRE 245
VERMONT 95
NEW YORK 42,619
PENNSYLVANIA 5,608
VIRGINIA 2,703
WEST VIRGINIA 262
NORTH CAROLINA 2,258
SOUTH CAROLINA 1,383
FLORIDA 19,464
GEORGIA 5,700
OHIO 2,906
KENTUCKY 671
TENNESSEE 1,455
ALABAMA 1,267
MISSISSIPPI 1,046
MICHIGAN 2,588
INDIANA 1,345
ILLINOIS 6,313
WISCONSIN 941
MINNESOTA 1,046
IOWA 313
MISSOURI 2,487
ARKANSAS 652
LOUISIANA 3,048
NORTH DAKOTA 24
SOUTH DAKOTA 28
NEBRASKA 248
KANSAS 546
OKLAHOMA 904
TEXAS 14,475
MONTANA 86
WYOMING 53
COLORADO 2,025
NEW MEXICO 460
WASHINGTON 2,788
OREGON 1,277
IDAHO 111
UTAH 474
NEVADA 896
ARIZONA 1,566
CALIFORNIA 38,329

0 miles 300
0 kilometres 500

© Martin Gilbert 1993

124

IMMIGRATION TO THE UNITED STATES, 1991

Between 1820 and 1991, 56 million immigrants were admitted to the United States. Most came as refugees from persecution and poverty, or in search of freedom and opportunity. This map shows the main countries of origin in the year 1991, when 704,005 immigrants were admitted. In addition, 1,123,162 aliens with temporary resident status became eligible for naturalization in 1991 under the Immigration Reform and Control Act (IRAC) of 1986

Most of the Soviet immigrants in 1991 were Jews. A further 300,000 Soviet Jews went to Israel that year. More than 2,000 Syrian Jews, allowed to leave for the first time in many decades, were also admitted to the United States

Temporary residents granted naturalization in 1991 (where more than 10,000 were from a single country):

Mexico	893,301
Haiti	35,191
El Salvador	32,479
Guatemala	19,374
India	13,899
Pakistan	11,846
Dominican Republic	11,228
Colombia	10,073

■ Countries from which more than 2,500 immigrants were admitted as permanent residents to the United States in 1991

More than twice as many immigrants were admitted from Vietnam (55,278) in 1991 as from the whole of Africa (22,618). Immigrants came, in smaller numbers than shown on this map, from almost every country in the world

The total number of immigrants admitted to the United States from Mexico and Central and South America, or granted naturalization, in 1991, was 1,134,194 (62% of the total)

POPULATION OF THE UNITED STATES
1980:   226,504,825
1991:   248,709,887

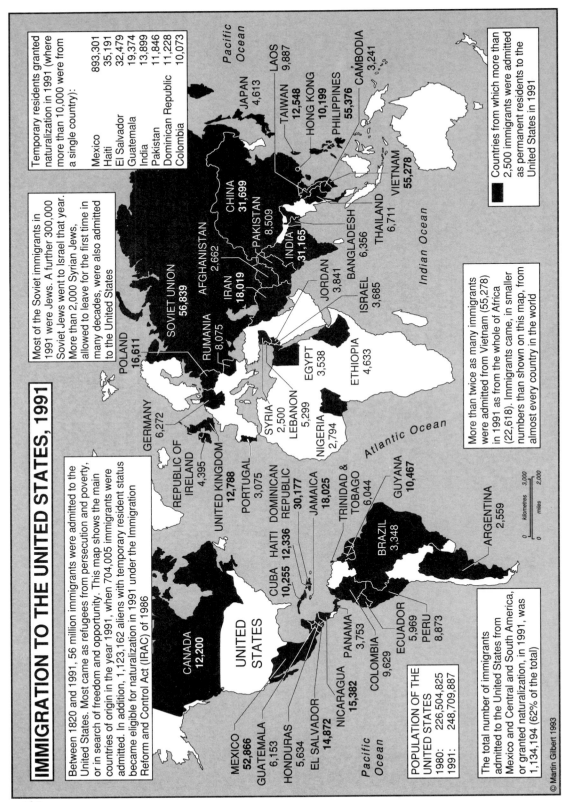

Pacific Ocean

Indian Ocean

Atlantic Ocean

Pacific Ocean

LAOS 9,887
JAPAN 4,613
TAIWAN 12,548
HONG KONG 10,199
CAMBODIA 3,241
PHILIPPINES 55,376
CHINA 31,699
PAKISTAN 8,509
VIETNAM 55,278
THAILAND 6,711
BANGLADESH 6,356
INDIA 31,165
AFGHANISTAN 2,662
IRAN 18,019
SOVIET UNION 56,839
JORDAN 3,841
ISRAEL 3,685
POLAND 16,611
RUMANIA 8,075
ETHIOPIA 4,633
EGYPT 3,538
NIGERIA 2,794
SYRIA 2,500
LEBANON 5,299
GERMANY 6,272
REPUBLIC OF IRELAND 4,395
UNITED KINGDOM 12,788
PORTUGAL 3,075
GUYANA 10,467
BRAZIL 3,348
ARGENTINA 2,559
CUBA 10,255
HAITI 12,336
DOMINICAN REPUBLIC 30,177
JAMAICA 18,025
TRINIDAD & TOBAGO 6,044
CANADA 12,200
UNITED STATES
MEXICO 52,866
GUATEMALA 6,153
HONDURAS 5,634
EL SALVADOR 14,872
NICARAGUA 15,382
PANAMA 3,753
COLOMBIA 9,629
ECUADOR 5,969
PERU 8,873

0   kilometres   3,000
0   miles   2,000

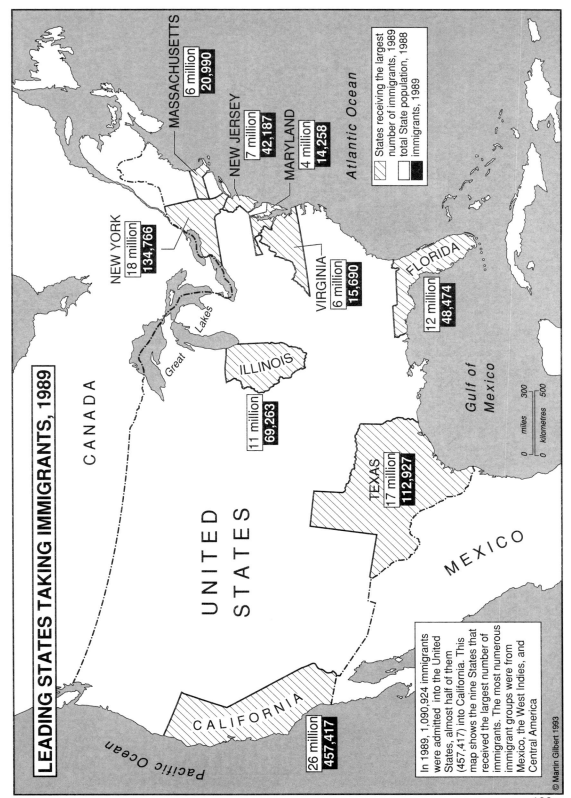

LEADING STATES TAKING IMMIGRANTS, 1989

CANADA

UNITED STATES

MEXICO

Pacific Ocean

Atlantic Ocean

Gulf of Mexico

Great Lakes

MASSACHUSETTS
6 million
20,990

NEW JERSEY
7 million
42,187

MARYLAND
4 million
14,258

NEW YORK
18 million
134,766

VIRGINIA
6 million
15,690

FLORIDA
12 million
48,474

ILLINOIS
11 million
69,263

TEXAS
17 million
112,927

CALIFORNIA
26 million
457,417

States receiving the largest
number of immigrants, 1989

total State population, 1988

immigrants, 1989

In 1989, 1,090,924 immigrants
were admitted into the United
States, almost half of them
(457,417) into California. This
map shows the nine States that
received the largest number of
immigrants. The most numerous
immigrant groups were from
Mexico, the West Indies, and
Central America

0   miles   300
0   kilometres   500

© Martin Gilbert 1993

126

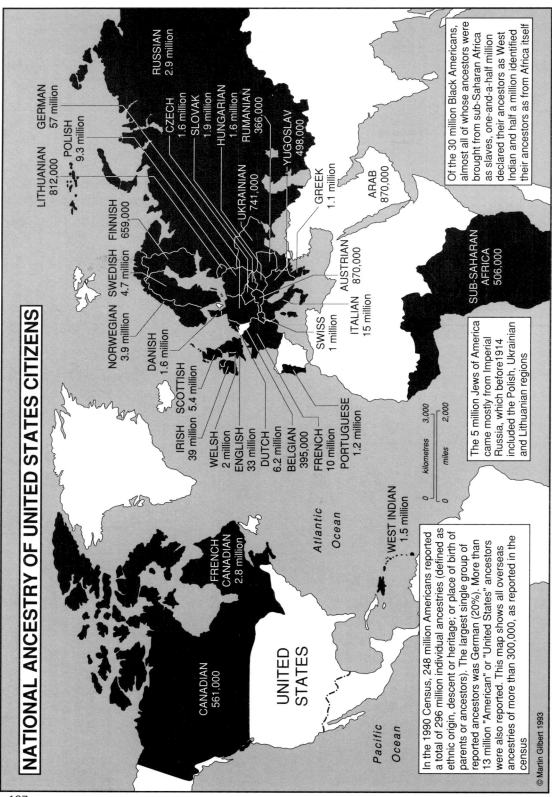

NATIONAL ANCESTRY OF UNITED STATES CITIZENS

LITHUANIAN
812,000

GERMAN
57 million

POLISH
9.3 million

RUSSIAN
2.9 million

CZECH
1.6 million

SLOVAK
1.9 million

HUNGARIAN
1.6 million

RUMANIAN
366,000

UKRAINIAN
741,000

YUGOSLAV
498,000

GREEK
1.1 million

ARAB
870,000

FINNISH
659,000

SWEDISH
4.7 million

NORWEGIAN
3.9 million

DANISH
1.6 million

SCOTTISH
5.4 million

IRISH
39 million

WELSH
2 million

ENGLISH
33 million

DUTCH
6.2 million

BELGIAN
395,000

FRENCH
10 million

PORTUGUESE
1.2 million

AUSTRIAN
870,000

SWISS
1 million

ITALIAN
15 million

SUB-SAHARAN
AFRICA
506,000

Of the 30 million Black Americans, almost all of whose ancestors were brought from sub-Saharan Africa as slaves, one-and-a-half million declared their ancestors as West Indian and half a million identified their ancestors as from Africa itself

The 5 million Jews of America came mostly from Imperial Russia, which before1914 included the Polish, Ukrainian and Lithuanian regions

WEST INDIAN
1.5 million

FRENCH
CANADIAN
2.8 million

CANADIAN
561,000

Atlantic
Ocean

Pacific
Ocean

UNITED
STATES

kilometres 0 / 2,000 / 3,000
miles 0

In the 1990 Census, 248 million Americans reported a total of 296 million individual ancestries (defined as ethnic origin, descent or heritage; or place of birth of parents or ancestors). The largest single group of reported ancestors was German (20%). More than 13 million "American" or "United States" ancestors were also reported. This map shows all overseas ancestries of more than 300,000, as reported in the census

© Martin Gilbert 1993

CITIES WITH LARGE ETHNIC GROUPS

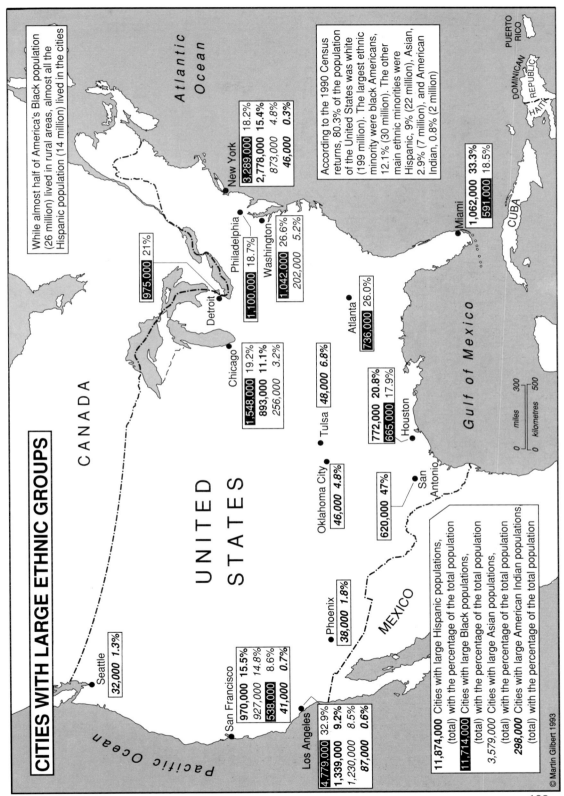

Atlantic Ocean

Pacific Ocean

Gulf of Mexico

CANADA

UNITED STATES

MEXICO

CUBA

PUERTO RICO

DOMINICAN REPUBLIC

HAITI

While almost half of America's Black population (26 million) lived in rural areas, almost all the Hispanic population (14 million) lived in the cities

According to the 1990 Census returns, 80.3% of the population of the United States was white (199 million). The largest ethnic minority were black Americans, 12.1% (30 million). The other main ethnic minorities were Hispanic, 9% (22 million), Asian, 2.9% (7 million), and American Indian, 0.8% (2 million).

New York
3,289,000 **18.2%**
2,778,000 **15.4%**
873,000 4.8%
46,000 **0.3%**

Philadelphia 1,100,000 18.7%

Washington 1,042,000 26.6% 5.2%
202,000 5.2%

Detroit 975,000 21%

Chicago
1,548,000 19.2%
893,000 **11.1%**
256,000 3.2%

Atlanta 736,000 26.0%

Miami 1,062,000 **33.3%**
591,000 18.5%

Tulsa *48,000* **6.8%**

Houston 772,000 20.8%
665,000 17.9%

Oklahoma City *46,000* **4.8%**

San Antonio 620,000 47%

Phoenix *38,000* **1.8%**

Seattle *32,000* **1.3%**

San Francisco
970,000 **15.5%**
927,000 14.8%
588,000 8.6%
41,000 **0.7%**

Los Angeles
4,779,000 32.9%
1,339,000 **9.2%**
1,230,000 8.5%
87,000 **0.6%**

11,874,000 Cities with large Hispanic populations, (total) with the percentage of the total population
11,714,000 Cities with large Black populations, (total) with the percentage of the total population
3,579,000 Cities with large Asian populations, (total) with the percentage of the total population
298,000 Cities with large American Indian populations, (total) with the percentage of the total population

miles 0 300 500
0 kilometres

© Martin Gilbert 1993

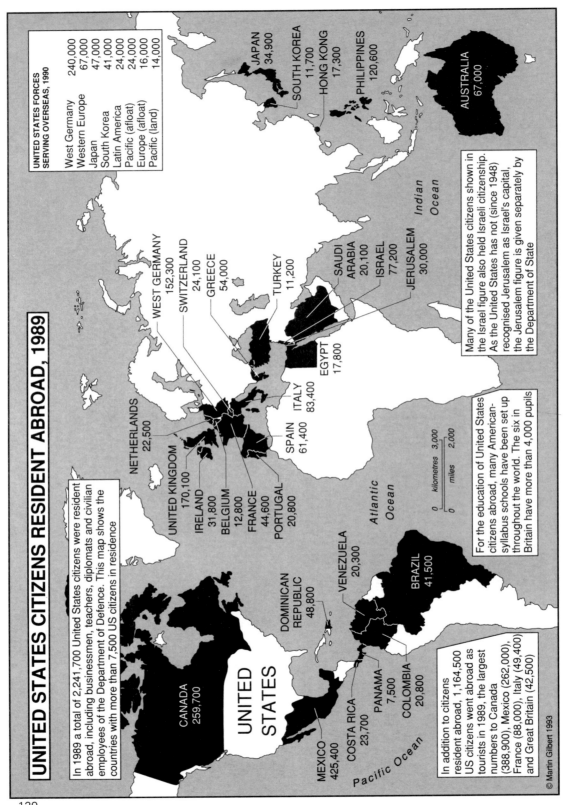

UNITED STATES CITIZENS RESIDENT ABROAD, 1989

In 1989 a total of 2,241,700 United States citizens were resident abroad, including businessmen, teachers, diplomats and civilian employees of the Department of Defence. This map shows the countries with more than 7,500 US citizens in residence

UNITED STATES FORCES
SERVING OVERSEAS, 1990

West Germany	240,000
Western Europe	67,000
Japan	47,000
South Korea	41,000
Latin America	24,000
Pacific (afloat)	24,000
Europe (afloat)	16,000
Pacific (land)	14,000

JAPAN 34,900

SOUTH KOREA 11,700

HONG KONG 17,300

PHILIPPINES 120,600

AUSTRALIA 67,000

Indian Ocean

WEST GERMANY 152,300

SWITZERLAND 24,100

GREECE 54,000

TURKEY 11,200

SAUDI ARABIA 20,100

ISRAEL 77,200

JERUSALEM 30,000

EGYPT 17,800

ITALY 83,400

SPAIN 61,400

Many of the United States citizens shown in the Israel figure also held Israeli citizenship. As the United States has not (since 1948) recognised Jerusalem as Israel's capital, the Jerusalem figure is given separately by the Department of State

NETHERLANDS 22,500

UNITED KINGDOM 170,100

IRELAND 31,800

BELGIUM 12,800

FRANCE 44,600

PORTUGAL 20,800

For the education of United States citizens abroad, many American-syllabus schools have been set up throughout the world. The six in Britain have more than 4,000 pupils

VENEZUELA 20,300

BRAZIL 41,500

Atlantic Ocean

0 kilometres 3,000
0 miles 2,000

DOMINICAN REPUBLIC 48,800

CANADA 259,700

UNITED STATES

COSTA RICA 23,700

PANAMA 7,500

COLOMBIA 20,800

MEXICO 425,400

Pacific Ocean

In addition to citizens resident abroad, 1,164,500 US citizens went abroad as tourists in 1989, the largest numbers to Canada (388,900), Mexico (262,000), France (88,000), Italy (49,400) and Great Britain (42,500)

© Martin Gilbert 1993

THE VISA LOTTERY PROGRAM, 1990-1993

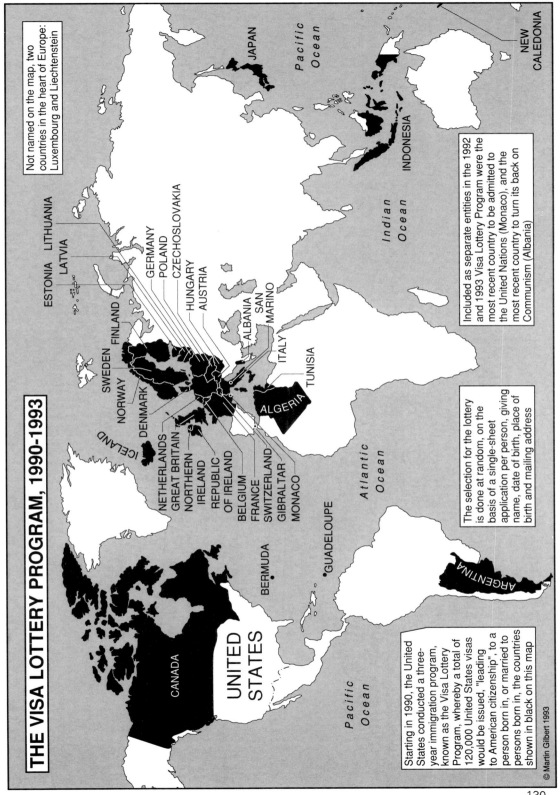

Not named on the map, two countries in the heart of Europe: Luxembourg and Liechtenstein

Included as separate entities in the 1992 and 1993 Visa Lottery Program were the most recent country to be admitted to the United Nations (Monaco), and the most recent country to turn its back on Communism (Albania)

The selection for the lottery is done at random, on the basis of a single-sheet application per person, giving name, date of birth, place of birth and mailing address

Starting in 1990, the United States conducted a three-year immigration program, known as the Visa Lottery Program, whereby a total of 120,000 United States visas would be issued, "leading to American citizenship", to a person born in, or married to persons born in, the countries shown in black on this map

ESTONIA LITHUANIA LATVIA GERMANY POLAND CZECHOSLOVAKIA HUNGARY AUSTRIA ALBANIA SAN MARINO ITALY TUNISIA ALGERIA

SWEDEN FINLAND NORWAY DENMARK ICELAND NETHERLANDS GREAT BRITAIN NORTHERN IRELAND REPUBLIC OF IRELAND BELGIUM FRANCE SWITZERLAND GIBRALTAR MONACO GUADELOUPE BERMUDA

JAPAN INDONESIA NEW CALEDONIA

Pacific Ocean Indian Ocean Atlantic Ocean Pacific Ocean

ARGENTINA

CANADA UNITED STATES

© Martin Gilbert 1993

130

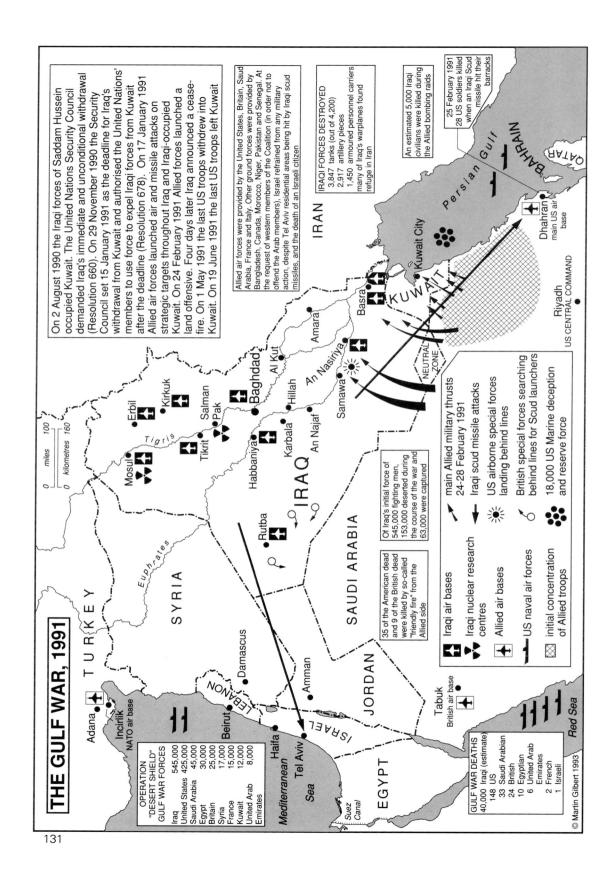

THE GULF WAR, 1991

On 2 August 1990 the Iraqi forces of Saddam Hussein occupied Kuwait. The United Nations Security Council demanded Iraq's immediate and unconditional withdrawal (Resolution 660). On 29 November 1990 the Security Council set 15 January 1991 as the deadline for Iraq's withdrawal from Kuwait and authorised the United Nations' members to use force to expel Iraqi forces from Kuwait after the deadline (Resolution 678). On 17 January 1991 Allied air forces launched air and missile attacks on strategic targets throughout Iraq and Iraqi-occupied Kuwait. On 24 February 1991 Allied forces launched a land offensive. Four days later Iraq announced a cease-fire. On 1 May 1991 the last US troops withdrew into Kuwait. On 19 June 1991 the last US troops left Kuwait

Allied air forces were provided by the United States, Britain, Saudi Arabia, France and Italy. Other ground forces were provided by Bangladesh, Canada, Morocco, Niger, Pakistan and Senegal. At the request of western members of the Coalition (in order not to offend the Arab members), Israel refrained from any military action, despite Tel Aviv residential areas being hit by Iraqi scud missiles, and the death of an Israeli citizen

IRAQI FORCES DESTROYED
3,847 tanks (out of 4,200)
2,917 artillery pieces
1,450 armoured personnel carriers
many of Iraq's warplanes found refuge in Iran

An estimated 5,000 Iraqi civilians were killed during the Allied bombing raids

25 February 1991
28 US soldiers killed when an Iraqi Scud missile hit their barracks

OPERATION
"DESERT SHIELD"
GULF WAR FORCES

Iraq	545,000
United States	425,000
Saudi Arabia	45,000
Egypt	30,000
Britain	25,000
Syria	17,000
France	15,000
Kuwait	12,000
United Arab Emirates	8,000

Of Iraq's initial force of 545,000 fighting men, 153,000 deserted during the course of the war and 63,000 were captured

35 of the American dead and 9 of the British dead were killed by so-called "friendly fire" from the Allied side

GULF WAR DEATHS
40,000 Iraqi (estimate)
148 US
33 Saudi Arabian
24 British
6 Egyptian
6 United Arab Emirates
2 French
1 Israeli

main Allied military thrusts 24-28 February 1991

Iraqi scud missile attacks

US airborne special forces landing behind lines

British special forces searching behind lines for Scud launchers

18,000 US Marine deception and reserve force

Iraqi air bases

Iraqi nuclear research centres

Allied air bases

US naval air forces

initial concentration of Allied troops

© Martin Gilbert 1993

TURKEY · Adana · Incirlik NATO air base

SYRIA · Damascus · LEBANON · Beirut · Haifa · Tel Aviv · ISRAEL · Amman · JORDAN

Mediterranean Sea · Suez Canal · EGYPT · Red Sea · Tabuk British air base

Mosul · Erbil · Kirkuk · Tikrit · Salman Pak · Baghdad · Al Kut · Amara · Habbaniya · Karbala · Hillah · An Najaf · Samawa · An Nasiriya · Rutba

Tigris · Euphrates

IRAQ · SAUDI ARABIA · Riyadh US CENTRAL COMMAND

KUWAIT · Kuwait City · Basra · NEUTRAL ZONE

IRAN · Persian Gulf · BAHRAIN · QATAR · Dhahran main US base

0 miles 100
0 kilometres 160

131

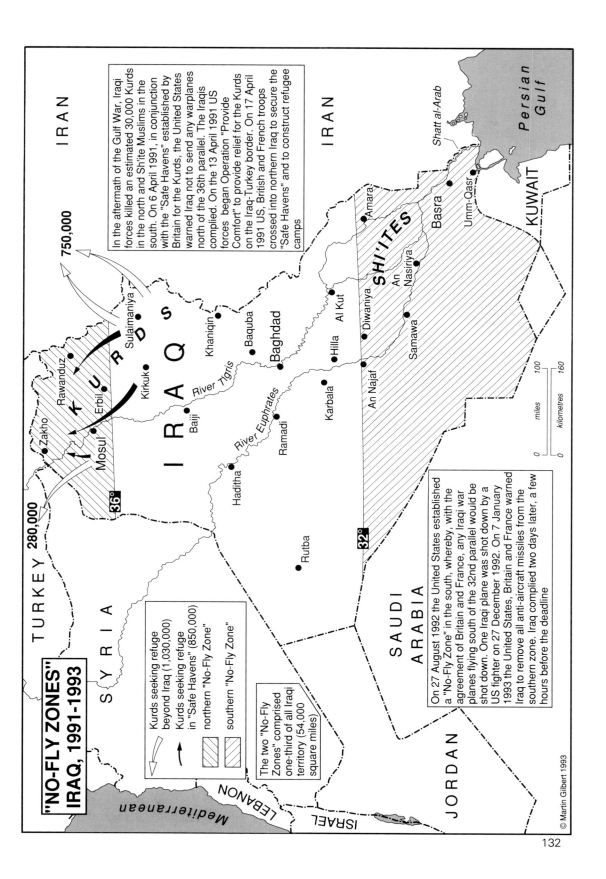

"NO-FLY ZONES"
IRAQ, 1991-1993

In the aftermath of the Gulf War, Iraqi forces killed an estimated 30,000 Kurds in the north and Shi'ite Muslims in the south. On 6 April 1991, in conjunction with the "Safe Havens" established by Britain for the Kurds, the United States warned Iraq not to send any warplanes north of the 36th parallel. The Iraqis complied. On the 13 April 1991 US forces began Operation "Provide Comfort" to provide relief for the Kurds on the Iraq-Turkey border. On 17 April 1991 US, British and French troops crossed into northern Iraq to secure the "Safe Havens" and to construct refugee camps

On 27 August 1992 the United States established a "No-Fly Zone" in the south, whereby, with the agreement of Britain and France, any Iraqi war planes flying south of the 32nd parallel would be shot down. One Iraqi plane was shot down by a US fighter on 27 December 1992. On 7 January 1993 the United States, Britain and France warned Iraq to remove all anti-aircraft missiles from the southern zone. Iraq complied two days later, a few hours before the deadline

Kurds seeking refuge beyond Iraq (1,030,000)

Kurds seeking refuge in "Safe Havens" (850,000)

northern "No-Fly Zone"

southern "No-Fly Zone"

The two "No-Fly Zones" comprised one-third of all Iraqi territory (54,000 square miles)

IRAN

TURKEY 280,000

750,000

SYRIA

KURDS

Zakho · Rawanduz ·
Mosul · Erbil · Sulaimaniya ·
Kirkuk ·
Baiji · Khaniqin ·
Baquba ·
Haditha · **Baghdad**
Ramadi · Hilla ·
Karbala ·
An Najaf ·
Al Kut ·
Diwaniya ·
Samawa ·
An Nasiriya ·
Amara ·
Rutba ·

I R A Q

River Tigris

River Euphrates

SHI'ITES

Basra ·
Umm-Qasr ·

36°

32°

SAUDI ARABIA

KUWAIT

Persian Gulf

Shatt al-Arab

IRAN

JORDAN

ISRAEL

LEBANON

Mediterranean

0   100 miles
0   160 kilometres

© Martin Gilbert 1993

UNITED STATES ARMS SALES, 1992

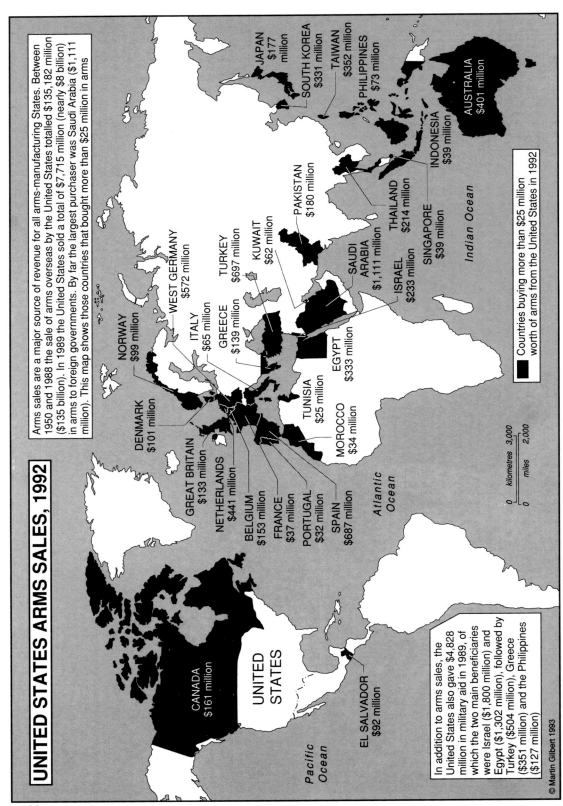

Arms sales are a major source of revenue for all arms-manufacturing States. Between 1950 and 1988 the sale of arms overseas by the United States totalled $135,182 million ($135 billion). In 1989 the United States sold a total of $7,715 million (nearly $8 billion) in arms to foreign governments. By far the largest purchaser was Saudi Arabia ($1,111 million). This map shows those countries that bought more than $25 million in arms

JAPAN
$177 million

SOUTH KOREA
$331 million

TAIWAN
$352 million

PHILIPPINES
$73 million

AUSTRALIA
$401 million

PAKISTAN
$180 million

THAILAND
$214 million

INDONESIA
$39 million

SINGAPORE
$39 million

Indian Ocean

SAUDI
ARABIA
$1,111 million

KUWAIT
$62 million

ISRAEL
$233 million

NORWAY
$99 million

WEST GERMANY
$572 million

TURKEY
$697 million

ITALY
$65 million

GREECE
$139 million

EGYPT
$333 million

TUNISIA
$25 million

MOROCCO
$34 million

DENMARK
$101 million

GREAT BRITAIN
$133 million

NETHERLANDS
$441 million

BELGIUM
$153 million

FRANCE
$37 million

PORTUGAL
$32 million

SPAIN
$687 million

Atlantic
Ocean

Countries buying more than $25 million
worth of arms from the United States in 1992

0   kilometres   3,000

0   miles   2,000

CANADA
$161 million

UNITED
STATES

EL SALVADOR
$92 million

Pacific
Ocean

In addition to arms sales, the United States also gave $4,828 million in military aid in 1989, of which the two main beneficiaries were Israel ($1,800 million) and Egypt ($1,302 million), followed by Turkey ($504 million), Greece ($351 million) and the Philippines ($127 million)

© Martin Gilbert 1993

MAIN RECIPIENTS OF UNITED STATES ECONOMIC AID, 1992

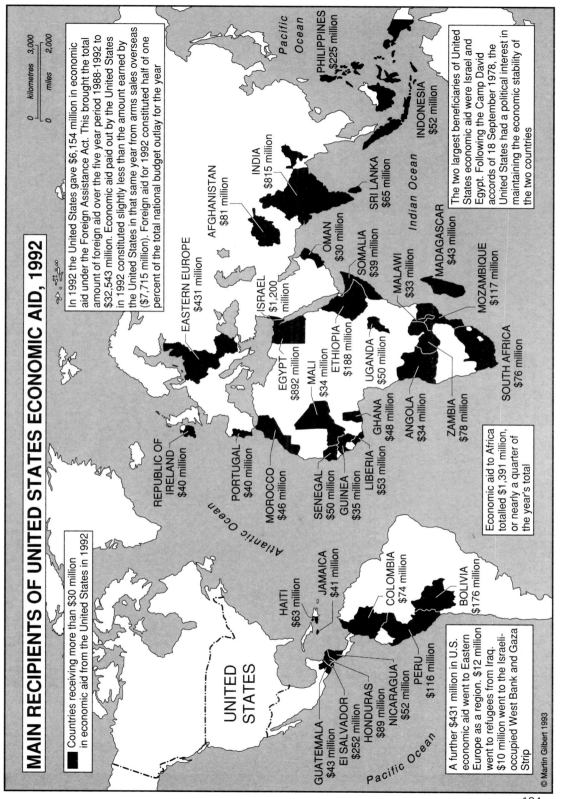

■ Countries receiving more than $30 million in economic aid from the United States in 1992

In 1992 the United States gave $6,154 million in economic aid under the Foreign Assistance Act. This brought the total amount of foreign aid over the five year period 1988-1992 to $32,543 million. Economic aid paid out by the United States in 1992 constituted slightly less than the amount earned by the United States in that same year from arms sales overseas ($7,715 million). Foreign aid for 1992 constituted half of one percent of the total national budget outlay for the year

The two largest beneficiaries of United States economic aid were Israel and Egypt. Following the Camp David accords of 18 September 1978, the United States had a political interest in maintaining the economic stability of the two countries

Economic aid to Africa totalled $1,391 million, or nearly a quarter of the year's total

A further $431 million in U.S. economic aid went to Eastern Europe as a region. $12 million went to refugees from Iraq. $10 million went to the Israeli-occupied West Bank and Gaza Strip

PHILIPPINES $225 million

INDONESIA $52 million

INDIA $815 million

AFGHANISTAN $81 million

SRI LANKA $65 million

Indian Ocean

MADAGASCAR $43 million

OMAN $30 million

SOMALIA $39 million

MALAWI $33 million

MOZAMBIQUE $117 million

ISRAEL $1,200 million

EGYPT $892 million

MALI $34 million

ETHIOPIA $188 million

UGANDA $50 million

GHANA $48 million

ANGOLA $34 million

ZAMBIA $78 million

SOUTH AFRICA $76 million

EASTERN EUROPE $431 million

REPUBLIC OF IRELAND $40 million

PORTUGAL $40 million

MOROCCO $46 million

SENEGAL $50 million

GUINEA $35 million

LIBERIA $53 million

Atlantic Ocean

Pacific Ocean

UNITED STATES

HAITI $63 million

JAMAICA $41 million

COLOMBIA $74 million

BOLIVIA $176 million

GUATEMALA $43 million

EL SALVADOR $252 million

HONDURAS $89 million

NICARAGUA $52 million

PERU $116 million

Pacific Ocean

0 — kilometres — 3,000
0 — miles — 2,000

© Martin Gilbert 1993

134

DEFENCE PREPAREDNESS ON LAND, 1991

From 1945 to 1990 the main thrust of United States defences was in the confrontation with the Soviet Union. With the collapse of Communist power from 1990, and the demise of the Warsaw Pact, defence priorities were under continuous scrutiny. This map shows the location of Air Force Tactical Fighter Wings, and of the Strategic Offensive Forces, in 1991. Further cuts in bases were made in 1992 and 1993

- ⊙ Air Force Tactical Fighter Wings
- ◪ Strategic Offensive air bases
- ■ Strategic Offensive naval bases
- ▣ Strategic Offensive missile sites

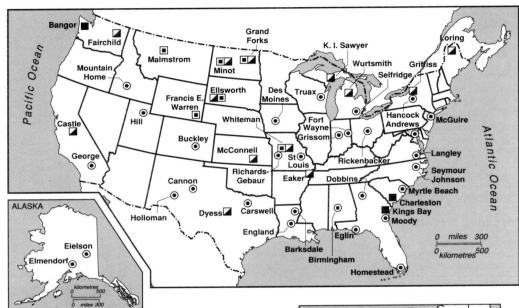

Pacific Ocean

Bangor ■
Fairchild ◪
Mountain Home
Castle ◪
Hill
George
Malmstrom ▣
Francis E. Warren ▣
Buckley ⊙
Ellsworth ▣◪
Minot ▣◪ ▣
Grand Forks ▣
Whiteman ⊙
McConnell ⊙
Cannon ⊙
Holloman ⊙
Dyess ◪
Richards-Gebaur
Carswell ⊙
England ⊙
Des Moines
Fort Wayne
Grissom ⊙
St Louis ⊙
Eaker
Barksdale
Birmingham
K. I. Sawyer
Truax ⊙
Wurtsmith ◪
Selfridge ⊙
Rickenbacker ⊙
Dobbins
Eglin
Homestead ⊙
Loring ◪
Griffiss ⊙
Hancock Andrews ⊙
Langley ⊙
McGuire ⊙
Seymour Johnson ⊙
Myrtle Beach ■
Charleston ■
Kings Bay ⊙
Moody ⊙

Atlantic Ocean

0 miles 300
0 kilometres 500

ALASKA

Eielson ⊙
Elmendorf ⊙

kilometres 0 500
0 miles 300

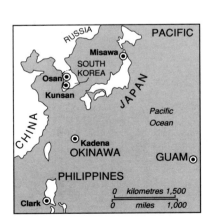

PACIFIC

RUSSIA
Misawa ⊙
SOUTH KOREA
Osan ⊙
Kunsan ⊙
JAPAN
CHINA
Kadena ⊙
OKINAWA
Pacific Ocean
GUAM ⊙
PHILIPPINES
Clark ⊙

0 kilometres 1,500
0 miles 1,000

EUROPE

Holy Loch ■
Atlantic Ocean
Upper Heyford ⊙
BRITAIN
Lakenheath ⊙
Bentwaters ⊙
GERMANY
Bitburg ⊙
Spangdaheim ⊙
Hahn ⊙
Ramstein ⊙
SPAIN
Torrejon ⊙
ITALY
Mediterranean Sea

kilometres 0 500
0 miles 300

On 30 July 1991 the Department of Defence announced the shutting down of 72 United States military installations in Europe, and reduced operations at seven others

BASES TO BE CLOSED	
Germany	38
Britain	13
Italy	8
Turkey	7
Spain	5
Netherlands	1

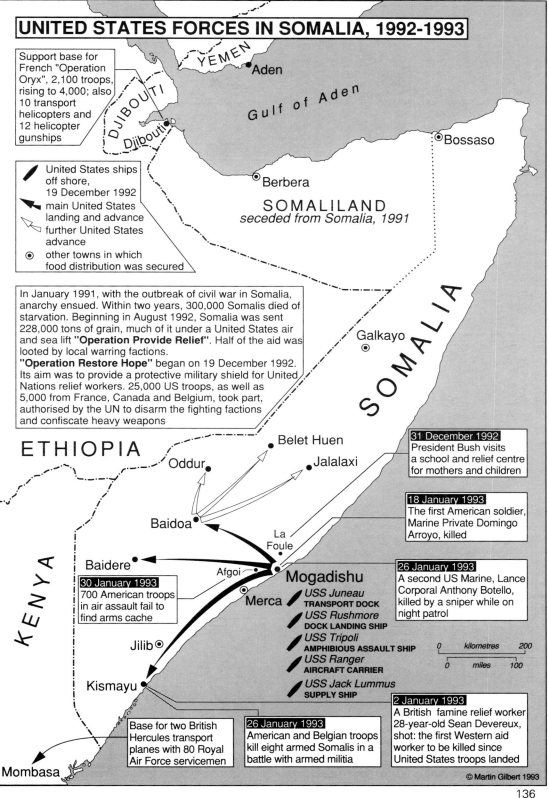

UNITED STATES FORCES IN SOMALIA, 1992-1993

Support base for French "Operation Oryx", 2,100 troops, rising to 4,000; also 10 transport helicopters and 12 helicopter gunships

United States ships off shore, 19 December 1992

main United States landing and advance

further United States advance

⊙ other towns in which food distribution was secured

In January 1991, with the outbreak of civil war in Somalia, anarchy ensued. Within two years, 300,000 Somalis died of starvation. Beginning in August 1992, Somalia was sent 228,000 tons of grain, much of it under a United States air and sea lift **"Operation Provide Relief"**. Half of the aid was looted by local warring factions.
"Operation Restore Hope" began on 19 December 1992. Its aim was to provide a protective military shield for United Nations relief workers. 25,000 US troops, as well as 5,000 from France, Canada and Belgium, took part, authorised by the UN to disarm the fighting factions and confiscate heavy weapons

YEMEN

Aden

Gulf of Aden

DJIBOUTI

Djibouti

Bossaso

Berbera

SOMALILAND
seceded from Somalia, 1991

Galkayo ⊙

SOMALIA

ETHIOPIA

Belet Huen

31 December 1992
President Bush visits a school and relief centre for mothers and children

Oddur

Jalalaxi

18 January 1993
The first American soldier, Marine Private Domingo Arroyo, killed

Baidoa

La Foule

26 January 1993
A second US Marine, Lance Corporal Anthony Botello, killed by a sniper while on night patrol

Baidere

Afgoi

Mogadishu

30 January 1993
700 American troops in air assault fail to find arms cache

Merca

USS Juneau
TRANSPORT DOCK

USS Rushmore
DOCK LANDING SHIP

USS Tripoli
AMPHIBIOUS ASSAULT SHIP

USS Ranger
AIRCRAFT CARRIER

USS Jack Lummus
SUPPLY SHIP

KENYA

Jilib ⊙

0   kilometres   200

0   miles   100

Kismayu

2 January 1993
A British famine relief worker 28-year-old Sean Devereux, shot: the first Western aid worker to be killed since United States troops landed

Base for two British Hercules transport planes with 80 Royal Air Force servicemen

26 January 1993
American and Belgian troops kill eight armed Somalis in a battle with armed militia

Mombasa

© Martin Gilbert 1993

136

EXPLORING THE SOLAR SYSTEM, 1962-1992

Beginning in 1962, the United States took the lead in exploring the solar system, starting with the launch of an unmanned *Mariner* spacecraft towards the planet Venus. On 3 March 1972 the unmanned, nuclear-powered spacecraft *Pioneer 10* was launched towards Jupiter: twenty years later it had travelled five billion miles from Earth

On 25 April 1990 the Hubble Space Telescope was launched, to study distant stars and galaxies, and to search for evidence of planets in other solar systems

26 January 1986
Voyager 2 passes, sends back details of planet's composition

URANUS

2 March 1992
Pioneer 10 reaches five billion miles from Earth, the furthest distance travelled by any man-made object

3 December 1973
Pioneer 10 gives first close-up pictures
4 March 1979
Voyager 1 discovers rings and details of sixteen moons

3 February 1992
Ulysses flies to within 235,000 miles (and 416 million miles from Earth). Its signals take 37 minutes and 15 seconds to get back to Earth

1986
Pioneer 10 becomes the first man-made object to escape the solar system

29 March 1974
Mariner 10 takes 2,800 photographs

8 December 1992
Galileo, while bound for Jupiter (due 1995) passes within 200 miles of Earth. Its instruments detect signs of intelligent life on Earth!

PLUTO

JUPITER

NEPTUNE

MERCURY

SUN

EARTH

VENUS

MARS

14 December 1962
Mariner 2 passes 21,648 miles from surface
5 January 1969
Soviet space craft lands on surface and returns

13 June 1983
Pioneer 10 crosses the orbit of Neptune

8 November 1968
Pioneer 9 achieves sun orbit

28 November 1964
Mariner 4 trajectory passes Mars and sends 22 pictures from 6,100 miles above the planet's surface
13 November 1971
Mariner 9 in orbit 862 miles above planet's surface

SATURN

November 1980
Voyager 1 sends photographs, reveals winds of 1,100 miles an hour at Equator and a total of 17 moons

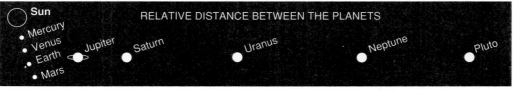

Sun — RELATIVE DISTANCE BETWEEN THE PLANETS — Mercury, Venus, Earth, Mars, Jupiter, Saturn, Uranus, Neptune, Pluto

DEFENCE PREPAREDNESS IN SPACE, 1992-1993

On 31 December 1992 the United States Department of Defence awarded 6-year contracts to develop the "Brilliant Eyes" satellite. Each satellite was intended to carry sensors to monitor both space and Earth. Between 20 and 40 "Brilliant Eyes" would orbit at less than 1,000 miles above the Earth, in contrast to the 22,000-mile altitude of existing Early Warning satellites. This whole programme was cancelled by President Clinton on 13 May 1993 when he announced "the end of the Star Wars Era": a final affirmation of the end of the Cold War

In January 1992, Russian President Boris Yeltsin called for the United States and Russia to establish a Global Protection System. Following his call, talks began for the establishment of a Joint Missile Warning Centre that would receive data on missile launches

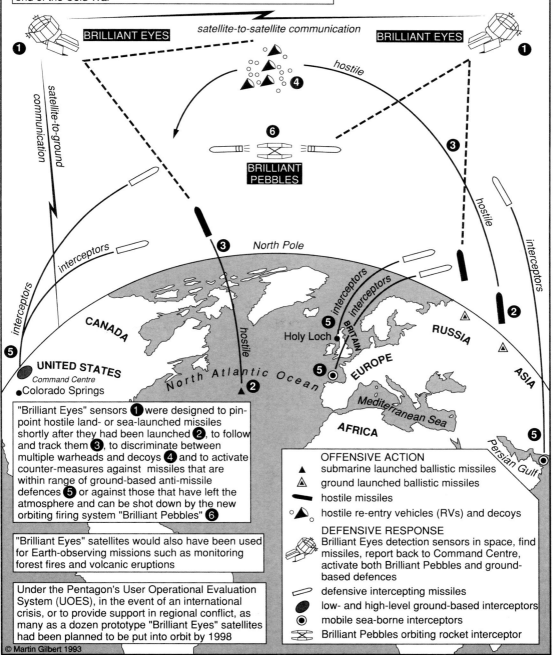

BRILLIANT EYES

satellite-to-satellite communication

BRILLIANT EYES

hostile

satellite-to-ground communication

BRILLIANT PEBBLES

interceptors

North Pole

hostile

interceptors

interceptors

hostile

interceptors

CANADA

Holy Loch

BRITAIN

RUSSIA

UNITED STATES
Command Centre
•Colorado Springs

EUROPE

ASIA

North Atlantic Ocean

Mediterranean Sea

AFRICA

Persian Gulf

"Brilliant Eyes" sensors ❶ were designed to pinpoint hostile land- or sea-launched missiles shortly after they had been launched ❷, to follow and track them ❸, to discriminate between multiple warheads and decoys ❹ and to activate counter-measures against missiles that are within range of ground-based anti-missile defences ❺ or against those that have left the atmosphere and can be shot down by the new orbiting firing system "Brilliant Pebbles" ❻

"Brilliant Eyes" satellites would also have been used for Earth-observing missions such as monitoring forest fires and volcanic eruptions

Under the Pentagon's User Operational Evaluation System (UOES), in the event of an international crisis, or to provide support in regional conflict, as many as a dozen prototype "Brilliant Eyes" satellites had been planned to be put into orbit by 1998

OFFENSIVE ACTION
▲ submarine launched ballistic missiles
△ ground launched ballistic missiles
▬ hostile missiles
°▲° hostile re-entry vehicles (RVs) and decoys

DEFENSIVE RESPONSE
Brilliant Eyes detection sensors in space, find missiles, report back to Command Centre, activate both Brilliant Pebbles and ground-based defences
⟋ defensive intercepting missiles
● low- and high-level ground-based interceptors
◉ mobile sea-borne interceptors
✕ Brilliant Pebbles orbiting rocket interceptor

© Martin Gilbert 1993

Kushka wishes a Happy Birthday to:

_____

THIS IS YOUR _____ BIRTHDAY!

YOU WERE BORN ON _____

YOUR FAVORITE COLOR IS _____

YOUR FAVORITE TOY IS _____

YOUR FAVORITE FOOD IS _____

WHEN I GROW UP I WANT TO BE A

_____

"Kush...ka, wake up sleepy head. Daddy has a **big** surprise for you today. We have lots of friends waiting to see you.

Come on Kushka time, *to get up!*"

2

"That's a good girl. Wake up it's time to get ready for school."

As Kushka's tail starts wagging, she...

stretches like a cat and is ready for a new adventure.

3

Kushka's daddy brings Kushka downstairs as he watches her to make sure she eats all of her breakfast. Mommy is there also to make sure Kushka "makes all gone."

Mommy asks Kushka if daddy told her that today is going to be a special day.

HAPPY BIRTHDAY KUSHKA!

4

As Kushka JUMPS in her bag and is ready to go off to school, her mommy gives her daddy a kiss and tells them to have a great day at school and have fun.

6

As Kushka and her daddy drive to school, Kushka is all excited, looking out the window, seeing people and smelling the fresh air.

Daddy reminds Kushka that, when we get to school, you need to show everyone that you have **good manners.**

no running in the parking lot.
Look both ways when you are crossing."

10

Daddy sees Ms. Davis and Mr. Jackson waving good morning to the two of them.

11

As we enter the school building, the principal is waiting for us at the front door. She greets us with a good-morning, as Kushka walks in with her **pretty pance**.

14

Daddy signs in Kushka as a visitor at the school, while several teachers greet Kushka.

One of the teachers tells Kushka that the boys and girls are so excited about her visit.

16

"Good morning, boys and girls. My name is Mr. K. and this is my special girl Kushka.

18

We are here to talk to you today about writing and how important it is to write well. The best part about writing is that you can write about anything you want.

19

Which one is your favorite hat?
I can write a story just about
Kushka's hats.

Kushka is going to show you how she dances. Kushka really enjoys spinning around and walking on two feet.

You can hear the children **applauding** in the background.

25

"That was wonderful, Kushka. Where did you learn to dance like that?" asks the principal. Kushka just smiles. Hmm, Kushka is wondering why we are not leaving the school building like we always do.

CLASS RULES
BE PROMPT
BE PREPARED
BE POLITE
BE PRODUCTIVE
BE POSITIVE

You can
LEARN
something new
EVERY DAY
if you
LISTEN

EXIT

GOOD MANNERS
BE A FRIEND
BE A GOOD LISTENER
BE KIND
HELP OTHERS
RAISE YOUR HAND
SAY "PLEASE" AND "THANK YOU"
TAKE TURNS

BEFORE Y
THI
T IS IT T...
H IS IT H
I IS IT I
N IS IT N
K IS IT K

The principal then asks Mr. K. and Kushka to please step into the gymnasium.

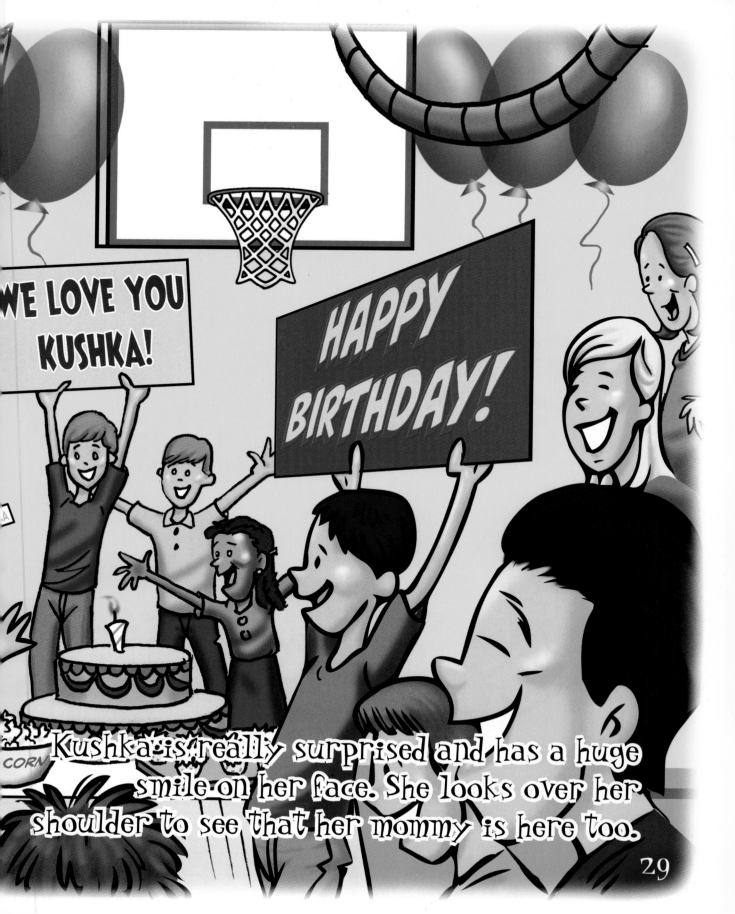

Kushka is really surprised and has a huge smile on her face. She looks over her shoulder to see that her mommy is here too.

Kushka quickly jumps into her mommy's arms and has a big smile.

Her mommy whispers into Kushka's ear, "Did you think we would forget that today is your birthday? We love you soooo much."

30

Kushka's daddy is busy passing out Kushka look-alike cupcakes to all the boys and girls. Kushka winks as if to say, "This was really a great day at school."

31

Kushka

WISHES ALL THE BOYS AND GIRLS

A SUPER HAPPY BIRTHDAY!